07.24.13

Kitty

Because you
must own this book!

Love You
Keith + Mary

Kaffe Fassett
Dreaming in Color

An Autobiography

STC Craft | A Melanie Falick Book

Stewart, Tabori & Chang
New York

For Brandon Mably

Page 1: A watercolor of decorative boxes I did in Holland in the 1980s. **Page 2:** Working in my painting studio. **Page 5:** A cabinet in my studio, packed to the brim. **Page 6:** My 1999 study of rose-covered objects.

Published in 2012 by Stewart, Tabori & Chang
An imprint of ABRAMS

Text copyright © 2012 Kaffe Fassett
All photographs and illustrations copyright © Kaffe Fassett unless otherwise noted on page 221.
Photograph of Nepenthe on page 22 by Morley Baer. © 2012 by the Morley Baer Photography Trust, Santa Fe. All rights reserved.

Library of Congress Cataloging-in-Publication Data

Fassett, Kaffe.
Kaffe Fassett : dreaming in color : an autobiography / Kaffe Fassett.
    p. cm.
"A Melanie Falick book."
ISBN 978-1-58479-996-2
1. Fassett, Kaffe. 2. Fashion designers—United States—Biography.
I. Title. II. Title: Dreaming in color : an autobiography.
TT505.F37F37 2012
746.9'2092—dc23

                                        2011049250

UK edition ISBN: 978-1-61769-007-5

Editor: Melanie Falick with Betty Christiansen and Sally Harding
Designer: Anna Christian
Production Manager: Tina Cameron

The text of this book was composed in Miller and Gotham.

Printed and bound in China.
10 9 8 7 6 5 4 3 2 1

Stewart, Tabori & Chang books are available at special discounts when purchased in quantity for premiums and promotions as well as fundraising or educational use. Special editions can also be created to specification. For details, contact specialsales@abramsbooks.com or the address below.

THE ART OF BOOKS SINCE 1949
115 West 18th Street
New York, NY 10011
www.abramsbooks.com

As I sit in my studio surrounded by my creative material—fabrics, yarns, paper prints, shelves of books, and collections of decorative objects—I can't help but reflect on the path that led me here. What astounds me the most is the confidence and faith in myself I have always possessed, from my early years as a free-spirited boy on the wild California coast, to a young man who strode into England and the world of design and made a place for himself. I never felt daunted by difficulties or blocked alleys. Somehow, I knew the path I was on was right, and my trust in that sense was stronger than the limitations of my own personal comforts or desires. If I ever doubted my direction or wanted to give up, key friends in my life encouraged me to press on.

Over the years I know I have had guidance from guardian angels, who have helped me at every turn. They have ranged from family members and collaborative partners to the colorful travelers who serendipitously crossed my path as they sought the beauty of Big Sur, California, my family home, filling my young imagination with impressions of the Old World and details of their eclectic lives. This education was more extensive than I could have known at that age. I conjured up a vivid land from all those tales told around the fire at our family restaurant. Since then, I have found a home in England, in the world of textile arts, and in a glorious life of my own design.

KAFFE Fassett

Opposite: In front of a painting I did of my Welsh dresser full of china. I've always had a passion for china, and London, with its great flea markets and antique shops, has been an excellent place to form a collection.

chapter one

1937–1956

Childhood in California

Above, left: School photo, aged 12, taken at my tiny Big Sur school. **Above, center:** My sister Dorcas and I dancing on the terrace of Nepenthe, the family restaurant in Big Sur. **Above, right:** The Fassett family trying out ballet positions on the Nepenthe bleachers, with our log cabin home in the background. **Opposite:** The magnificent Santa Lucia Mountains as seen from the terrace of Nepenthe. The patio is made of cut redwood rounds.

When I was nine, my parents built a stunning modern restaurant perched on the cliffs of Big Sur, California, where the whole family lived and worked. As a barefoot boy on the California coast, I loved the rugged terrain . . . redwood canyons, beaches, and steep mountains. This spectacular, isolated setting turned out to be a big draw for artists, writers, musicians, and actors, and our family-run business became a magnet for interesting people—both staff and visitors—from across the globe. Meeting these larger-than-life characters stimulated my young mind and was a powerful influence. Their confident personalities and colorful stories about the exotic worlds of Europe and the Orient filled me with longing to experience those places for myself. The progressive boarding school I attended as a teenager, which was full of cultured teachers and inquiring students, would further intensify my burgeoning enthusiasm for a creative life of my own.

My early years in San Francisco and Carmel

I was born on December 7, 1937, at 2:47 a.m., at the Children's Hospital in San Francisco—December 7 would later become the infamous Pearl Harbor day. My parents, Bill and Lolly Fassett, were both twenty-six at the time and already had a one-year-old in tow, my brother Griff. Dad and Mom debated about a name for me. Griff had been named after Dad's maternal grandfather, William Eliot Griffis, so Dad said, "Why not please your family and name him after *your* grandfather?" Mom had adored her maternal grandfather Frank Powers, and she readily agreed, signing my birth certificate "Frank Powers Fassett."

My antecedents were an eclectic mix of art philanthropists, entrepreneurs, academics, artists, suffragettes, and writers. This made my parents encourage creativity in anyone who crossed their paths. Mom was a great romantic and loved the color in life, and Dad loved drama. Neither had cultivated an art or craft, so they didn't impose any particular artistic discipline on their kids. Still, they were always keen to promote celebration and heightened fun.

Mom had been a very handsome young woman in her early life and had traveled around Europe with her painter grandmother, Jane Gallatin Powers, wife of Frank Powers. After Frank's death in 1920, Jane emigrated to Europe, taking her two youngest daughters— her oldest daughter, my grandmother, was already married and had had my mother by that time, so she stayed behind in San Francisco. At the age of seventeen, my mother left California and went over to join Jane. Mom would regale us with tales of her six years spent in Paris, Rome, and Capri. One story I loved was how on arriving at grand hotels, my great-grandmother would unscrew the door handles and replace them with her own more decorative ones.

Mom also told us about the dashing, unusual clothes she wore during her years in Europe. She often described an apple green satin dress she had worn, for which she had made one peacock blue shoe and one emerald green. Is it any wonder I should develop a passion for color with inspirational visions like that embedded in my memory? One of Mom's aunts married the governor of Capri, so Mom spent many summer days swimming and evenings attending receptions and dancing at grand balls.

My father was tall and handsome with a wicked sense of humor that gained more of a sadistic edge as he really got to know you. His personality would have made him a good twenty-first-century TV presenter, prying out embarrassing stories from unsuspecting people. He was also an eclectic and avid reader. Politics, religion, and the American Civil War were among his favorite subjects. He talked often of writing a great book, but those plans remained in the realm of talk—a sad fact that motivated me to act on my own dreams.

Dad's upbringing, mostly in California, was rather bohemian for the time, and after finishing Cornell University, where he studied hotel management, he returned to California

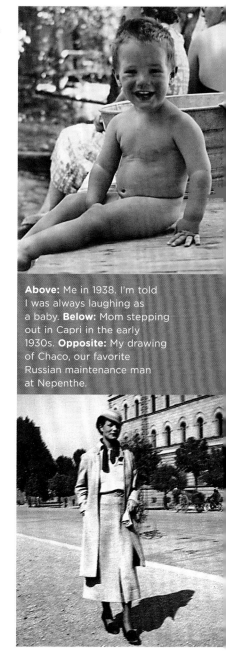

Above: Me in 1938. I'm told I was always laughing as a baby. **Below:** Mom stepping out in Capri in the early 1930s. **Opposite:** My drawing of Chaco, our favorite Russian maintenance man at Nepenthe.

and started working as a merchant marine. He lived next door to Mom in San Francisco, and it was only a matter of time before these two handsome people would get together. They were both born in 1911 and married at twenty-four.

At the time of my birth, my mother and father were living in the Powers family home on Steiner Street in San Francisco where my mother had grown up. Her maternal grandparents, Frank and Jane Gallatin Powers, were the founders of the artist colony in Carmel-by-the-Sea on the beautiful wild coast of California. They had bought a house on the edge of the Carmel beach called The Dunes when they were developing the colony, but they also had this San Francisco house, as Frank had his law practice there. Jane's father was Albert Gallatin, a wealthy California businessman who was an early pioneer of hydroelectric power and power transmission, and was the president of the largest hardware, iron, and steel company on the West Coast. A self-made man, he built himself a large house in Sacramento that later became the governor's mansion for thirteen California governors.

My father's antecedents were pretty impressive as well. His maternal grandfather, William Eliot Griffis, was a noted American Orientalist and writer who had been decorated in Japan for his work in education there. Dad's birth father was Edward Lee McCallie, whose family had founded the McCallie School, a renowned boy's school, in Chattanooga, Tennessee, but his mother, Kevah, divorced and remarried when he was still a baby. His wealthy stepfather, Newton Crocker Fassett, was William's best friend and the man who, by adopting Dad, gave our family their surname.

The past family glories didn't seem to offer my young parents much financial privilege. I always remember them struggling pretty hard to make ends meet during my childhood. But the advantage passed down to me was probably the cultured upbringing my parents had had—it ensured that I was exposed to the arts from a young age.

My very first memories are of the Powers family's Steiner Street house and its garden. The house seemed huge to me then, but it came down to size when I was to see it a couple of decades later—a kind of average-size four-story San Francisco Victorian. I lived there with my parents and older brother until I was four and Griff was five.

Being so young, I don't remember much about living on Steiner Street. What I do recall is the delicious feeling of lying down in my little red wagon and gazing up at clouds and the berries on the holly tree till I dozed off. The next thing I knew, my mother's voice was booming out of the upstairs window. "What are you doing? Come up to bed if you want to sleep." Naps were compulsory for Griff and me, and we hated having to take them. We were active boys and disliked being told, "Oh, you are overtired," whenever we complained about anything. One afternoon when we were really resisting shutting our eyes at naptime, Dad said, "You'll love having a nap one day." Indeed, I have come to treasure a short power nap during my working day in the studio. It need only be ten to fifteen minutes to set me up for an afternoon's hard work. Often when guests are here for lunch, I'll slip out as they are having a cup of tea after the meal and be back before they get up from the table.

A story I often heard my mother tell regarded my "real" name. When I was old enough to go to nursery school in San Francisco, my father signed me in there as Frank Powers Fassett. A year later, when I required a vaccination, the school needed my birth certificate, so they sent off for it. When it arrived, my astonished teacher rang my mother to ask, "Doesn't your husband even know his own child's name?"

1, 3, 4: My great grandmother, artist Jane Gallatin Powers, in Italy, where she lived and painted in the 1920s and 1930s, and two of her paintings from that era. **2, 5, 9:** Jane would have approved of my patchwork fabrics from the nineties—Bekah and Cloisonné—and my Fair Isle knitting from the eighties. **6, 8:** Mom in Capri in the early 1930s, when she was living with her grandmother; and Jane's portrait of her. **7:** Mom and Dad looking content on their wedding day in 1935.

"Why, what did he sign him in as?" she asked.

"Frank Powers Fassett. But I have his birth certificate in front of me, and it says Frank Havrah Fassett!" My mother had never heard the name Havrah, so she called Dad at his office to get an explanation. My father was so shocked when he heard the story that he dropped the phone. When Dad was born to his astrologically obsessed mother, Kevah, she gave him the middle name Havrah, a name thought to have great stability because it had an "h" at each end. Dad hated it as he grew up and never used it or told anyone about it, including Mom. Kevah had passed away a few years before I was born, but my mother always felt she must have wanted the name Havrah in the family so much that she had "arranged" it from the other side. I feel sure that Kevah was a forceful creature, capable of doing that. Educated at Vassar in the early twentieth century and quite a bohemian, she was divorced twice and married three times in the days when divorce was a very rare occurrence. She became active in the early movement for women's rights and worked with Margaret Sanger, the founder of Planned Parenthood.

Our family had another addition in 1941 when my sister Dorcas Jane Fassett was born, and in the same year we moved to a ranch just outside Marin City, a couple of miles northwest of downtown Sausalito. With three small children under five, my parents were trying to make a go of running a horse ranch, and Dad joined the World War II effort working in the Sausalito shipyards, at the north end of the Golden Gate Bridge. Housing in Marin City itself was building up rapidly at the start of the war to accommodate more than 70,000 shipyard workers flooding into Sausalito to work in the Marinship Shipyard. My strongest war memory is Dad coming home with a gas mask on and sending our family dog, Dewsy, into a frenzy of barking.

My sister Holly Fassett was born during the war in 1943, and shortly after it ended we moved to a rambling house in Carmel. It was a warm-hearted abode only a block from the beach, so we could swim before and after school. My mother wrote of it as a "marvelous old Spanish-style house with a huge living room and a fireplace." Dad took various jobs, but found his vocation when he started a magazine called *What's Doing*, which featured the Monterey Peninsula happenings. An aspiring writer, he was much more in his element doing this than working in the shipyards. The new job also put him in touch with all the movers and the shakers of the area, which would be a great advantage when he and my mother took up their next adventure.

1947
Arriving in Big Sur

In 1947, my parents had the foresight and good fortune to buy a spectacular piece of coastal property—a twelve-acre hilltop about thirty miles south of Carmel that was crowned with a log cabin. The cabin had a forty-mile view of coastline along Big Sur. A ninety-mile stretch of coast between San Francisco and Los Angeles, Big Sur had been an inaccessible wilderness until Highway 1 was finished in 1937 (shortly before my birth), linking it to towns north and south. Before then, Big Sur had been accessible only by foot or horseback. Despite its remoteness, the unique landscape always attracted hikers and lovers of unspoiled wilderness. The log cabin, built in the 1920s by the Trails Club of California (the precursor of the Sierra Club), was a pivotal base for them. This area, with the stunning Santa Lucia Mountains tumbling gracefully and dramatically down to the Pacific Ocean, is considered one of the most beautiful coastlines in the United States. Much of the wild nature there is luckily still protected by vast federal and state parks along the coast. My mother had spent childhood holidays on the beach below the log cabin where she and her grandfather Powers had had picnics, roasting corn on log fires on moonlit nights.

Dad bought our log cabin and its twelve acres from Orson Welles, who had purchased the property in 1944 as a honeymoon present for Rita Hayworth, but the couple never actually stayed there. Since this rugged coastline had only had its highway since 1937, and the war had interrupted any substantial development, by the time the Fassett family arrived, it still had no electricity and very few inhabitants.

Above: Our rugged log cabin home before our restaurant, Nepenthe, was built next to it. The woods below drop dramatically down to the Pacific. **Below, left:** The family brushed up for a photo in 1941, before we started our adventure in Big Sur—Mom and Dad, with me (left), my brother Griff, and our new sister, Dorcas. **Below, right:** My sister Holly's painting of our beautiful Big Sur coastline as seen from the restaurant terrace. **Right:** My handwoven fabric called Caterpillar Stripe, designed in the 1990s, in shades of the ocean that dominate Big Sur.

Coming from the small seaside town of Carmel, my sisters, older brother, and I took to this rugged new home with great enthusiasm. Surrounded by oak trees and redwoods, our log cabin was perched 800 feet above the Pacific. At the beginning, we lived outdoors for the most part—chopping wood for our stone fireplace, climbing up the near-vertical hills, and tumbling down long canyon trails to our stunning deserted beach. What a perfect child's adventure it was for us, like having a huge park all to ourselves, one that was full of new smells and sights. We would run naked in the surf, arrange stones and shells in decorative patterns on the sand, and climb the miniature waterfall up the creek, picking wildflowers. When I think of how cosseted and supervised kids are today, I'm amazed by and grateful for the trust our parents had in our independent exploring.

My three sisters, Dorcas, Holly, and Kim—at six years, four years, and nine months old—were the "little kids" when we moved into the log cabin. I was nine and my brother Griff was a very grown up ten and a half. We had a tight friendship for a brief period, before he found pals his own age and suddenly saw me as the annoying little brother. Soon after we arrived, Griff and I did a quick survey of the properties surrounding our plot and explored the terrain until we were scared off by warning shots from a neighboring landowner.

When we kids were not climbing and frolicking on the beach, I would often have the job of looking after my little sisters while my parents were occupied with settling in to our primitive accommodations. Sometimes, to keep them and me amused, I'd dress them up in romantic costumes, dreaming we were in the time of Shakespeare's *Henry V*.

I'd recently seen the Laurence Olivier film, and my young imagination had taken in every detail of the sets and costumes. My father had a record of the key speeches from the film, which we'd listen to over and over, picturing the vivid scenes and savoring the language: "This day is called the feast of Crispian."

I'd drape my sisters in scarves and strings of beads and push them around in our old wheelbarrow, transforming them into the grandest of ladies in fine coaches, or we'd wrap bandannas around our heads, put on loincloths, and become Native Americans. We built improvised theaters with bedspread curtains and played music from a windup record player, all under our big oak tree. That oak tree—like a huge elephant on whose back and trunk we'd climb, squealing with delight—was a living entity for us. We spent hours on the swings hanging from its branches.

When the rains (which could be torrential) struck on frosty winter days, we'd make puppet theaters in our rooms and beg any adults to come watch our latest productions. My mother saw from an early age that I had a creative talent, and she gave me every encouragement. Each year, about a month before Christmas, while my siblings slaved at chores like cutting wood, cleaning, and filling kerosene lamps, I was planted at the dining-room table to hand-paint the many Christmas cards we sent out. I loved this task, and I got more and more imaginative and detailed as I worked through the piles of colored papers making my poster-paint images. It was a joyous job I looked forward to every year.

Aside from encouraging my painting, my mother attempted to introduce me to other arts on offer in Monterey, thirty-five miles north of us. She took me to any colorful piece of theater and film she could. I remember the surprising vision of a Kabuki troupe, Balinese dance performances, and classic films like David Lean's *Great Expectations* and, later, Powell and Pressburger's *The Red Shoes*. These productions became a rich education for me. My brother also started to find his own intense interests. He discovered classical music through friends of the family and through our father, who loved romantic orchestral pieces, often filling the house with great rolling symphonies.

My fondest early Big Sur memories of Dad are of him reading stories to us kids as we gathered in our pajamas in front of a roaring fire. He always read what interested him as well as us. Satirist and short story writer Ambrose Bierce was one of his favorites, as he was steeped in the American Civil War and writings about that period. He also read us *The Wonderful Wizard of Oz* and many English children's books—*Winnie-the-Pooh*, *The Wind in the Willows*, *Alice's Adventures in Wonderland*, and, best of all, the Mary Poppins series by P. L. Travers.

Building the Fassett family restaurant

My parents had different opinions about what they wanted to do to make a living with their Big Sur property. Dad seemed happy to set up a roadside hamburger and coffee stand, but my mother thought they should build unique cabins on the site and rent them out. Eventually they decided to build a huge modern restaurant just below the log cabin so the world could share our spectacular view—which included the sun rising over the Santa Lucia Mountains and spectacularly setting over the Pacific. Finding someone to design the building took a little time, but they finally met Rowan Maiden, a sensitive architect who lived in Monterey. Mom realized he understood her vision for the unique restaurant she wanted to build. Rowan had studied with Frank Lloyd Wright and was one of Wright's three favorite apprentices.

Coming to an agreement about what the restaurant should look like wasn't easy for my parents. My mother was definitely the visionary in the family, while my father, with his hotel management training, was the practical one. Because he had a very male approach to many things and was not particularly aware of aesthetics, my mother had an uphill struggle to keep her unique vision untainted. Their fights were legendary even before we embarked on the restaurant. I remember bottles of milk being smashed against the walls as we children tried to eat our breakfast and, most memorable, a stack of glass ashtrays crashing on a concrete floor.

To construct the building, Mom and Dad turned to two brother contractors whose father had built our log cabin, Frank and Walter Trotter. They were big, powerfully built guys, sympathetic to the design of the building. To finance the construction, Dad went to his uncle Stan. Stanton Griffis had made a fortune as an investment banker, then later ran Paramount Pictures and owned Brentano's bookstore in New York. During the President Truman years, he had also been the U.S. ambassador to Poland, Egypt, Eva Perón's Argentina, and Franco's Spain. Maybe his own sense of adventure helped him to understand my parents' attempt to set up a business in the beautiful backwoods like this.

I remember Uncle Stan arriving in a big car. He stepped out looking pasty and old to me, and dressed in a very exotic three-piece suit—everyone I knew in those days wore casual clothes. After looking over our property, he had mumbling conversations with Dad. As he was preparing to leave, my little six-year-old sister Dorcas, realizing he was about to back

The great modern structure of the restaurant takes form, with me trying to help the workmen.

our dream business, tried to make polite small talk. She gestured to the looming mountain behind us and said, "Isn't that a beautiful mountain, Uncle Stan?" This elderly, balding New Yorker gazed up at the sight and said, "Do you want me to buy *that* for you, too?"

By hook or by crook, Mom got Dad to agree to her dream, and her rustic modern structure started to materialize. My parents both contributed to the actual construction process. Dad worked for the Trotters for a while doing building labor. Although Mom had her hands full with five kids to look after and meals to make for all involved, she still found time to help work on the restaurant. When big bricks were needed for the outdoor fireplace and a retaining wall below the log house, she made her own version of them using local pinkish gravel and cement. Mom's boots and work clothes were often stiff with splattered cement.

We kids were fascinated by the building of the restaurant and were

allowed to help. My brother and I shoveled earth from the kitchen area, which was carved out of a hillside behind the main dining terrace. As the great trusses that formed the skeleton of our building went up, it was like a huge stage set for me. It was thrilling to watch the wide south-facing concrete terrace and mammoth stepped seating area that led down from the log house being poured.

As my parents were looking for a name for their restaurant, the name Nepenthe came from our family friend Daniel Harris, a Hungarian-American artist who had dubbed himself ZEV ("wolf" in Hebrew). *Nepenthe* is Greek for "isle of no care," and my mother thought that a place meaning basically "house of no sorrow" fit in with her picture of creating a beautiful haven for all to enjoy. ZEV had studied art in Hungary and at the Academy of Design in New York, and he and his wife, Gertrude, had built a fantasy of a house called Crazy Crescent in Seaside, just north of Monterey. They had used wonderful found objects to make it a little palace of delights. Mill-end floors of odd shapes of wood set on end, walls made of old bottles creating a stained-glass effect, and mosaics of crockery and pebbles all added enchantment.

To us kids, ZEV was a magician. He had a whimsical grin and dancing, fun-filled eyes. He was always drawing or making something, or digging in his treasure chests to find us a memorable present. These chests were full of little boxes and pretty cloth bags of ZEV's favorite things—beads, china, coins, paintbrushes, pens. He was a big kid who squirreled away his magic talismans.

One day ZEV announced he would make special mosaic tables for inside the restaurant and outside on the terrace. He found some glass tiles in brilliant colors—kingfisher blue, gold, purple, ruby red—and added to those some of his prized strings of beads, glass inkwells, and keys. We watched spellbound as he danced about, brimming over with creative joy. The resulting tables were eye-catching and delightful, the bright collection of a magpie. My love of mosaic started there.

ZEV also drew a wonderful phoenix bird for Nepenthe, which became the symbol of the family enterprise. He wrote a ditty to put on the menu: "Forget all your worldly cares at Nepenthe's gay pavilion—where the Phoenix Bird repairs and is feeling like a million." I recall his delight in Nepenthe's early costume parties, where he arrived one year sporting a skin-tight pair of knitted shorts (a child's outfit he found at a thrift store, stretched over his muscular legs), a sailor's hat, and a huge grin. ZEV gave us kids drawing pens and paper for Christmas, always encouraging us to be as productive as we could be.

Though ZEV was married, his unbridled joie de vivre and kooky sense of humor revealed a free spirit that was never going to be tamed by the heterosexual world. I once overheard my parents arguing about ZEV's homosexuality having a possible influence on us kids. They needn't have worried in my case; I'd instinctively known from an early age where my strongest interests lay. As much as I adored the girls and women in my life, I knew that men were the attractive ones for me.

From the time we arrived in Big Sur, Mom had started making Sunday-night dinners in her big kitchen in our private quarters in the log cabin, to which all kinds of interesting neighbors and friends were invited. She continued these as the restaurant went up, and they became famous over the years. One reason Dad gave for agreeing to build the restaurant in the first place was that they were already feeding everyone in the vicinity. The dinners drew in local artists, writers, and antique dealers—Big Sur, Carmel, and Monterey were home to many creative types, and my vivacious parents attracted them into their circle. The table was always full of laughter and gossip, as well as split French loaves of garlic bread, pasta or hearty stew, big tossed salads, and lots of good wine. Mom's adoring dinner guests wore colorful clothes matched by her own big-print oriental-style tops and oversized earrings.

Aside from being allowed our outdoor ramblings, my school-age siblings and I were signed up for the local school a couple of miles north of us on Highway 1. To us kids, it was a large house, but it was actually a pretty small place to accommodate first through eighth grades. The youngest kids were in a side room while the rest of us were in the main room with our one teacher. There was a big blackboard at the end of the room, and we sat in little wooden desks—seats attached to a writing surface that opened to store our schoolbooks. One wall was mostly large glass windows that looked out on a playground and a road that curved around to the front of the school.

The end-of-year photo from our small schoolhouse in Big Sur. I'm the fourth from the left in the middle row; my sister Holly is to my right in the same row; and my sister Dorcas is the sixth from the left in the top row.

PFEIFFER
SCHOOL
BIG SUR CALIF
FALL 1950
MISS
ANDREWS
PRINCIPAL

1, 5, 10: Mirage, a knit I remember designing on a trip to India; my Paperweight ribbon design; and my fabric Millefiore—inspired by my mother's passion for color. **2:** The entrance to Nepenthe restaurant. **3:** I loved the costume parties at Nepenthe. Here I am in 1956, wearing a hula skirt and an Egyptian tapestry that made me into a Kabuki character. **4:** The restaurant was designed by architect Rowan Maiden. **6:** Our artist friend ZEV dancing at Nepenthe's first Halloween party. **7:** Nepenthe, finished and ready for business. **8:** The phoenix bird, which is a symbol of Nepenthe, made into a door decoration by ZEV. **9:** Another joyous end-of-season Halloween party at Nepenthe; after this party the restaurant would close for the winter. I would often appear in several costume changes during the evening, sometimes quite dramatically under a huge silk parachute. It gave me a taste for dramatic happenings on the world's stage.

6

7

8

9

10

The only grandparent who played a significant role in our lives was my mother's mother, Madeleine Powers Ulman. My brother, sisters, and I called her Nona and visited her frequently. She had a very different style than my mother's and lived in a grand country house, with lush gardens and a fruit orchard, situated on the Carmel River. We loved romping in those gardens, but entering her house was a nightmare for country kids. "Don't touch the wallpaper! Don't touch the banisters!" was the constant cry.

On one of her visits to our Big Sur home, Nona was reading us an Oscar Wilde story when she suddenly started to weep. My father happened to stick his head in the door at that instant, and he asked, "Why are you crying?"

"Because the words are so beautiful," she replied tearfully. Then she turned back to us children and her tears stemmed instantly as she yelled, "Kick it, kick it!" pointing to our dog. Startled, we looked at our sweet dog lying at our feet, lazily licking his balls. I gently took him out the door instead. When I came back and sat down, Nona drew herself up to her full height and declared forcefully, "A dog always reflects the habits of its master."

Nona was very grand looking, like a Gibson girl—red hair piled up on her head and usually topped off with a bold garden flower. We nicknamed her the Duchess. She would make points by closing her eyes with her head held high. When an actor friend met her some years later, he said, "When she closes her eyes, it's like the curtain descending at the Met!"

My grandmother's spacious house was lavishly furnished with antique carpets and textiles, and handsome furniture, some passed down from her father, Frank Powers. Big brass trays and Italian pots stand out in my memory, as do the murals, done by a local artist, in her sunroom, which overlooked the gardens leading down to the river.

One day as we were playing croquet on Nona's lawn, I suddenly focused on the beautiful, big, shiny leaves of her magnolia tree. The suede brown undercoating of these waxy leaves transfixed me. As I gazed in wonder at their size and contrasting textures, my grandmother murmured, "You like the leaves, but you didn't see the flowers." She reached up with her croquet mallet and pulled down the most enormous bloom I'd ever seen. Huge, creamy petals surrounded the golden center of a flower the size of a punch bowl, or so it seemed to my young eyes.

Nona's fruit orchard was at the side of the house, and I also have wonderful memories of climbing her apricot tree, picking the fruit, and nearly swooning at the sight of the orange apricots with deep pink blushes against the sapphire blue sky. I recalled these orchard impressions to make conversation with Nona after she had been divorced and was living in a much smaller house in Carmel. "Don't rub it in! I was kicked out!" she bellowed at me.

Above: The Nona quilt I designed in memory of a cloth my maternal grandmother, Madeleine Powers Ulman, gave me. **Opposite:** The oil painting I did of my grandmother in the early 1960s. She arrived for the sitting with a bucket of garden roses, a decorative cloth, and her striped muumuu.

Nepenthe starts up

The building of Nepenthe lasted for more than a year, and the restaurant opened in 1949 with a fire-lit evening. There was music, a playwright reading his play, and folk dancing on the terrace. The place was a great success from the start. Dad's role was crucial—the financial management and the running of the business. But he was hurt and even jealous at the number of compliments Mom received for the concept and visual details that made the restaurant unique in its time.

From the beginning, Nepenthe attracted people from many different worlds who lived nearby or were passing through. Because we were either working in the restaurant or hanging around it, we kids got the benefit of soaking up culture from every corner of the globe through our contact with these visitors. The bar, the restaurant, the stunning surroundings, and the company of my interesting, vibrant parents were all big attractions. Right away, Nepenthe was considered a relaxed and welcoming place by local residents. The entertainment my father organized was a draw, too. Dad would stage harpsichord and dance performances and poetry and play readings on Nepenthe's grand terrace. There was always a great welcoming fire burning inside the restaurant, as well as one outside on the terrace to greet guests as they arrived. When some professional event wasn't scheduled, we kids would occasionally put on fantasy costumes and dance our hearts out during the evenings, inspiring the customers to get up and join in.

One good thing about residing in a challenging, rugged countryside with no electricity and far from civilized town life is that you are surrounded by self-sufficient souls as well as creative ones—writers, actors, potters, painters, and sculptors. Big Sur was the perfect place for those seeking a different lifestyle and a place to peacefully get on with their writing or artwork. One vivid character in the artistic set on the coast was the renowned author Henry Miller. My father had known him before the restaurant opened, and he was one of the first famous regulars at Nepenthe.

Henry had come to Big Sur in 1944 and had lived in our log cabin before Orson Welles bought it. After his time in the log cabin he moved farther down the coast to Anderson Creek. The houses at Anderson Creek were constructed as a camp for prisoners who were employed to build the precipitous coastal highway. Several cabins were left standing and could be rented out, but they had no heat or power. Henry lived in the deserted mess hall. The makeshift oil-drum stove inside it provided barely enough heat to warm the big drafty space in winter. As it was right on the sea, the views from the mess hall were fabulous, and it was surrounded by clumps of narcissus that perfumed the air in spring. On nights when gales occurred and the wind whistled though the rafters and floorboards, Henry and his visitors bundled up in blankets and sipped wine before the fire. When anyone got unbearably cold in Big Sur, there was always relief at Henry's favorite place, the hot sulphur springs that were just down the road. A bath in those would warm your bones right through the night.

By the time Nepenthe opened, Henry was in his late fifties and a very well-known writer whose daring work was inspirational to the upcoming Beat Generation of poets and authors. Even though Henry had already written some of his most notorious books, recounting his sexual adventures and the joys of life in Paris and Greece, he was struggling to make ends meet at that time. His money was evidently difficult to get from his publishers in war-torn Paris. He was married then to a pretty young Polish woman named Lepska, and they had two very small children, Valentine and Tony. A fan of his had given them a house and property on Partington Ridge, a bit north of Anderson Creek, to live in free till they could afford to pay for it.

What I recall of this wiry little man with a deep voice and New York accent was his enthusiasm for life, and especially for art. He adored painting, saying, "To paint is to love again." When I got a little older and started producing large portraits of my family, Henry was my most enthusiastic audience, cheering me on. Aside from frequenting the bar and restaurant, he was also often around at Nepenthe while he was reading his work onto long-playing records. The sleeve on one of these says, "Recorded at Nepenthe, Henry's nearest neighbor with electricity." Henry also mentioned our family later in his book *Big Sur and the Oranges of Hieronymus Bosch*. He talks about my parents running the restaurant and their brood of children, and notes that all five of the young Fassett kids "specialized in raising hell."

Henry's own house on Partington Ridge was full of delightful colors (predominantly pink), bits of mosaic, colorful mobiles, children's artwork, and a motley collection of the crockery found at charity shops. As a child, I can't recall ever seeing a house that boasted a complete matching set of china for the table. Even our restaurant had plates of a dozen different colors.

During those early years, running the restaurant was like being in the theater for

my parents. They would wind up high on adrenalin after dealing with full houses. If there were interesting people around after most had gone home, a moonlight trip to the sulphur baths was laid on. The ocean spray wafting up in the cool night while the soothing candlelit hot springs warmed your body was a touch of nirvana that people never forgot.

Even with Nepenthe up and running, Mom was still raising us on a shoestring, as most of the money she could coax out of Dad went to her next building project. We always needed more space for storage or housing for staff members, so there was an ongoing series of small buildings being put up on the property. My mother would hear of a job lot of timber or building materials going and would have a house built by traveling workmen needing a job.

Above: Henry Miller, drinking with Mom and Dad. He was a frequent visitor to our log cabin, where he'd lived in the 1930s. **Right:** One of Henry's gouaches. He used to say, "To paint is to love again." **Left:** A quilt from my book *Simple Shapes Spectacular Quilts* that echoes the fabric on my mother's bold smock. **Below:** My Chevron Stripe fabric.

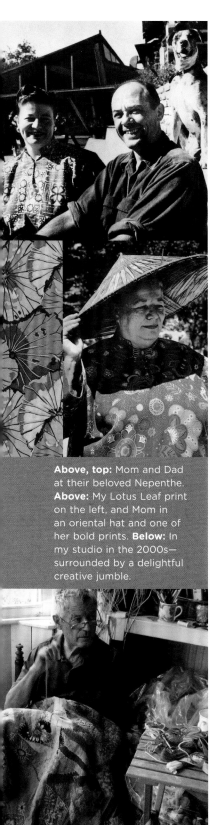

When the wooden bridges on our highway were replaced with concrete ones, she bought as much of the reclaimed timber as she could.

As the physical work of the building was nearing completion, Mom saw Dad skipping off on one affair after another, and she found solace in food. She discovered the nutritionist Adelle Davis, as many did in that era, and was very careful to eat healthy foods, but secret hoards of candy were to be found wherever she went.

Memories of my mother could fill a book, but one that sums up her spirit and warmth for me is this tale: When I was about fourteen, a tramp came knocking on her kitchen door begging for a little food. She rushed to me, saying, "I'm heating up some nourishing soup for this guy, but what can I put it in for him to take it on the road? I don't want to give him a bowl, as I'll never see it again. Oh, I know, I'll give it to him in a can." She quickly opened a can of plums, poured the contents into a bowl, and ladled the soup into the empty can for him. "What can he eat it with?" was the next question. She went to her drawer, fished out her best wedding-gift silver serving spoon, and plunked it into the can. "He can sell it afterward—I don't have a lifestyle for this now." Then she opened the back door and handed the astonished hobo his can of hot soup with a huge ornate silver handle sticking out of it. This wasn't Mom's first or last act of kindness, and she quickly garnered a reputation with locals for feeding and lending money to hard-up passersby in Big Sur.

Living in our rugged outpost wasn't always upbeat and jolly or, conversely, full of drama. After the big costume party celebration that was held at the restaurant every year for Halloween, the restaurant was routinely closed for the winter, not to open again till April. My parents used this time for necessary repairs and renewal. Some of the staff took this opportunity to retreat to Mexico for the season. So even though my mother still held her Sunday dinners for friends, and certain events were put on for selected locals, the winter months meant everything wound down to a slower pace, at least it seemed to for us kids. We would often set up a ping-pong table in the restaurant and play throughout the winter.

I recall many lonely times, isolated as we were. And as I grew into an adolescent, there were, for me, times of introspection. I didn't have too many fears of bogeymen in dark places, but I had a huge anxiety as a child about whether I would be able to remember things later in life. It had overpowering strength emotionally and was somehow linked to my fear of not being able to organize and keep a tidy home. This fear was quite real to me—the difficulty of dealing with the avalanche of chaos that life brings in its wake. "Could I ever be grown up and lead a normal, organized life?" I wondered. The funny thing is that as I write this book at the age of seventy-three, I do have trouble remembering the dates and places of the events of my life, but most of my treasured stories are astoundingly vivid in my mind, such as seeing my mother's aghast look when she would come into my room and behold the chaos of my child's worldly goods around me. She would pick up the closest misplaced item and hurl it across the room in no particular direction to try to get me to make an effort to tidy it all up! I still create a mess around me wherever I am working—yarn, books, paints, paperwork, sketches, knitting needles, fabric scraps—but I usually know where to find what I need.

One thing I did learn in those solitary days of wandering the countryside was to look at things more intensely if I got bored or sad. There was always something to light me up— even the grayest of rocks revealed delightful hidden shades when studied closely.

Spreading my wings outside Nepenthe

By the fall of 1952, when I was nearly fifteen, I had gone as far as I could in the local one-room schoolhouse and started ninth grade at Monterey High School. It was a big change for me, as I was entering a more conventional atmosphere than I was used to. I was already a budding artist and took art very seriously. During the early years at Nepenthe, my mother and the bohemian guests at our restaurant who noticed my interest in the arts often encouraged my artistic leanings.

Many of our changing staff were also creative types. At one point, two women had come to work for us: gentle, feminine Janet with glasses, and big, broad-shouldered Anna, who had a wicked drawing line. Anna often did telling cartoons of the various characters at Nepenthe. I'd see her broad shoulders hunched over a quill-pen work, her blond ponytail quivering, a giggle escaping from the side of her mouth. A beady-eyed drawing of Dad had the caption, "There's nothing to fear now the crisis is here." She did one of Tyke, our chef's wife, with a pointed nose, squinting eyes, and a large carving knife in her bony hand. We all agreed it captured her to a tee. She watched my growing creativity and advised me intensely, "Draw every day—any object around you. A coffee cup, a piece of fruit, your hand . . ." I carried this message with me as I arrived at my teenage years, and it still rings in my ears.

While I was in ninth grade, my path toward the arts got a further boost from artists Liam O'Gallagher and Bob Rheem, who often spent time at Nepenthe. They were well-traveled, erudite men who loved the restaurant and all of us kids dancing and dressing up. Liam taught art part-time at a private school down the coast in Ojai (just south of Santa Barbara) called Happy Valley School and told my father this was the place for me. When Dad protested he couldn't afford the fees, the school offered a very good scholarship, and in the fall of 1953, off I went to boarding school to start my sophomore year there. Dad broke down in tears as he delivered me, saying it was just the sort of school he wished he had gone to.

Happy Valley School was very different from the usual conventional high schools of the 1950s. It was founded in 1946 by philosopher Jiddu Krishnamurti, author Aldous Huxley, Vassar philosophy professor Guido Ferrando, and Rosalind Rajagopal, a member of the theosophical circle. The school was built on more than 500 acres of land in the idyllic Ojai Valley that had been bought by Annie Besant many years before. Its back history is fascinating. Besant was born in London in 1847 and spent most of her young life as a prominent social activist. In middle age she turned, to the surprise of her socialist cohorts, to the spiritual, quasi-mystical beliefs of theosophy and moved to India in the 1890s.

In India, Besant became involved in establishing a Theosophical Society whose aim was to prepare humanity for the "world teacher" when he appeared again on earth. Jiddu Krishnamurti was the humble Indian boy a member of the society discovered in 1909, who was assumed to be this awaited "savior." He was tutored privately and eventually sent to Europe for an elite education, where he learned to speak several languages and mixed with the upper echelons of society. Although Krishnamurti later separated himself from the theosophists and denounced the idea that there should be a world teacher, he remained a philosopher and educationalist his whole life and close to his adoptive "mother," Annie Besant. Besant's California property passed to Krishnamurti's charge on her death in 1933. When the Happy Valley School started, followers of Krishnamurti would flock there to be near him and would work for peanuts teaching and doing administration. They shared his view of holistic education, providing children with a noncompetitive environment where they could freely develop their emotional, creative, and intellectual potential—a radical concept in 1950s America.

Because I had an operation for a hernia just as the Happy Valley term was about to start, I missed the first couple of weeks of school. All the other students had settled in and were making friends. They looked at my empty bed and empty place at the dining table and began to speculate about who this missing boy was. They finally all agreed—I was going to be a seven-foot-tall black boy called Ralf. "Ralf?" I cried when I arrived. "I hate that name!" It was even worse than Frank. For a few years, I had begun to dream of the artistic life that seemed to be opening up for me, and I started to feel that "Frank" lacked spark—it just didn't suit me. Then, when I was about fourteen, I came across a children's book called *Boy of the Pyramids* by Ruth Fosdick Jones. The book was set in ancient Egypt, and a drawing of the Egyptian teenage hero was featured on the dust jacket. It was the cover that caught my eye. The boy looked like me! Since my early grammar school days, I'd worn my hair in sort of a pudding-basin style, or "bowl cut," and this son of a pharaoh had exactly the same look. I totally identified with him. When I opened the book and read that his name was "Kaffe," I felt it fit me like a glove. Up to this point, I had never had the courage to actually change my name. Now was my chance. "If you are going to change my name, 'Kaffe' is what I want to be called," I told my classmates. That name appealed to them, and I was called that by everyone in the school thereafter. When I got home, I announced my new identity to my family, who surprisingly took to it with no fuss.

Happy Valley School was small, funky, creative, and free! We could wear whatever we liked, so we wore colorful clothes we'd find in charity shops, went barefoot, and sometimes even tucked flowers behind our ears. We were way ahead of our time with our relaxed, pre-hippie look. I loved the atmosphere, so I didn't mind at all being sent to boarding school. It was a great adventure, where I could be with people who understood me. I also considered how lucky I was not to have been sent, like my older brother Griff, to my grandfather's McCallie School in Tennessee. At the time, it was a strict military academy, like many private boys' boarding schools in those days. Griff had been involved with speeding cars and other teenage-boy misdoings before he was sent off to McCallie. Perhaps I was fortunate never to have learned to drive!

There was bound to be the exception to the rule of our colorful dressing, because everyone was encouraged to express their own personality. That exception was fifteen-year-old Joan Watts—she wore bobby socks, two-tone brown-and-white shoes, immaculate pleated plaid skirts, and neat blouse-and-sweater combos. Her hair was done up in the current high school coifed look. In short, while the rest of us ran about thumbing our noses at conventional America, she was the nonconformist Doris Day look-alike. And that's not the most surprising thing—her father was the renowned British philosopher Alan Watts, who wrote *The Spirit of Zen* in 1936. He had moved to California in 1951 and became the main popularizer of Eastern philosophy in the United States and one of the figureheads of the Beat Generation and hippies.

I recall vividly when Watts came to Happy Valley for a school lecture once. Holding up a piece of chalk he asked, "What's this?" We students offered a few suggestions, to which he added, "It could be makeup or something to stop a squeaky hinge, but it's none of these things. It's THIS!" He hurled the chalk into the midst of the audience—shocking, exciting! We loved it.

Krishnamurti and Huxley gave talks, too. Huxley's niece Olivia was one of my best friends at the school. But our favorite teacher was Ronnie Bennett, a dashing drama and dance coach who directed us in a Shakespeare play each year. The first year I was there it was *The Tempest*, in which I played Ferdinand. I loved the language and helping with costumes, sets, and makeup. Ronnie and I would have long talks in his little MG car to get away from the hubbub of the school. He had the head of a young Shakespeare with blond hair brushed back, a small goatee, twinkling blue eyes, and that director's sharp gaze. He wore handsome knitted sweaters, tweedy turtlenecks that looked excitingly timeless on him, and he could silence us rowdy teenagers in an instant with his powerful actor's voice: "NOW PEOPLE!"

I roomed with a tall, fierce-looking boy named Erik de Steiguer. He would have made a perfect Dracula with his pointed eyebrows and square jaw and was aptly cast as Prospero in *The Tempest*.

In spite of his tall, menacing looks, Erik was quite innocent and naïve. His younger brother, Kim, on the other hand, was good-looking and very precocious, leading me—without too much resistance, I must admit—to the bushes, after lights out in the dorm. Those spring and early summer nights were quite an education. Some of the brighter sparks in the senior class set up a mill to make gin, bringing juniper berries from the desert to flavor it. Many drunken nights followed that; it's a wonder we didn't all go blind. I recall the speed with which we could set up and dismantle our still in the communal showers between our dorm father's inspections. Even in the bohemian environment of Happy Valley, where we called our teachers by their first names and went barefoot to class, we still were meant to follow certain rules!

Above: My roommate Erik de Steiguer as Prospero in *The Tempest* at Happy Valley School—a boarding school I went to that nurtured creative spirit. **Overleaf:** Ukranian wedding dance at Happy Valley in 1954. I'm waving a flag, center back. Above and below are ribbons I designed in 2010 that could easily have been used on our costumes.

One of the best things I studied at Happy Valley was folk dancing. We learned the dances of many countries, but concentrated on those from Russia, especially the Ukraine. Our troupe was formed for exhibition dancing, so we practiced assiduously. The boys wore black billowing trousers and leather boots with a smocklike white shirt. We embroidered panels on the sleeves and bibs of these shirts in geometric cross-stitch patterns. Given a personal choice of colors, I chose an autumn palette of rusts, golds, and moss greens for my shirt. This was my first serious attempt at embroidery, and obviously I loved it, as I remember my color palette to this day.

The girls wore full skirts, boots, and large-sleeved blouses with similar embroidered panels on the sleeves and the fronts. In their hair they sported wreaths of flowers with long colored ribbons hanging down the back. These scarlet, cobalt, and saffron ribbons contrasted excitingly with the crisp black and white of the boys' outfits.

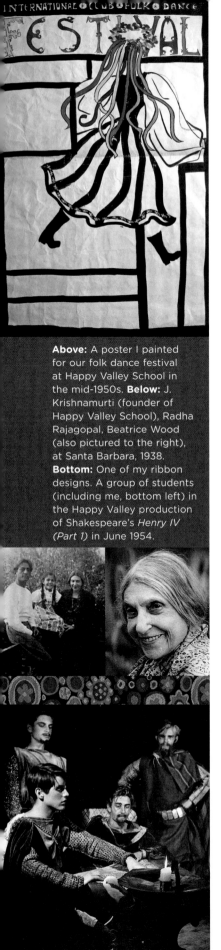

Above: A poster I painted for our folk dance festival at Happy Valley School in the mid-1950s. **Below:** J. Krishnamurti (founder of Happy Valley School), Radha Rajagopal, Beatrice Wood (also pictured to the right), at Santa Barbara, 1938. **Bottom:** One of my ribbon designs. A group of students (including me, bottom left) in the Happy Valley production of Shakespeare's *Henry IV (Part 1)* in June 1954.

As we danced to the rhythmic Ukrainian music, the skirts whirled out, and we boys did intricate, energetic leaps and squat-kicks with our Russian-style *prisyadkas*. I did *prisyadkas* so enthusiastically that I cracked the cartilage in my knees on two occasions and had to have hours of therapy to put it right. Once our troupe was in its stride, we took these polished performances onto local television a few times and into a women's prison on one occasion. The inmates developed instant crushes on us male dancers—and on some of the girls, too.

The folk dancing and the plays and modern dance we performed helped us get over our stage nerves and speak and move unselfconsciously in front of audiences. This was great preparation for facing audiences later in my career.

Classes progressed, and I learned a lot in my first year at Happy Valley.

The free atmosphere helped, as did being among a collection of bright kids from interesting, cultured families. Parents had to be fairly enlightened to send their kids to this highly unconventional school.

It was exciting to have our Shakespeare plays to design and act out, as well as music to explore. We also did our own creative writing, painting, and pottery. Talks by Krishnamurti, Alan Watts, Aldous Huxley, and architect Richard Neutra opened our minds to the vast world within each of us. There were always characters of great individuality visiting our classrooms. They demonstrated to us how rich and fulfilling a creative life could be.

The famous potter Beatrice Wood was the most vivid visitor. She was about sixty at that time and, living nearby, was a frequent presence in our lives. She wore big, colorful skirts and red leather boots. I once heard her say to someone, "I sleep in these boots!" Before she died in Ojai at 105, she wrote her autobiography, titled *I Shock Myself*, which brings her big personality to life. She was a prolific potter, creating a world of subtle but exotic color and texture like ancient Byzantine metallics. When I was at Happy Valley, I didn't know of her colorful past life. She had been an actress in Paris in the 1910s and was at one time the lover of Marcel Duchamp and, simultaneously, Henri-Pierre Roché. Roché wrote the book *Jules et Jim*, which was inspired by their bohemian threesome and later became a famous French film of the early 1960s. Before becoming a potter, Wood had also worked on the first *Dada* magazine in New York and gained the nickname "the Mama of Dada."

My French teacher at Happy Valley, Kate de Nagy, also had an accomplished artistic past. Known as Käthe von Nagy, she was born in Hungary in 1904 and became an acclaimed movie star in France and Germany before World War II, making the jump from silent films to talkies. She appeared in scores of 1920s and 1930s films.

Of course, the adults at school had an impact on me, but the strongest

memories are of my peer group. Cappy Peake was a classmate I remember fondly. A fascinating gazelle-like creature, she had huge eyes, delicate hands, and a hesitant boyish charm that really appealed to me. She could also draw like Michelangelo.

One day, Cappy took me to meet her family. Her father, Channing Peake, was a well-known artist who had studied fresco muralism with Diego Rivera. They lived on a working cattle and horse ranch just north of Santa Barbara. Their house was enchanting. Filled with Indian rugs and big wooden furniture, it had a bold western style. In pride of place in the dining room was a large canvas by the renowned Mexican painter Rufino Tamayo. It was the first time I'd seen a really famous painting in a private house.

My roommate Erik also invited me to his family home, which was in the desert. I loved the look of his parents' place—good colors, paintings, rugs in a sort of New Mexico style. One day during my visit, we took a long walk into the desert to see an abandoned dam. As we neared the base, I was amazed how huge the dam was. I felt it must be as tall as a New York skyscraper. Erik said, "I've climbed it before. Let's do it now!"

With enthusiasm, we started climbing the metal rungs embedded in the dam wall. The wall slanted away from us for about two-thirds of the way up, then became vertical. Not thinking to pace myself, I quickly pulled myself up hundreds of rungs. By the time I reached the vertical section, I felt nearly drained of energy. I realized I hadn't the courage to go back down, and Erik had already reached the top, so I struggled on. Very near the top, I suddenly ground to a halt—my arms were weak as a baby's. Because I felt helpless to move in either direction, a huge wave of terror swept through my body. "I can't move," I told Erik.

He peered down from the top rim of the dam. "You only have a few feet to go, Kaffe, then you can jump up on top," he said encouragingly.

"I can't. I haven't got the strength," I replied. Fear paralyzed me more with each small movement, and I realized I didn't care if I fell. In fact, it would have been a relief to just let go and stop straining; even holding on to the rung was just about beyond my capabilities. I tried to imagine the fall—the terrible descent waiting for the crunch of impact. The wind was howling up my legs, urging some sort of action. I could now not feel anything in my arms.

Erik talked to me quietly. "Just take a deep breath and rest, then put your hand and foot on the next rung." I realized I hadn't taken a breath in some minutes, and that was a large part of my paralyzed state. Slowly, a tiny bit of strength returned to my useless hands, and I took the next rung. Somehow, with Erik's encouragement, I got my leaden body up over the edge.

That scene has played in my mind many times as I enter some dangerous episode in my life that makes me feel helplessly vulnerable. "I survived that dam," I say, "and somehow I'll get through this."

I spent my junior year at Happy Valley as well and enjoyed it just as much as my first year there. Although I missed out on some of the goings-on at our family restaurant during these two years of boarding, I still went home for holidays and summer vacation. One year Erik visited me at Big Sur, and we spent the summer bussing tables and peeling potatoes for the restaurant. We'd had many laughs together, but one of the best ever was after a near disaster one busy night in the restaurant. We were clearing a large party's dishes away, and I was holding a tray as Erik placed the used plates and glasses on it. The guests at the table were at that drunken stage where everything anyone said evoked roars of laughter and loud responses. Eager to get away from them quickly, I rested the edge of the tray on something and hurriedly helped Erik pile it high. Suddenly, I wondered what the tray was resting on. Looking down into the candlelit shadows, I saw it was resting on a poor woman's shoulder. In her inebriated state, she didn't seem to notice. But she must have wondered why she was sinking lower in her chair. I gently lifted the tray and Erik and I rushed back into the kitchen, where we both exploded with laughter.

After our long hours working, at each night's end Erik and I would join other dancers on the terrace to release wound-up energy, and I would wonder if Erik would hook up with any of my sisters. That didn't come to pass.

My Russian folk-dancing lessons at Happy Valley were a boon to Nepenthe. The simple dances were wonderfully easy to teach to guests in the restaurant. This added to their enjoyment, as they could join in for a memorable night of after-dinner dancing under the stars in Big Sur. Whatever the staff were doing on the property, every one of us who knew the dances would run to the terrace when we heard the music start up. It was such a seductive sound. I loved seeing the salad chef in his apron, one of the bartenders, and the dishwasher all joining hands with us kids to do a rhythmic line dance from Israel, the Balkans, or Greece. A favorite by the early 1960s was a lilting Greek dance to the song "Never on Sunday" from one of the epic films of that era.

For a spell during the mid-1950s, the salad chef at Nepenthe was a young actor from Oregon named Lewis Perkins. This lighthearted fellow with a large head and delicious sense of humor was a big influence on my development. A typical teenager, I had a tendency to brood over perceived problems and sulk if I didn't get my way or was criticized (which was often, it seemed, in those developing days). Lewis took everything in his stride, had a wonderful use of language, and could affect a fruity, deep voice to quote a poem or sing a phrase of opera or a popular song to lighten any tense moments.

This incident illustrates Lewis to a tee: My father was being bombastic (a regular occurrence), stressing about something in the running of the restaurant and directing his tirade at Lewis. Dad's words, as usual, were delivered in a powerful, bullying tone. When he stopped to draw a breath, Lewis, who was standing in front of a large bed that served as a couch in our living room, cried out in a plaintive voice, "Kiss me!" I was shocked, and frightened how macho Dad would take this cheeky invite. For a moment he scowled in astonishment, then burst out laughing and fell against Lewis so they both took a tumble onto the couch. It was just the sort of drama my father actually loved and why he fit in so well with Big Sur's extrovert characters.

The main thing I remember about Lewis was that he often carried about a bag of knitting and would be working on a cardigan or jumper of many colors. Some of his yarn was retrieved from unraveled sweaters from the Goodwill store, and he called his concoctions "dump sweaters." I have vivid recollections of broad stripes of teal, wine, mustard, and pink. This was the first knitting that attracted my attention and made me start to think about taking up needles. My mother knit solid-colored things that I took hardly any notice of, but Lewis's creations were tantalizing. It would be nearly twenty years before I would actually learn to knit.

Senior year at Monterey High School

As much as I loved Happy Valley, it strengthened me with so much belief in myself that I became curious to see what I could get out of the ordinary Monterey High with my newfound self-esteem. And, indeed, it was much better for me when I returned there for my senior year. Feeling more grown up at seventeen, I got to know my teachers much better than I had in my freshman year and was able to decorate for parties at the school and have

Opposite: The Fassett family poses on the bleachers of Nepenthe's terrace, around 1952, with our log cabin home above.

37

really meaningful talks with my peers. I also liked the ethnic mix of Portuguese fishermen's kids, Mexicans, and lots of black kids with their energy and rhythm and quirky sense of style. My best friends were Francis Dauer, a short Japanese boy who had a German mother, and Vito Danis, a tall, handsome guy from Lithuania.

Inspired by the artists I had met at Nepenthe and Happy Valley, I continued to wear as much color as I could find when I returned to Monterey High. I still wore secondhand charity-store finds, but I also splashed out on a new pair of brilliant orange corduroys. I dyed my white tennis shoes bright pink to go with them and found a kelly-green sweater to complete the outfit. I was a total freak at our conventional school—but what else was new?

My teachers there were much straighter in appearance than those relaxed Happy Valley folk, but I found some of them to be very creative under their conventional clothes and short haircuts. Our English teacher surprised us all one day as we stumbled into his class in our usual sleepy, bored state. The room was in darkness with a few candles burning around a little open coffin in the middle of the room. As we came up to look in, sad funeral music cast a spell on us. In the little silk-lined coffin lay the huge silhouette of a comma cut out of black paper. As we all looked on in puzzlement, our teacher intoned mournfully, "This is the death of the comma." He then handed out our latest essays, in which there was universal disregard for the poor comma in our writing. I'm probably not the only student who has never forgotten this class.

My parents continued in their sometimes-stormy relationship throughout my high school years. I remember especially when Germaine Maiden moved to Nepenthe. She and her husband, architect Rowan Maiden, had become friends with my mother and father when Rowan designed Nepenthe. Germaine had, in fact, become Mom's closest confidante. She had met Rowan when he was working with Frank Lloyd Wright at Taliesin, where her father was Wright's garden designer. Germaine was a real beauty, with hair worn like someone's from Chopin's age—pulled back with large, attractive curls hanging down to frame her beautiful, chiseled face and green eyes. She moved and spoke in a dreamy, always-enthusiastic way. I don't ever recall her being angry or down. Full skirts were the rage then, and she wore hers with panache.

Like all the creative people in our lives, Rowan and Germaine lived on meager earnings but seemed to make the most of it. They were building a house on Huckleberry Hill near Monterey, and when they were nearing completion, Germaine decided to throw herself a party to celebrate years of living on a building site finally coming to fruition. She baked wonderful food all day, cleaned, and decorated. When the first guest arrived—a handsome writer friend—they shared a glass of white wine and a glorious waltz. After that, she said, "I'll just have a little rest before the party. If anyone else comes, please let them in." When she woke, the party was over, the food and wine were devoured, and she realized she had totally missed the festivities. Her response to the fact that no one thought to wake her resulted in a rare instance of Germaine losing her temper.

The year Rowan was accidentally killed, falling from a roof, Germaine moved to Nepenthe. She worked as a hostess and waitress in the restaurant and shared a room in the log house with her three children. All of us Fassett kids benefited from her sunny spirit in our lives, but, unfortunately, so did Dad. It was a double blow to Mom when my father had a very public fling with Germaine. He took Mom's best friend and confidante off on trips where they would spare no expense to pleasure themselves. This was especially galling for my mother, as she was, as always, trying to make ends meet raising us, and the restaurant still had to borrow money during the winter months to tide us over while it was closed.

The mid-1950s saw Nepenthe's popularity growing. It was by then open for lunch as well as dinner. Both *Architectural Forum* and *Arts & Architecture* had featured photos of the restaurant in 1950, which alerted a wider audience to its existence. Mom's love of vibrant color served to humanize the dark line of modern architecture. She scattered cushions covered in brightly colored burlap along the redwood benches, chose canvas director's chairs in many colors, and selected dinner and salad plates in a multitoned palette.

My parents had made the place more and more enjoyable for the guests, creating a homey yet exciting center for Big Sur. The homeyness came from our large family working in the restaurant and the staff all acting like welcoming hosts. The excitement came from the bohemian atmosphere of the family, staff, and guests alike, as well as the special events. As much as Dad protested that he knew nothing about art, he was quite an entrepreneur, putting on concerts, poetry readings, and dance evenings on the restaurant terrace. One of my favorite performances was a harpsichord recital played with great style and verve by an attractive woman. I visited her one day in her house down the coast when I was about sixteen. We talked all day about art and life. I told her I loved Scarlatti, as he was one of the few piano composers I'd noticed and learned the name of at that age.

At the next concert she gave at Nepenthe, she played a Scarlatti piece, which I recognized and loved. When I told her afterward how much I had enjoyed it, she said, "Yes, that was especially for you, Kaffe." I was shocked and deeply thrilled—a gawky teenage kid being honored by a brilliant, beautiful performer. The present I got from that unexpected acknowledgment stayed with me for years.

On nights when no special events were staged, we played folk music and every sort of dance music from rock and roll (Elvis Presley hit our world with a bang at this time) to dreamy Glenn Miller tunes. To this day, if I hear Glenn Miller, I'm transported back to warm nights of slow dancing on the terrace, with cocktail glasses clinking in the background.

As well as artists and writers, Nepenthe also drew in the Beats and the Hollywood set. There was always a frisson running through the restaurant when a celebrity was dining there. From the early years, I recall seeing Ramón Novarro, Gloria Swanson, and Steve McQueen. Ted Turner and Jane Fonda were frequent visitors. I first met Jane at Nepenthe when we were both nineteen. After a wild night of dancing, she complimented me on my movement. I was a total fan of her father's films. And recently, reading her story, I realized we were the same age, having parallel lives all these years. Her acting has always involved my full attention, so I return her early compliment.

On certain memorable occasions, my parents would throw private parties in the winter months. The one I'll never forget was held for Olivia De Havilland in the 1950s. We heard the film star was visiting Big Sur and was looking forward to experiencing the great Nepenthe she had heard so much about. Mom said, "We must not disappoint her. Let's invite everyone on the coast for a party in her honor." Many local people had no idea who this Olivia was, but entered the spirit of the evening—dancing and having a glorious time. When I ran into her ten years later at a New York party, her eyes glowed with excitement recalling that evening. Those magical times at the house of no sorrow are not easy to forget.

The Nepenthe bleachers with the cushions Mom collected to add color and comfort. The bleachers are a great vantage point to view the dancing or special events on the restaurant terrace.

chapter two

1956–1964

Striking Out
On My Own

Above, from left: My favorite drawing of my good friend Charles Heim, who opened so many doors for me as an artist. My first oil painting, done when I was attending the School of the Museum of Fine Arts in Boston, in 1958. My wash drawing of a Victorian building in San Francisco, from the early sixties right before I left for England. Me putting on clown makeup at a Big Sur beach around the same period. **Opposite:** Making myself at home in actor Alvin Epstein's apartment in New York in 1960, with my papier-mâché mirror in the background.

After finishing high school in the summer of 1956, I was ready to strike out on my own and excited by the prospect of leaving my California comfort zone. My mother's stories of her Italian adventures and all those visitors from Europe to Nepenthe made me yearn to explore that old world, where I saw myself one day dancing in the streets in bright costumes and creating wonderful works of art or theater. On my way to that dream, I first studied acting at a performing arts camp in Colorado, then took a trip to explore Paris and Rome for a few months, and finally went to study fine art in Boston and New York. These East Coast cities were as exotic to me as Europe, and I soaked up everything they had to offer. Deciding where to focus my scattered energy and creativity was difficult at first. When I saw *Auntie Mame* in New York and heard Rosalind Russell say, "Life is a banquet, but most poor sons of bitches are starving to death," I wholeheartedly agreed. I was deliriously tasting every dish that life presented!

Pursuing Acting
and Traveling to Europe

My early experiences in theater productions—learning those
Shakespeare lines from *The Tempest* and *Henry IV* at Happy Valley—made me think
I might be a budding actor. During my last year at Monterey High School, I'd seen the
Perry-Mansfield Performing Arts School do an amazing dance performance to Beethoven's
Pastoral Symphony and longed to be up on the stage and part of that expressive world.
A few months after that, Mom arranged for me to take classes at Perry-Mansfield in
Steamboat Springs, Colorado, for the summer following my graduation. I took to it as easily
as I did to Happy Valley School. There I was among a group of seriously talented young
actors and dancers, and it was thrilling to wake each morning looking forward to rehearsals
and exercise classes with like-minded students from all over the country. My days at Perry-
Mansfield became a powerful part of my education.

The school had a fantastic reputation. The actress Julie Harris had attended Perry-
Mansfield some years before, and their new theater was named after her. The teachers were
the big draw. The great modern dancer Helen Tamiris, who had choreographed dances
for *Show Boat* and other famous Broadway shows, was teaching and directing a dance
production when I was there. She used Stravinsky's *Rite of Spring* and set the action on the
streets of New York. The same age as I was, Dustin Hoffman was studying there at the time
as well, bringing his distinctive swagger to the proceedings. I remember all of us thinking,
what a pity such a talented guy will never make it. We thought him too short and not
handsome enough. Funny how he has gotten more attractive as his immense talent proves
itself in film after film.

As I was saying good-bye to Helen at the end of her time teaching us, I said, "I think
I'll move up to the intermediate class in dancing next week."

"Don't fool yourself, Kaffe," she said. "I think you should stick to your artwork." I was
thunderstruck, but bowed to her insight. We had worked closely together for weeks, and
somehow art didn't seem so bad if I was lacking in the dance department, which I could see
was a very hard life.

Because I was tall and had a certain look, I was cast as the lead in the play the school
produced that summer. I was terrible. I remember Dustin quipping, "Kaffe couldn't act his
way out of a wet paper bag."

When I was back in Big Sur that fall, after acting camp, a Hollywood writer
friend convinced me to go have a screen test. My lack of success at Perry-Mansfield didn't
really deter me. Dad contacted his uncle Stan, who was chairman of the board of directors
of Paramount Pictures at that time, so he could arrange everything for me. During the trip

Opposite: A drawing I did
of artist Alba Heywood, my
mentor in Big Sur, who I
studied with in 1961 and 1962.

down to Hollywood, my writer friend regaled me with horror stories of the hardship involved in an actor's life—beginning with getting up at 4 a.m. every day to go in and be made up. He went on to explain how prescribed your life becomes as you get famous, and how everyone watches every detail of your life to glean juicy slip-ups for gossip columns. It seemed less and less glam. When I got a coach and started learning a script to do my screen test, my nerves set in, and I was quite relieved when Uncle Stan informed me I should start at the bottom and work up. He offered me a job in the mailroom at the studios. "That's it?" I asked myself, my dream of stardom evaporating before my eyes. "I am out of here if that's all my connections afford me."

From L.A. I went to stay with my father's sister, my aunt Katy, in Laguna Beach. To earn my crust, I gave children art lessons and taught them yoga classes on the beach. The months seemed to pass aimlessly. Feeling very adolescent and at a loss, I suddenly decided to join the army. God knows why. I suppose I needed structure and couldn't manage it myself.

When I informed my dad that I had joined the army, he had an unexpected reaction. "I can't bear to think of you in the army," he said. "If you can get out of it, I'll send you to Europe." I couldn't believe it! I skipped off to the army board and begged to be let go. "I have a chance to study in Europe," I lied. Thank God my interview was conducted by two older women who said, "We approve of education and travel. We will see what we can do."

The next month, October 1956, I was off to New York to board a Holland America ocean liner to sail to France. It was my first real trip out of the West, and New York City was a thrilling shock to the system. First of all, there were the tight rows of houses, the crowds of well-dressed people, the shops and museums! Buses, subway trains. Being able to transport myself quickly and cheaply around a dense city was ecstasy!

When I first hit New York, I devoured it with every sense in my country boy being. The Museum of Modern Art was a must on my list. I rushed through it, seeing Picassos, Matisses, and many famous Impressionists. These paintings were so familiar that they were like wallpaper to me, as I'd studied them all in books and magazines in Big Sur. My mother had always cut out artwork from periodicals and put them in scrapbooks for us. However, one large painting stopped me in my tracks and made me halt my art rush. It was about seven feet square and featured a tree that filled the canvas with its gnarled roots and branches. Heads and bodies of children were emerging from the shadows created by the foliage in the tree. As I studied it, I realized the tree was actually a gigantic hand with veins running up the back of the hand and out along the fingers. (It wasn't until I reached Rome that I would find out who painted this intriguing canvas.)

I took in as many tourist stops as I could fit in. I took a boat trip to the Statue of Liberty (in those days you could go climb up into her crown), went up to the top of the Empire State Building, and to many more museums.

Going to the theater was also a treat. A Polish Jew called Louis Golubovsky, whom I met walking in Central Park, liked my enthusiasm and took me to the shows he had seen and loved. We saw all the exciting productions in that 1950s era. The musical *Bells Are Ringing* with Judy Holliday is the sparkler that remains with me.

I was staying on the West Side with my "aunt," Helen Kelly Rand. We always called her our aunt, but the actual family connection was that her daughter was married to Uncle Stan's son Nixon Griffis, who managed Brentano's bookstore for him. Helen ran a private bar called the Sun-Up Club, which employed high-class ladies to entertain tired-out businessmen after hours. She was a Mae West sort of character—a big Irish woman with blond hair piled up high and a large crimson mouth. She dressed in black lace and a mink stole and often sported a voluptuous purple orchid. Aunt Helen would take me to any film or play I wanted to see, and then sleep through the performance at my side.

When it was time to board the ship to Europe, I could hardly contain myself. If New York was amazing, think what Europe would be! Could my pulsating heart take the strain? During the days it took to cross the Atlantic, I got to know several fellow passengers quite well. One of them was a sensitive writer with whom I had many philosophical talks on the breezy decks or over a brandy before retiring. Then I caught the eye of a dashing Frenchman—tall, handsome, with bedroom eyes. We ended up in his room, and he asked why I was always seen talking to the writer. "He is very interesting," I explained.

"He should have been made into a lampshade," my Frenchman murmured under his breath. It was my first encounter with anti-Semitism, and I couldn't understand what he meant. When I told the writer later, he explained with a pained expression, "There are people in this world who feel we Jews should not be allowed to live." I was in a state of shock and avoided the anti-Semite for the duration of the trip.

After the boat landed, my first stop was Paris. When I got there, I was thrilled but very nervous, being so new to this world. I had the name of a good inexpensive hotel, which I went to and settled into a room. What a miserable night that was! My naïve fear of being robbed in my sleep made me put my camera, passport, and wallet under my pillow, leading to a very restless, lumpy night.

When I ventured into the Paris streets, the smells and sights got right under my skin. What struck me most was the relaxed humanness of it all. I felt as if I were in Big Sur, yet this was a big, important city in Europe. The feeling was so strong that the many times I've returned to Paris, I get the same frisson, and powerful sense memories of those first impressions return.

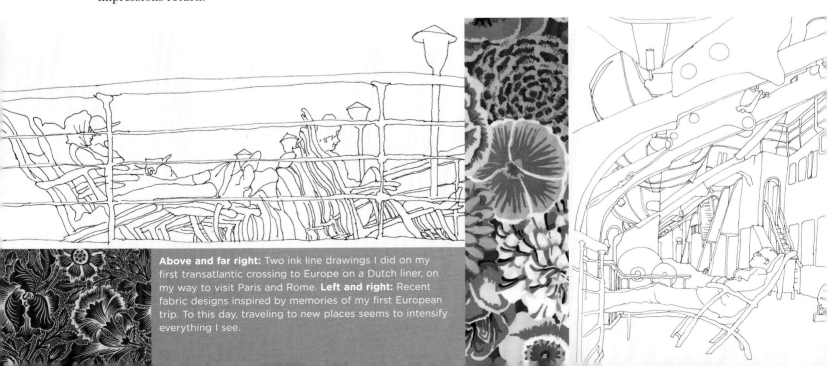

Above and far right: Two ink line drawings I did on my first transatlantic crossing to Europe on a Dutch liner, on my way to visit Paris and Rome. **Left and right:** Recent fabric designs inspired by memories of my first European trip. To this day, traveling to new places seems to intensify everything I see.

Right: Odilon Redon's painting *Bouquet of Wild Flowers*. I saw a show of his work in Paris when I was 18, and his glorious use of color has fed me ever since. **Above and below:** My knitting, needlepoint, rag rugs, wall painting, and fabric prints inspired by Redon's brilliant, smoldering colors.

I found a small hotel on Rue des Saints-Pères called Rive Gauche and moved there. It was surrounded by workingmen's cafés, where all the artists ate, among them American and English expats. Meals were delicious, jolly, and lingered over with stimulating conversations. The red-and-white-checkered tablecloths, loaves of chewy bread, carafes of good inexpensive wine, and warmhearted but no-nonsense waitresses bustling about made each meal memorable.

Before I left Paris, I went to see a museum exhibition of the work of the mystic artist Odilon Redon. It introduced me to one of my first huge color influences. This painter, whom I'd never heard of, had an electric effect on my senses that has stayed with me all my life. I think it's to do with the rich, tinted mists he creates around his studies of figures, shells, and, best of all, richly colored flowers that pierce my imagination so deeply. Every time I study Redon's work, even in bad repros, I'm moved to a vibrant world where color is tangible. I heard that Redon painted almost-dead flowers so their color would be more intense.

The next stop on my European tour was Italy. Our family friend ZEV was in Rome, and I was to meet him and his wife, Gertrude, there. What a relief to have them to show me around. The train ride from cold winter Paris to the sunny south was wonderful. When we crossed the border into Italy, people started singing as they felt the sun.

ZEV and Gertrude were staying in artist and stage designer Eugene Berman's flat off the Piazza Navona, and I joined them there. On my second night, they gave a dinner party for me, and Gertrude told me a very famous Russian painter was coming to the dinner. "He has work in the Museum of Modern Art," she said.

"Oh, damn!" I said. "I'm afraid I rushed through that place and can only recall one work. It was a big hand that looked like a tree with baby faces in it."

She smiled and replied, "Tell our guest that. It will interest him." When I was introduced to Pavel Tchelitchew that night, I told him the only work I'd been stopped by was this tree painting. He, too, smiled—it was his 1942 painting called *Hide and Seek*.

ZEV's delicious, zany humor was a tonic. He turned out to be a fantastic guide, knowing weird and wonderful little shops, the great museums, and lesser-known ones. We took side trips to Pompeii and other places. ZEV also knew good, inexpensive restaurants and made up hilarious stories about the statues and paintings we'd see on our tours. I began to feel so at home there, especially when I met loads of people I wanted to get to know better. Not wanting to leave, I wrote to Dad, asking for more money so I could stay on in Rome. His blunt refusal was a shock. That was a good lesson to learn early on—make your own money so you can do as you please, not be controlled by someone in charge of the purse.

Passing through New York on my way home to Big Sur, I went to a fabulous Christmas party given by Leo Lerman, the famous magazine editor who worked for Condé Nast, among others. Leo was one of the most delightful characters I met in a city crammed with colorful people. He had an unpompous self-confidence and a very original eye for the exotic. The Christmas tree he decorated for the party made such a vivid impression on me that it was foremost in my mind when I was asked to decorate the tree at the Victoria and Albert Museum in London fifty years later. All over his tree, Leo had placed lacy cut-paper fans in many sizes, ranging from about fourteen inches across up to very tiny at the top of the tree; they were virginal white with touches of bright color—a veritable wedding cake!

A Christmas tree I decorated with cloth-covered fans for the Victoria and Albert Museum in London in 2005, inspired by a tree I saw at a party given by Leo Lerman in New York in the 1950s. A large team of volunteers spent six months creating the 600 fans. Mine were in saturated colors, but Leo's fans were pure white with light touches of color.

Leo's legendary parties were always full of creative types—artists, writers, musicians—so the company was stimulating. At one of them, a jolly black man caught my eye and said, "Hello, I'm Louis Armstrong." A few nights later, I was walking near Radio City Music Hall when I heard a pure trumpet solo coming from a dressing room window. As I stopped to listen, an African American man on the street looked up and murmured, "That's Satchmo!" As I basked in the golden sound, I thought New York was a magical city.

Starting life as a young artist on the East Coast

After my second brief stay in New York, I went back to Big Sur. I was nineteen and pretty much determined to continue my artwork and give up my misplaced acting ambitions. I soon met poet and playwright Lyon Phelps, who was then in his mid-thirties. He was in California visiting his parents on Partington Ridge. Lyon's father had been a missionary and scholar in China for thirty years, so Lyon spoke Chinese and was very well read. We talked books, and about Europe and the East Coast, where he spent most of his time.

Although Lyon was a bit of a dreamer, he had practical advice for me—he convinced me to move East and go to art college. We went to New York together and found an apartment there. I look back on it as a very exciting time. Lyon introduced me to painters like Larry Rivers, and poets and writers such as Frank O'Hara and his lover, Joe LeSueur. It was an education for me being around bright, ambitious artists and writers. I was growing up culturally and socially. At one stage, Lyon took me to a one-night-only performance of his play *The Gospel Witch*, which was on in a prominent New York theater. I had a martini before the play, ensuring I slept soundly through it. Another lesson: Don't drink before the theater.

Because Lyon had gone to Harvard, he was always interested in what was happening in Boston and Cambridge and knew what the area had to offer. He encouraged me to apply for a scholarship to the School of the Museum of Fine Arts in Boston, which I did, and I received a generous one. We moved to a little house near the school.

I adored Boston. With the cobbled streets on historic Beacon Hill, it felt older than New York. It also moved at a slower pace, and had shops and coffeehouses everywhere. People seemed to live relaxed lives. Houses full of paintings, books, and colorful old carpets stimulated my greedy eyes. At one dinner party hosted by a very posh friend of Lyon's, I got talking to a handsome woman about fifty. When I told her I was interested in portrait painting, she asked, "How do you get a likeness?" I held forth for the whole evening about my experiences painting my family and friends. When she left, I asked my hostess, "Who was that very nice lady who listened so attentively?"

"Oh, she is the best portrait painter in Boston!" Mental note: must ask questions before pontificating next time!

Lyon became the theater and film critic for the *Boston Globe*, and we attended many previews of films and plays. I loved the small poetry readings and student productions, as well as the glamorous first nights of big pre-Broadway shows.

Meanwhile, my classes at the Museum School progressed. In the beginning, I learned as much from fellow students as from the instructors. But after about three months there, when we started seriously studying the color wheel, I rebelled. Color is instinctive, I told myself. I didn't want to dissect it in a scientific way, so I decided to withdraw and teach myself. The school was very disappointed at my giving up, as I was a scholarship student they had high hopes for. My father's reaction was not unexpected. He told me, "If you don't finish college, you'll be a dishwasher the rest of your life."

Nonetheless, I was determined to make progress as an artist. I drew every day and painted as much as I could on my own. Needing more room in my little rented house, I took a hammer to a dividing wall between the living room and a tiny side bedroom. That gave me more room and extra light from the bedroom window. The poor landlord nearly dropped dead when he came to check the flat, screaming, "Where is my wall?" I handed him a sack full of plaster dust and sticks. How do we get so brazen and insensitive in our ignorant youth? I blanch to think of scenes like this now. I don't know why we weren't kicked out onto the street immediately.

One day during the beginning of our time in Boston, Lyon got word that a great friend, the folk singer Odetta, was coming to town to give a concert. I was amazed when I heard Lyon had offered her a place to stay while she was in Boston. Our abode consisted of a tiny kitchen, three cramped rooms, and no proper bathroom. We just washed at the kitchen sink.

Lyon was reviewing a film, so I was sent to attend Odetta's concert and bring her back to our place afterward. I will never forget her powerful performance. It was totally engrossing. Her face was full of pathos, her voice as deep as Paul Robeson's as she sang spirituals to her gutsy guitar. The audience went wild. Odetta's expressive voice had captivated them. It's no wonder that she soon became known as the queen of American folk music, inspiring Joan Baez, Bob Dylan, and Janis Joplin.

The powerful singer Odetta, whom I met in the late 1950s when I was in art school in Boston. She stayed overnight at the apartment Lyon Phelps and I shared.

After the concert, I went backstage to find Odetta surrounded by fans five or six layers deep. "How will I compete with all this to get to her to come home with me?" I wondered. As I stood behind her at the edge of the enthusiastic crowd, a long black arm appeared through the throng and grabbed my hand. She remembered meeting me the year before with Lyon.

My abiding image of Odetta's stay was seeing her in a little nightdress, washing at our humble kitchen sink. Although she was much younger than my mother, she was like her in many ways—large, shy, talented, and full of love and passion. I remember Odetta's laugh when Lyon played her a recording of Edith Sitwell reading her poem series *Façade*, and it came to the part about Negresses. When she showed us pictures of her new brawny boyfriend, she said, "Can you imagine me with this handsome guy? Sure wasn't looking for someone that handsome. I always thought, who needs it?"

A couple I got to know very well during my Boston years were the Cohens. They lived in Cambridge in a huge Victorian family house with a massive garden. Bobbie was a photographer and Freddy an architect. They had three young children who were growing up fast, and Bobbie longed for a new baby to cuddle. She was thin and hyper with a nervous laugh. Wanting a mural to entertain her kids in the living room, which they used as a big playroom, Bobbie commissioned me.

I devised a highly detailed fantasy of clown figures roaming a strange land and worked laboriously on my vision with small brushes. It was my first proper mural, and I loved doing it. Not knowing how to price my work, I charged far too little. It's hard to think about the mural now, because after I worked months and months to complete the piece, a psychiatrist friend commented to Bobbie that she thought it would give the kids nightmares. The next time I visited the Cohens, the walls were painted white. All trace of my work was gone! I should have charged more than five dollars per eight-foot square panel, I told myself, then she might have valued it. Unfortunately, there are no photos of the mural. It was the late 1950s, and we were less camera-happy in those days.

While I was still working on the mural, Lyon and I were looking for a house in a run-down (therefore cheap) part of Boston. I found an area of the city called Roxbury that really appealed to me. In the late 1950s, Roxbury was full of wonderful rows of old multicolored Victorians in various states of disrepair. One particular stone house with a rather Swiss-type green roof caught my eye. I asked a little boy in the street if anyone lived there. "Just a minute, I'll see," he said. And picking up a rock, he threw it through the window. "Nope. No one's there," he said.

I learned that the house had been foreclosed by the bank, which was willing to sell it for $3,000. It had four stories and eleven garages that could be rented out, so was a steal. I called Dad, begging for finance to purchase this bargain. "Don't touch it—it's a bad deal," said my adventurous father. So I raised the money from a friend and we moved in.

Making the house habitable was a struggle, to be sure. Fortunately for us, however, a large part of nearby Boston was being torn down to make space for a whole new spate of modern development. We were somehow given carte blanche to wander about the demolition sites, helping ourselves to whatever we could salvage. Sinks, wiring, doors, windows, pipes—all covered in the dust of ages—made it possible to start patching up Daimon's Lair, our name for our new house. Lyon was very well versed in the classics, so I'm sure he called our house Daimon's Lair thinking of the guardian angel or guiding spirit of the Greeks. (Bobbie, on the other hand, called it Cold Comfort Farm after Stella Gibbons's hilarious comic novel of the 1930s.)

Once settled in our Roxbury house, I finally had generous space for a studio, so I started working like mad on a series of still lifes of large bowls, platters, and cups. One of them was hanging in our living room when my father flew in for a visit and to view the "bad investment." He stood back in shock when he saw the canvas. "That's the sort of painting people would put on their walls!" he gasped in amazement. The poor man had been raised with all of us kids producing little artworks that everyone cooed over, but he never really got it—that any of us would ever take art up seriously was beyond his reckoning. As for the house, he was glad I was settled but didn't rate the neighborhood.

Dad would have been more impressed by the manor house my friend Eduardo took me to visit while I lived in Boston. I had met garden and interior designer Eduardo Tirella in California a few years earlier. For a while, he had shared a house with dress designer Edmund Kara in Laurel Canyon near Hollywood, then they both moved to Big Sur when Dad decided to rent them a property near the restaurant, which he had just acquired for its water rights.

Eduardo used to drop by Daimon's Lair from time to time when he was in the area for jobs. For the last few years, he had been working for tobacco heiress Doris Duke. Doris was then one of the wealthiest women in the world, spoke nine languages, and devoted her time to the arts, philanthropy, and improving her many grand houses and gardens. Eduardo collaborated with her on decorating several of her homes and was, among other things, designing the gardens of the world for her family estate, Duke Gardens, in New Jersey.

At one point, Doris sent her private plane to fetch me and take me to meet them at her other family estate on the ocean in Newport, Rhode Island, called Rough Point. It was a stormy night, but my flight got through. Eduardo and Doris were held up in New York and would come in the next day. I wandered around alone in the huge eighty-five-room mansion—it was vast with large, high-ceilinged rooms. Later, I ate dinner on a long antique table, waited on by her staff—very lonely and strange. I tried to imagine what it would be like to own this and her other houses in Hawaii and L.A.

When Doris and Eduardo arrived, the house came alive—dogs, music, conversation. Eduardo told me that as soon as Doris had inherited the house from her mother, she immediately had the dark wood-paneled walls painted white—shades of Miss Havisham when Pip pulled the heavy curtain down. Eduardo lit a chandelier at one end of the house, and as we walked through the many rooms to the other end, he turned out lights so we could look back through a dozen rooms and see the light shining like a candle in the far cavelike distance.

Eduardo adored the gardens he was working on there and showed me through the ones done and in construction. We wandered from there out onto a little beach near the house, and I smoked my first pot, seeing with heightened vision the little plants on colored stony cliffs as Eduardo impressed on me his love for the natural world.

Doris allowed me free run of the house to paint anything I wanted, so I set up my easel in a corner of the enormous kitchen and did a study of brown and white dishes and fruit. She quipped to Eduardo, "He has a pick of all the fabulous European antiques I have collected, and he chooses the kitchen bowls!" I also painted a huge bouquet of flowers Eduardo had gathered from Doris's garden.

In the evenings, Doris would practice her singing. Her dream was to be a big jazz singer. She had a very high voice that was barely audible, but felt hard done that no one in the industry would give her a chance to perform. She was convinced she wasn't getting that break because they thought she didn't need the work.

Eduardo told me he grew up in New Jersey, and his family would occasionally drive past the great walls of the Duke house and vast gardens nearby. He used to wonder wistfully what it would be like to be in there and longed to have a look. And that little boy Eduardo found himself years later on the other side of the wall becoming an indispensable part of Doris Duke's life.

This reminds me of my friend Gayle Ortiz, whom I met years later in California. She used to pass a house she loved in her neighborhood and would often put her hands on the gates and say, "One day you will be mine!" When it came on the market unexpectedly years later, she was first in line and bought it. So those youthful dreams and yearning can materialize. Gail now has a great bakery near Monterey in Capitola and has filled her house with her brilliant mosaics. After one of the area's earthquakes, she circulated the neighborhood asking, "Any breakages?" I learned mosaic techniques from her and now often find myself on the scrounge, just like her.

1: My painting of Doris Duke's Rough Point kitchen, done in the late 1950s. "He has the pick of all my fabulous antiques, and he paints the kitchen bowls," she commented. **2:** The sprawling Duke mansion, Rough Point, in Newport, Rhode Island, which I visited with Duke's garden designer Eduardo Tirella. **3:** A pen drawing I did of Eduardo sitting under one of his sumptuous flower arrangements at Doris Duke's home. **4:** A young Doris Duke in a fetching fur outfit. **5, 6, 7, 8:** My fabric designs echo the magical palette of French artist Pierre Bonnard's shimmering painting. **9:** Bonnard's *Le Déjeuner*, 1932. This incandescent Bonnard convinced me that color was the way to go in my own work.

Because Lyon was a critic for the *Boston Globe*, my life in Boston was peppered with many invitations to interesting cultural events—music, plays, exhibitions. One of the most exciting concerts I was lucky enough to happen upon was the first Newport Folk Festival in Newport, Rhode Island, in July 1959. It was when I first heard Joan Baez. Folk singer Bob Gibson was scheduled to do a fifteen-minute performance, and he gave up half his time to introduce a new talent he had come across. Out stepped a barefoot eighteen-year-old girl with long black hair in a homespun dress, a virtual unknown to most of the audience. She opened her throat and made history.

In 1960, after a few years in the Roxbury house, I realized my heart wasn't in the reconstruction side of things, and that Lyon and I would never really finish it to any comfortable standard. Lyon wanted to write, and I wanted to paint, so we never quite focused on the task at hand. After I decided to leave Boston and move to the more artistically vibrant New York, Lyon stayed on in Daimon's Lair for a while. But eventually we sold the place for $8,000, which made our poor artist buyer happy, and we were glad to move on. My father was probably right that it wasn't a particularly wise long-term investment. When I went back to Boston some years after selling the house and told a taxi driver I wanted to go see it, he said, "Hope you aren't planning to stay there on your own. It's not safe." Unfortunately, by the late 1960s, Roxbury had become famous for its race riots.

Just before I left Daimon's Lair to live in New York in 1960, I decided to take mescaline with Lyon. It wasn't quite the swinging sixties, but drug taking was starting to enter the bohemian world. We had all read *The Doors of Perception* written by Aldous Huxley in 1954. Lyon and I were very curious to enter that inner world, yet very nervous because of all the horror stories we had heard of people becoming addicted to heavier drugs or hitting terrible depths of depression or even dying.

We cleared our calendar, and on a warm summer morning, with a friend to sit with us for the day, we dropped our pills. What followed is difficult to put into words, but the main impression left in me was that everything in life is deeply significant and beautiful if we experience it with an open enough perception. It's a tall order with our constantly chattering minds full of conditioned reflexes and attitudes. I remember seeing two street boys talking to each other on a corner. I didn't hear their conversation, but just watched their bodies as they talked. The total affection and connection was clear to see, yet I'm sure they were ordinary heterosexual guys. At one point, I was leaning out the window watching the light on the leaves of the tree next to our house when I felt our sitter grab me back into the room. He was sure I'd let myself sail down through those leaves, and I felt no sense of danger, so I am glad he rescued me. Later, I thought a lot about that experience and decided it was worth taking time to let the significant beauty in the world around me surface, as I knew it would if I gave it that time. Drugs never interested me again after just a couple of experiments like this.

Lyon had reviewed a series of Shakespeare plays during his time with the *Boston Globe,* one of which starred Alvin Epstein. Alvin was a stage actor in his early thirties, already well known for playing the part of Lucky in Beckett's *Waiting for Godot* on Broadway opposite Bert Lahr's Gogo in 1956, and the Fool in Orson Welles's *King Lear* in the same year. When I met him backstage in the late 1950s, he had a warm twinkle in his eye, and we got along famously. He invited me to visit him in New York the next time I was down, and I stayed with him there a few times while I was still in Boston. When I moved to New York, Alvin generously told me I was welcome to share his West 14th Street apartment.

Once established in New York, I continued with my artwork, painting Alvin, his friends in the theater, and still lifes. I also made papier-mâché angels after seeing some German carved wooden ones on the Metropolitan Museum of Art's Christmas tree.

One of my favorite still lifes that I did in New York was heavily influenced by Pierre Bonnard. I'd discovered him a year before, while flipping through a book of the French painter's work. The glowing colors astounded me. I think that was when my fierce love of color really started to rear its head. I was particularly struck by Bonnard's use of orange and cool lavender. To prepare for the still life, I first spread an orange oilcloth over our dining-room table, which had an overhead lamp that bathed the area in a pool of light. The subjects I placed on the table included marmalade jars, soft blue-gray cups, and plates of fruit. The reflected light from the orange cloth onto the blue-gray pottery and the grapefruits enchanted me. I can't remember where we ate as I labored for a week or so on the painting. "Don't touch the still life," was a refrain often heard in my kitchen studio. Poor Alvin—with me taking over his life like that—but he never complained (and we're still friends).

There are two stories of Alvin's that always remind me what America was like in the late 1950s and early 1960s when I was in New York. In 1962, he had a part in a play starring the tall, elegant, and talented actress and singer Diahann Carroll. It was a musical by Richard Rodgers called *No Strings* about an African American woman and a white man—played by Diahann, and Richard Kiley—who meet up in Paris as lovers. This was a very progressive theme in that era. The delicious episode Diahann told Alvin sums up the racial attitudes of the time. A year before, she was booked to sing in a hotel in Florida. She got there, settled into her room, and called down to book a table for a preshow dinner. "Where would you like that, Miss Carroll, in your room or in the kitchen?" she was asked. Without batting an eyelid, she replied, "I'll have it wherever you would like the show, in the kitchen or in my room, it's all the same to me."

At that time, there was also a deathly fear in the United States of Russia and its people. They were supposedly our entrenched enemy, who would do us in if we ever let our guard down. Alvin's father, a well-established doctor in New York, had as a patient William Z. Foster, the chairman of the Communist Party of America. Foster needed a big operation that he couldn't afford to have done in the United States, so he went to receive treatment in Russia, and Alvin's father accompanied him there. We had just lived through the McCarthy era, when so many creative people in theater and film had been blacklisted and lost their careers and reputations for having supposedly communist leanings. When Alvin's father returned from Russia, he was aglow with impressions of life in the Soviet Union. Learning and books were freely available, he said, people happy and warmhearted. He'd been to such great theater and ballet, and on and on. How could this be? We heard everyone was crushed under the heel of that oppressive regime, and no happiness or freedom was to be found.

I began to understand how the truth could be twisted. Later, I realized how repressed some Russians were and also how they were brainwashed into believing we Americans were the oppressed and miserable masses—our poor begging in the streets, medical treatment for only the rich, and no culture. Both sides used propaganda.

In 1960, when Alvin had time off, which was rare, we traveled across America in a Volkswagen bus and loved it. We were both greedy for the sights of the vast landscapes and the fascinating towns in the "flyover states" that you never hear much about. Alvin loved Big Sur when we reached the West Coast, and I introduced him to my parents and the stunning views of the wild coast from our family restaurant.

When we visited Deetjen's Big Sur Inn a short distance down Highway 1 from Nepenthe, they were playing Joan Baez's first album. It was a perfect combination: Joan's English and Scottish ballads soaring out of an old Norwegian inn among the towering redwoods in Big Sur. The combination of a rich, heart-stopping voice and a cool self-contained persona makes Joan one of the deepest fascinations in my life. Her vibrant voice has popped up in California and London throughout my years, always enchanting. How lucky I felt to have seen her historic début at the Newport Folk Festival!

Back in New York, I met many creative, famous, and working theater people through Alvin. He had received a Ford Foundation grant to start his own theater group, and with it, for rehearsals, he rented a huge loft in the Meatpacking District near our 14th Street apartment. This area is now very desirable, but it was a real backwater then.

We gave several amazing parties in that loft to break it in. At one I recall meeting Siobhan McKenna, whom I had seen some years earlier starring in George Bernard Shaw's *Saint Joan*. She left me totally smitten with her rich Irish voice. Celebrities like the comic duo Mike Nichols and Elaine May, and actor Eli Wallach also added sensational dash to the event. But the most memorable meeting that night was with legendary composer Leonard Bernstein. I had seen and adored *West Side Story* on Broadway and was fascinated to actually meet the creator of its musical score. Imagine my emotions as he pressed my hand, looked longingly at me, and said, "How does it feel to be the most handsome man in the world?" I'm sure he was a bit drunk and said that line to many people, as I've learned he was a passionate soul who ate alive the world he encountered. Still, I thoroughly enjoyed my moment with him.

When Alvin got in his stride developing the first production for his theater group to showcase for producers, I suggested he hire Dustin Hoffman, who was living in New York and who I'd heard was looking for work. They rehearsed the play *The Bacchae*, and Alvin was quite pleased with Dustin till the night of their presentation—Dustin never showed. When Alvin met him a couple of years later and asked why he hadn't bothered to come, Dustin quipped, "Because I really want to make it." Which as we all know, he certainly did to great acclaim when he appeared in the film *The Graduate* in 1967.

Dustin Hoffman in the late 1970s, around the time my friend Alvin Epstein cast him in a play he was directing and before he made it in the movies. Dustin and I had attended the same acting school a few years earlier, where he had observed, "Kaffe couldn't act himself out of a wet paper bag." Luckily, visual arts had a stronger pull for me!

To continue my art studies in New York in 1960, I started attending the Art Students League on West 57th Street. It was, and still is, an atelier school where students can take studio classes taught by international artists. Painting and drawing there was hugely stimulating. However, in my still life class, the subjects were mostly pedestrian bowls of fruit with draped cloths. Hardly inspiring. I asked if I could set up the next arrangement for us to paint, then went down to the Lower East Side, where I found vacant lots with piles of rubbish. Gathering up the rusty buckets and tools, old broken window frames, and corrugated metal I collected there, I arranged a landscape of dereliction. It was the start of my love affair with the rich tones of rust.

When we weren't painting still lifes, we worked from live models. One day, a middle-aged, plumpish woman took the stand. As we painted away, our instructor, Mr. Dickenson, stuck his head through our door and commented, "There is not one muddy shadow on her body, students. They are all silver." Later, when our model had donned her robe and left the room, Mr. Dickenson informed us that she had modeled for the fountain in front of New York's Plaza Hotel (which has since been converted to fancy apartments). I think of her every time I pass that corner on my New York visits.

Working as an artist on the West Coast

In my early twenties and forever restless, I packed my bags sometime in 1961 and moved back to Big Sur, eager for new experiences. California looked suddenly fresh and new after my four-year absence.

I was lucky enough to rent the old mess hall at Anderson Creek where Henry Miller had lived in the 1940s. My sister Holly and her husband, Tony Gafill, lived in a cottage below me. Tony was a beautiful, bright, barefoot boy, with huge, dreamy eyes and a tall, lanky body. He used to wear a scarlet nightshirt all the time, and I remember seeing his naked legs sticking out from under his car, which seemed to need endless repairs. When Holly had her first child, they found a Victorian book called something like *Caring for Baby*. This baby's care was a steep learning curve for Holly. As Holly said of those days, "Babies don't come with instructions." Tony had wanderlust and soon drifted away after their second baby, Erin, was born. Like many children deprived of a father's attention, she developed a deep imaginary picture of Tony and longed to meet him as she was growing up.

I painted a lot of still lifes and family portraits in my new big studio. There was no heat except for an oil drum cut to accommodate logs. It actually threw off quite a good heat if there wasn't too hard a gale blowing. Wild cream narcissus, orange calendulas, and the delightful round leaves and flowers of nasturtiums surrounded the mess hall. The salty scent of the pounding sea below us mingled with the perfume of the flowers. Sunrises and sunsets were glorious, and it was mostly an intensely happy time.

Sometimes, however, I did feel isolated. Not wanting the expense of running a car, I didn't drive, so I had to hitchhike thirty miles into town to shop, and often had a long wait getting back unless I could corral a friend into giving me a lift. What saved me from drowning in loneliness for several months was an intense relationship I was having with a man my age from back East who had a strange sense of humor. Eventually, we split up over some misunderstanding, and I felt glad to be on my own in my big studio house at Anderson.

Some weeks after the breakup, I was woken up in the middle of the night by voices in my kitchen. It was my ex-friend saying to a stranger, "Oh, you can sleep anywhere here. Kaffe won't mind." As I ran into the kitchen I flew into a rage at the presumption of it. "How dare you come barging in here acting like you own the place?" I shouted. Then I turned to the poor stranger, a quiet man with a black mustache who was cringing in embarrassment. "I'm not angry with *you*," I said. "Please do stay!" My embarrassed guest turned out to be

I'm proud of my sister Holly, who came to painting late in her life and handles color so well.

Steve Lovi, an artist from Chicago living in San Francisco at the time. During breakfast the next morning, his gentle intelligence impressed me—yet I had no inkling what a huge role he would play in my life some years down the road.

I continued painting away in my studio, entertaining the occasional visitor and trying to keep myself motivated. One day not many months after my return to the West Coast, I heard a big four-wheel-drive car pull up outside. I looked down my long studio room and through the open door at the other end. A tall man in white silk pajamas sprang out of the car. The only colors on him were paint smudges around his crotch. I knew that syndrome—nervously grabbing yourself as the excitement of painting took hold. He announced in his proud voice, "You don't know me. I'm Alba Heywood.

1: One of my first Fair Isle knits from the 1970s. 2: A painting I did of the prisoner's mess hall that became my studio in Anderson Creek, CA, in 1961, when I returned from the East Coast. 3: The wild Fassett tribe in the sixties with a new generation of nieces and nephews. 4: Such a romantic; a cow's pelvis on my head and wearing Ethiopian beads. 5, 6: Portraits I did while at Anderson Creek: local character Margeret Lial sitting in a field of mustard flowers, and Mom in her green velour bathrobe.

I live up the hill, and you are coming to paint with me." Something about his assertive manner made me collect my paints and join him—the beginning of my two-year study with this established artist.

Alba had the look of a hero in the Napoleonic war paintings. Tall, thick brown hair parted in the middle, piercing eyes, and eagle-sharp features. Born into a prominent oil family in Louisiana, he was in his early thirties when I met him. He shared his Big Sur home with his Dutch lover Loet Vanderveen, whom he had met in New York. They both had had successful careers that they threw over in 1960 to move to Big Sur and live the dream. Loet became a ceramicist and sculptor, and Alba concentrated on his painting. Alba taught me many things in the next months, often sweeping me off to go to exhibitions in Monterey or San Francisco when not painting day after day in his studio.

Being a southerner, Alba was full of stories and drama. One day in San Francisco, we were walking down a street when he suddenly lit up, grabbed a passing young woman by the face, and said in a breathless voice, "Kaffe, look at these eyes. Have you ever seen anything so beautiful?" The poor creature went from terror to melting under his appreciative eye. One thing Alba taught me that really took hold was: "Paint as well as you can. Don't worry about your style. It will arise from the weakness you can't correct."

While I was working away at Anderson Creek, Eduardo Tirella used to

drop by occasionally. It was through Eduardo that I also came into contact with movie star Kim Novak and singer Peggy Lee. He was good friends with both. (His friend Edmund Kara used to make dresses for Peggy Lee in the early 1950s.)

At some point, Eduardo took me to Peggy's house in Hollywood Hills and talked her into sitting for me to paint a portrait. "But I don't have my paints with me," I protested.

"I'll buy you a new set," said Eduardo, and off we went to get paints, turpentine, brushes, and a canvas. It all added up to the price I'd charge for a painting. Another of life's lessons—one's materials can be replaced, and it's money well spent. I painted Peggy's portrait sitting in her garden in three hours and gave it to her. Recently, I met her daughter, who says she inherited the painting.

I was always fascinated by stories of the film actress Kim Novak. She was cool and beautiful with a passion and wildness sizzling just under her elegant serenity. I loved hearing that all her dressing rooms had to be painted lavender, as it was one of my favorite colors at the time. At one of Nepenthe's big Halloween parties, I spotted Kim sitting quietly, surveying the crowd of costumed characters. I grabbed a grapefruit from behind the counter and strode up to her table. "I'd like to present you with a prize for looking the most like Kim Novak," I said, bowing deeply. She laughed and asked me to join her. I'd seen a film she'd starred in about actress Jeanne Eagels, which I enjoyed a lot. She said she loved that part better than any other she had done, but the film was not a success and the studio was not proud of it. Because she had a house up the coast near Carmel, she was a frequent visitor to our family restaurant. It didn't really surprise me when she retired early from the dazzling limelight to raise horses.

One day when Eduardo was visiting my Anderson Creek studio, I began

complaining, saying I would love a little garden in front of my house but hadn't the time or energy to do anything about it. Eduardo was a passionate designer who felt anything was possible if you set your mind to it. "Are you free this weekend?" he asked with a determined look. "Yes," I said. "Well, let's make that garden!" He bundled me off to the beach, where we found driftwood logs and large stones, which we brought to the house. We then spent a day digging up a plot, planting succulents and other shrubs, and positioning wood and rocks. Presto, a garden in two days! It was a great illustration of "never say never" and what a burst of enthusiasm and confidence can achieve. Remember, this is forty years before the spate of instant garden makeover programs on TV. Eduardo would often stop in wonder at the beautiful mushrooms, ferns, and river stones as we hiked in Big Sur canyons, saying that no garden designer could make anything better. He made me value even more what was so familiar to me. When Alba met Eduardo, he said, "Oh, I expected you to be wrapped in cellophane!" I guess I'd gone on about him too much.

Although my life in my converted mess hall studio seemed natural to me, one event put into perspective how unconventional and bohemian it seemed to others. I had a visit from Michael Murphy, the cofounder of Esalen, a center for the study of human psychology that had just opened at our beloved sulphur springs down the road. He brought with him a group of ardent young students who were on a weekend course at the institute. They had come to study how a bohemian artist lives free of the restraints of society's conventions. There I sat in my big drafty studio, my oil-drum fire burning, and tried to answer questions about my bizarre (to them) life. Their well-ironed beige chinos, button-down collars, and neat haircuts were quite a contrast to my sandals and colorful shirt.

Many unconventional people were still being drawn to the unique life and setting of Big Sur in the early 1960s. One such was a boy named Archie, who was a street gypsy from San Francisco. Very bright and attractive, he appealed to men and women. My sister Kim rose to the challenge when he said he knew little about women. She would instruct him, she thought, and instantly became pregnant with her first son.

A painting I did during my days at my Anderson Creek studio of a view of little painted houses I loved at Krinkle Corner in Big Sur.

Archie and I got on well. My friend Lyon, by now back on the West Coast, liked him because he was intellectually curious and read what was recommended to him. One evening Archie, Lyon, Alba, and I were having a drink at Nepenthe when Alba suggested we continue drinks up at his house on the ridge. With Archie in the driver's seat, we began our long, winding journey up to Alba's place, 1,600 feet above sea level. Once we left the highway and started up the hill through Alba's canyon, Archie stopped the car for a pee. I stayed in the car, and Alba and Lyon jumped out and started walking on ahead. When Archie caught up with Alba and Lyon, he slowed the car down so they could jump up onto the front bumpers. As we neared the top of the ridge, Alba, feeling frisky, shouted, "Let's go! Hit the gas!" Obediently, Archie speeded up. Suddenly the car hit a deep rut and careered sideways off the road and over the cliff. Alba and Lyon jumped clear just in time. The car rolled over about eight times till it came to rest on a bush at the edge of a steep drop to the rocks below. As Archie and I had tumbled around in the car, I had felt nothing but exhilaration. I'd always wondered what a car accident would feel like, and here it was—whoopee!

When the car came to a stop on its side, I asked Archie if he was okay. Luckily, he had only one scratch on his head, and I wasn't injured at all. We quickly climbed out of the car and looked up the hill. Far above us we saw Alba and Lyon in tears, convinced we were done for. Once we were back up on the road we realized it was Alba who had been hurt jumping from the careering car. He had broken his wrist, which was now giving him pain as he emerged from shock. We drove into town to take him to the hospital. His frustration at not being as mobile the next month was very difficult for him.

Like all of us, Alba was lucky to escape the accident alive, but seven years later his luck ran out. In March 1969, he fell asleep with a lit cigarette in his hand. Having taken sleeping pills, he didn't awaken, and smoke inhalation sent him to a tragic early death—he was barely forty. As I was writing the first draft of this story, an old friend of mine showed up with a painting of Big Sur he felt sure I had painted. At first glance, I thought it was one of the

Left: A drawing I did of artist Alba Heywood in 1962 as he recovered from the car accident we survived. **Below:** A view of the Big Sur coast by Alba. **Right:** In costume again at a Nepenthe Halloween party in the very early 1960s. My makeup was poster paint—not good!

many studies of the coastline I produced in the early 1960s. But there was something about the way it was seen through a framework of planks that gave it a strong style I recognized as my old teacher's. Indeed, it was signed "Alba." I'm so grateful to have this tangible memento of a towering influence in my life.

Once again restless to explore more of the world, I moved up to San Francisco in early 1963, and Lyon gladly claimed my Anderson Creek studio. I took to the big city like a duck to water—I was never meant to remain a country boy. The rugged Big Sur coast is very seductive with its fresh, wild life in all senses of the word. But to be able to wander down streets of Victorian houses and climb hills looking at front gardens with all the variety man puts into his dwellings was irresistible to me. On top of that, there were the shops, museums, and chance meetings with people from all over the globe—stimulating in the extreme.

When I was first in San Francisco, I was lent a beautiful hilltop apartment on Nob Hill by Judy McBean, a socialite art lover who was going to Europe for a month or so. After settling in, I wandered down to the nearby North Beach area of the city, and the first person I met who appealed to me was an artist from a Danish American family—Charles Heim. We got talking, and I could see at once he was really into painting and knew about all the artists in the area. I brought him to my digs to show him my paintings and drawings. He responded in a very positive way to my work, wanting to show it to all of his rich collector friends.

Charles invited me to his house and studio on Potrero Hill. I was thrilled to be meeting another young artist who was bright, attractive, and really encouraging, finding me many contacts. He had an elfin quality, laughed easily when pleased, and was serious most of the time. His house was full of things I loved—oriental carpets, interesting furniture, paintings, and drawings.

In the next months, Charles and I spent a lot of time together. He was a great cook and made good meals for us. Music was a big part of our relationship, as Charles's ex-lover Jesse was training to be a concert pianist and shared the house. We talked nonstop about Europe, paintings, theater, and books. We ate in interesting restaurants. We went to every museum and quirky antique shop we could discover. We walked the city; planned murals, paintings, and exhibitions; and painted and drew together with gorgeous romantic music filling the studio. Charles told me of his European travels and instilled me with longing to return there.

This was the most stimulating period of my artistic life up to that point. Charles constantly brought me interested collectors who commissioned work and heaped encouragement on me. I began to feel like a proper artist under his enthusiastic eye. Charles himself worked for a printing firm and so could only paint seriously in the evening or on weekends. I swore, if I had to starve I wouldn't go that route. When I asked him why he didn't do art full time, he said, "I have to have a car. I couldn't afford to run it on an artist's earnings." I vowed then never to have a car till I could afford one on my creative pay. So I never properly learned to drive—one of the few citizens of California not to drive, I'm sure.

In San Francisco, I hung out mainly in a huge warehouse of a restaurant, called The Old Spaghetti Factory Café and Excelsior Coffee House, in North Beach. Freddy Kuh, a world traveler and confidently funny man, had built the restaurant up from scratch from the burned-out shell of a turn-of-the-century pasta factory. He lived above the business.

Above: My drawing of socialite and art lover Judy McBean, who lent me her hilltop apartment when I arrived in San Francisco in 1963. Below: Charles Heim painting on one of his rare days off. We sometimes painted together after I settled in San Francisco. Overleaf: A drawing from my sketchbook of The Old Spaghetti Factory Café in North Beach in San Francisco. It was a magnet for poets, artists, and theater folk at the time.

The place consisted of three vast floors filled with Freddy's auction-house finds. Masses of couches, overstuffed chairs, and dressers filled with china vied for space with paintings, sculptures, rugs, and all manner of objects. When you had tea with Freddy, you could pick the room set you fancied. There were at least a dozen completely furnished areas of chairs, settees, cabinets, and tables cheek by jowl to wander through. It was like an overcrowded vintage showroom.

After The Old Spaghetti Factory opened in 1957, it quickly became a haven for artists, theater folk, and Beat poets, as well as lotus-eaters of the burgeoning hippie movement. The restaurant served modestly priced food and wine and was imbued with atmosphere. Eccentrically decorated, colorful wooden chairs hung upside down from the ceilings; moose heads and other kitsch lined the walls.

Freddy liked my work and even bought a few of my still lifes and drawings. Eventually he asked me to do a large mural in the restaurant, depicting all the characters that frequented the place. It was eight feet square and done on Masonite. I loved my weeks of working on the painting, right on the wall where it would hang as you entered the main room. Freddy gathered the cast for the painting day by day: the little flower seller Millie; the great artist's model Flo Allen, who sat for me with bare brown breasts; and one of Freddy's best friends, the artist Joseph St. Amand. Even visiting poets like Thom Gunn were included.

When I was hesitant about what to charge for my mural, Freddy said, "I'll give you lifetime free eating and drinking at the Spaghetti Factory for it." What an offer, since I spent most of my food budget in that place. The trouble is I moved to England a month later, only having the occasional meal there on visits home. Years after Freddy died and the Spaghetti Factory changed hands, the painting showed up in an antique store in San Francisco. It was bought by a filmmaker who made a documentary about it for TV. He invited me and all the people in the painting (those still living) to be interviewed for his film.

During my life in San Francisco, I had some precarious times, trying to
support myself as an artist and getting very near the end of my funds. I had had one-man drawing shows at the Pantechnicon Gallery and the Legion of Honor museum, but I was still

Below: I painted this moody self-portrait in the window of my San Francisco apartment in 1964. **Right:** In my little San Francisco apartment, surrounded by my paintings.

struggling. Luckily, as close as I came to destitution, those angels never really let me down. Looking at my bank account at one point, I realized with real fear that I had only about five dollars left. I took out three dollars and bought bread, cheese, and eggs from a day-old shop that had real bargains for struggling artists like me. Then I called a drama critic friend who had expressed interest in my work. After inviting him to dinner in my studio room in the Fillmore District, I hung every painting I'd done three or four high on the walls.

We ate my simple meal (thank God for the bottle of wine he brought) and gossiped about San Francisco life. He never once seemed to look at my work, so as the meal ended and he was donning his coat to leave, I said to myself, "I guess I'll have to go back to live with my family in Big Sur!" Just as he reached the door, he turned and asked, "How much is that painting on the far right?" My heart leapt, and I knew that no matter how close I got, I'd always survive.

Another life-saving commission I got was from a very wealthy family friend, Hugh Chisholm. He called one day and invited me to draw his huge house in Hillsborough, just south of San Francisco. The area was very upmarket (the local yarn shop was called the Status Thimble). I sat drawing his grand house for a few days, and during that time was introduced to a visiting couple from England. Jeremy Fry was an inventor, successful engineer, and philanthropist, and Frances Chadwick (the wife of a famous sculptor) was having a fling with him. They were both tall, elegant, beautiful, and easygoing. Our lunch together was full of laughter and flirtation. The next day as I sat drawing, Hugh said, "You liked those people, didn't you? Well, I think you should go to England. You have many good qualities, but you could use some finishing touches, and England can do just that for you."

Suddenly, that did sound like a good idea. At a dinner party some weeks before, I had met English novelist Christopher Isherwood. He must have been about sixty-one then, but was so full of vim and vigor I didn't even think of his age. He was a small figure with dancing eyes blinking with intelligent wit. We got so engrossed in conversation, the whole party seemed to fade away. We talked about books—I'd just read W. Somerset Maugham's *The Summing Up*, a literary memoir written in 1938. Christopher thought Maugham hadn't been honest enough about his gayness. We also discussed art and perception, and about the coincidences that keep cropping up in regular patterns. Christopher was without a doubt one of the most stimulating and engaging souls I'd ever met. The next day, I bought as many of his books as I could find and devoured them. They were about England as well as the rest of the world, including Berlin and L.A., seen through his English eyes.

I was well stoked to take up Hugh's suggestion about going to England, and I found a cheap ticket on Icelandic Airlines—a propeller flight that took twenty-four hours if you were lucky.

In October of 1964, the night before I was to fly, I went to The Old Spaghetti Factory to have a farewell dinner. As I sat there before my huge multi-portrait—excited about the new world before me but sad to leave all this—the door burst open and in walked Jeremy Fry. He was on his way to the Far East to check on some of the remote-control valves that had made his fortune. "Guess where I'm going tomorrow?" I cried. When he heard I was flying to England, he was thrilled. "Do you have a place to stay?" When I said I hadn't arranged anything, he pulled a huge iron key out of his briefcase and handed it to me along with the address of his business flat in London. "I'll be there in a week's time," he said. "Once I arrive, we can go together to my home in Bath."

chapter three

1964–1969

England in the Swinging Sixties

Above, left: This study of shells on lace followed my early white paintings, with hints of the color and pattern to come in my next body of work.
Above, center: Fashion designer Billy Gibb and I on our first trip to California together. **Above, right:** A painting I did of my garden studio in an outbuilding at Widcombe Manor in 1964—shades of white studies to come. **Opposite:** A striped sweater I picked the colors for, knit for me by one of Billy's cousins in 1966. I'm painting a triptych of broken china on an antique patchwork quilt.

Many of my American friends had warned me about the terrible weather and lack of good food in England when I told them of my travel plans. One English woman in Boston had a different impression to impart to me. She got a faraway look of deep affection in her eyes as she said words that have come back to me often: "England has a pearly light." The year I arrived, London was having an Indian summer, with warm, sunny days that stretched late into autumn. The smells and sights kept me on a high for months. English childhood books, *Mary Poppins*, *Wind in the Willows*, et cetera, and impressions came flooding back to me. For most of my first year, I was in a state of ecstasy over gardens, people's amazing utterances, and the English way of life. I was recognizing a world that I belonged in.

A foreigner in this "green and pleasant land"

Off I traveled to London, with the big key to Jeremy's flat tucked safely in my pocket. My plane was delayed on the stopover in Iceland, so we got in at about 9:00 in the evening. By that time, all the banks were closed, and I was dumped off the bus at the terminal in the middle of London with no English money. I spotted a man in a bowler hat carrying an umbrella and asked if he knew how I could get to the address Jeremy had given me for his flat. He told me to take the number 15 bus and get off at Hyde Park Corner. "But I have no money," I told him. He proceeded to flag down a taxi. "Take this chap to this address," he said, and paid the driver. Thank you, angels—once again!

I was surprised to see the light on as I let myself into the apartment. On the second floor of the duplex, I found the terrified nanny who worked for one of Jeremy's business partners. She was holding a chair over her head, ready to brain the stranger who was creeping about the apartment. Luckily, she quickly calmed down when I explained that Jeremy had given me the key and was going to meet me in a week. The next morning, she gave me a fabulous tour of London. Unfortunately, I've never met this young Australian again to thank her for that warm welcome.

Even though it was late October, the days were balmy with golden light. I'd walk out each morning from Halkin Street and usually head for nearby Hyde Park to see the flowerbeds and the sunbathers at the Serpentine swimming pond. I loved drawing those bathers and the people on benches throughout the park. Fascinated by the ornate buildings, I also often sketched them before heading to museums or galleries. The smells of flowers, coffee, and bakeries enchanted me because they were so different from those of my Big Sur life.

I devoured all the sights around me on my daily jaunts: the plants, people, dogs, and wonderful English buildings. Window boxes exploding with colorful flowers on so many buildings, even banks, surprised and delighted me. Walking everywhere, I explored the little squares, old churches, museums. The Victoria and Albert Museum particularly had a deep significance for me from this very first visit. It contained so many things I was growing to love and identify with my life: the great oriental galleries with carpets, tiles, and pottery; the top floors of porcelains and clayware of every mood and period of history; the costume court with fashion going back to medieval times. The collections of miniature paintings from Mughal India and Persia were tiny bejeweled worlds that drew me in and would play a big part in my painting and knitwear inspiration.

After I had been in London a week, Jeremy showed up on schedule, and we drove down to his house in Bath, Widcombe Manor. It was an autumn evening, so it was

Above: A drawing I did at the Serpentine in Hyde Park in 1964, during my first days exploring the magic of London. **Opposite:** My drawing of a bedroom with ornate architecture and tented ceiling in Widcombe Manor, Bath. I set up my first artist's studio in England in an outbuilding on the property.

dark as we passed though many small villages on the way there. Finally, Jeremy said, "See this wall we have been driving alongside for some time? It's the wall around my property."

"What a beautiful stone wall," I commented.

"It needs constant repair," he said with feeling. We rounded the corner, the large gates opened, and I beheld the most elegant Georgian mansion behind a fountain courtyard. A wide expanse of lawn swept down from the house.

We had a drink and went straight to bed. I was put in a grand bedroom at the back of the house and was told, "This is where Tony Armstrong-Jones and Princess Margaret sleep when they visit." (I had heard of the British royals, but had yet to learn the significance of that remark.) When I awoke in the morning, I looked out my large Georgian window to see a stuffed elephant by a pond at the end of the garden. Jeremy informed me that Queen Victoria had ridden it while in India. The house, I learned, was steeped in history—Henry Fielding resided there when he wrote *Tom Jones* in 1749.

Camilla, Jeremy's wife, was away on holiday when I arrived, but I met his three children, Francis, Cosmo, and Polly. Polly was the youngest at four years old, a chubby-cheeked little girl who cried a lot, claiming, "It's not fair." Cosmo was handsome, robust, and full of confident charm at seven. Francis had the lean, handsome face of his father, but was a bit of a worrier at his tender age of eight or so.

I quickly settled into Widcombe Manor, moving to an attic bedroom where I could paint and draw. Camilla soon returned, and we got on well. Her father was quite a well-known painter in his south-of-England circle, and she herself had done a very competent still-life painting when she was young, but had never tried again. From her mother, who ran an antique shop, Camilla had inherited a great eye for the furnishings found in the many vintage shops England is famous for.

We played music, went to films, and had dinner parties, and I painted and drew every day. The old terraced buildings that lined the hills of downtown Bath fascinated me. I could see why it was considered one of the most beautiful towns in England.

Discovering the rolling countryside around Bath, I delighted in the long, narrow country lanes lined with dense foliage that formed cozy tunnels. They are the perfect entrances to the small villages of the Cotswolds. Those golden stone cottages, some with thatched roofs, are so human in scale. I felt I was born there when I saw them for the first time.

As I got to know this exotic land, there were so many little reminders that I was in a very foreign place. At the drugstore (the "chemist"), you'd get a bottle simply titled The Lotion, or The Tablets. They only needed a label saying DRINK ME to be totally *Alice in Wonderland.*

I remember watching two talking heads having a political discussion one day on TV. "That's not what the polls say," one said to the other. "Or do you pooh-pooh polls?"

"No, I don't pooh-pooh polls!" the other retorted sharply.

I was most delighted at large, fatherly men asking, "Shall I be mother?" as they picked up the teapot to pour the tea, oblivious to how strange this typical polite English refrain sounds to a foreign ear.

The fact that trucks were lorries also struck my fancy. *Lorry drivers* sounded so much gentler than *truck drivers*, as did *petrol pump* instead of *gas station*, *torch* instead of *flashlight*, and *car bonnet* and *boot* instead of *car hood* and *trunk*. When Shell Oil did

1: Piccadilly Circus, another drawing from my first week in London in 1964. **2:** Camilla and Jeremy Fry on vacation in Sienna in the sixties. **3:** Jeremy looking cool in front of a blue door in his beloved Malta. **4:** One of my rich blue quilts. **5:** With a romantic self-portrait I painted at the Fry's Widcombe Manor in Bath, where I lived and worked when I first arrived in England.
6: My drawing of Portobello Market for the *New London Spy*, a guidebook that came out in 1966.

a campaign imploring the English to "Put a tiger in your tank," I heard someone on the radio inquire, "Have you got a tiger in your tank?" The answer came, "No, but I've got a puss in my boot!"

I gradually began learning to put up with the cool reserve of the English. How could I ever forget the Frys' friend—writer and garden designer Alvilde Lees-Milne—who telephoned the house one day? She called because she'd heard the Frys had a houseguest, and this had aroused her curiosity. I answered the phone, as everyone was out, and said, "Hello?" Alvilde retorted in a very arched voice, "Oh, you're an *American*!" The emphasis on the word told me all I needed to know. What really got to me is that she knew my nationality from just the word *hello*.

A couple of years later, I had an encounter with another aristocratic woman, Lady Montagu, and I was greeted with a similar response. I told her, "I'm so glad to be in a country where one speaks the same language." She uttered with feeling, "That's the *theory*!" Later, when I told a New Zealander how paranoid I had become being American in a land where I wasn't really wanted, he shouted, "Don't be a pillock! The English are fascinated by Americans. Some of them feel insecure about them, or have deep-seated prejudices left over from the Second World War, but basically they are fascinated!" That was another important lesson, that there is often more going on than appears at first encounter.

In my early days at Widcombe Manor, Jeremy's lifelong friend Tony Armstrong-Jones paid a visit one evening. A photographer and filmmaker who was then married to Princess Margaret, Tony was shorter than Jeremy and me, and had a nervous intelligence that was riveting. We had a jolly time swapping stories, and after Tony left, Jeremy and Camilla filled me in on the adventures they had all lived through in early 1960. Tony had used out-of-the-way Widcombe Manor when wooing Princess Margaret in the late 1950s. Then, after the couple decided to have a royal wedding in 1960, they asked Jeremy to be the best man. Upon the announcement of the wedding, the press, not liking Princess Margaret, dug around to see if they could dish the dirt on her in any way. They were delighted to find an old newspaper article about Jeremy's early slipup—as a young man he had been arrested for cruising in a public toilet in London and let off with a two-pound fine.

When the story was about to break, Jeremy was on a skiing vacation in Switzerland, unaware that the press had uncovered his youthful indiscretion. While on the slopes enjoying his sport, he noticed a young fellow falling over on his skis and went over to offer him advice on his technique. Impressed by Jeremy's kindness, the guy guiltily admitted, "You are really quite nice. I think I should tell you that I am one of several reporters here to record your reaction when the story of your past hits the newsstands tomorrow."

In a panic, Jeremy rushed to a plane, and flew home as the news broke in the papers. Speeding down the highway to Bath, a traffic cop pulled him over. Jeremy leaned out of his car window, saying, "You can see who I am. The press are on my tail. Could you see your way to letting me off this time?"

"Of course," replied the cop, seeing what a pickle Jeremy was in. "I'll let you go with a warning." The next day a second headline blared, "Jeremy Fry, Second Offence, LET OFF!" The Palace rang Widcombe Manor to request Jeremy play ill and not attend the wedding, and he complied.

Painting in my studio at the bottom of Jeremy Fry's garden in Bath in 1964. At the age of 26, I was already interested in patchwork quilts!

For years and years after, this high-society story was rekindled by the press. Camilla herself was cornered while shopping, and journalists camped on their doorstep, so even going for a walk in their garden was too dangerous. Once when Camilla was rung up by a journalist who asked for an interview, she said, "No comment," and hung up. The paper then printed a full-page interview making up the entire story. She sued and won after a couple of years' battle.

I did eventually meet Princess Margaret as well. One day Jeremy had something to drop off for Tony, so he took me with him to Kensington Palace in London, where the couple lived. I'd been told I would have to bow to her when we met, so I was quite nervous. But instead of any formalities, Jeremy just rang the bell, which was answered by a servant. The next thing we knew, Princess Margaret was at the door saying, "Jeremy darling," and giving him a big kiss. In the flush of this affection, I was introduced as a friend and shook her hand. Then she said merrily, "I've just been given a harmonium." And she dragged us enthusiastically to a lower room where she sat down and banged out "Alexander's Ragtime Band," singing it loudly to both of us. She had the most beautiful large green eyes, and they really glowed as she showed me her wonderful John Piper paintings, among others. The visit was such a pure delight, and Margaret was so easygoing, that when I met her formally much later at an exhibition she was opening, I got confused at her frosty public face and actually curtsied instead of bowing!

I ran into Tony Armstrong-Jones again as well, maybe two years after our meeting at Widcombe, when I was modeling for *Brides* magazine. The location for the shoot was Beaulieu House, part of the Montagu Estate in Hampshire. I had to wear a gray suit and top hat and ride in one of the vintage cars in Lord Montagu's collection. As I was breaking for tea, the flower girl's guardian, who was a large, rather upper-middle-class matron type, looked through the window and said, "Now you will be able to see one of our royals." ("You poor little colonial," she might just as well have added.) Just then Tony walked in and said, "Hello, Kaffe. How have you been? How is Jeremy?" When he left, the guardian muttered, "You might have *told* me you knew him already!"

"I honestly didn't think he would remember me," I blustered.

Jeremy was a great guide to the intelligentsia and upper strata of English society. We would drive miles to visit people, view gardens at grand estates, or go sailing in Cornwall. One day he said he had an invitation to a party at photographer Cecil Beaton's place. I was thrilled, as Beaton was one of my heroes, having seen his photographs and read his books. We drove through a snowstorm for hours to get from Bath to Salisbury. When we finally staggered up the steps of Beaton's manor house and knocked, we heard someone on the other side of the door saying, "Oh shit, someone has arrived!" Jeremy looked at me and asked, "Shall we disappear?" I couldn't bear it—to be so close, then to just leave after coming all that way. So we stayed and were welcomed in and given a quick tour of the house. My memory of Beaton's home was of opulent flowers and golden light, colorful details. But we got very quickly tipsy and were rushed off to a special dinner at the nearby house of music and dance critic Dicky Buckle. The conversation was sparkling and witty. Years later I read in Cecil's published diaries that he met "a handsome man from Big Sur." Could this have been me?

I got used to frequent rainstorms in the West Country of England, but the shortness of them, and often the sun shining through after, brought me a sense of hope. When it rains in California, it can be torrential and go on for days. The light English rains I came to almost enjoy. I loved the way people didn't panic if spots of rain fell. Instead of instantly deserting a picnic or a walk in the park, they would step under a tree or a shop doorway and wait patiently to see if it would pass over—which it usually would.

One of my fondest, most English of memories in my Bath days was Jeremy driving a small car through a rainy day, with me and three other English people in the car. The radio was on, and suddenly the hymn "Jerusalem" started up—England's most popular patriotic song. Without a second's hesitation, everyone (except me) burst into full song, knowing every word and singing in tune! I was properly gobsmacked and in ecstasy at such a total harmony of a moment. To hear the passion in the voices of these otherwise contained people was moving. I can see the raindrops on the windshield and the sun breaking through as the rich history of the English was stirred to full-blooded life. "I will not cease from mental fight . . . Till we have built Jerusalem/In England's green and pleasant land."

Years later, the memory of this episode resurfaced when I invited an English friend down the Grand Canyon on a ten-day whitewater-rafting excursion. There were sixteen of us on the trip, organized by my nephew Kirk. When we all gathered around a campfire a week into the trip, and each performed a well-practiced "party piece"—a favorite song, poem, or other routine—my English friend, film prop-maker Keir Lusby, stood up and simply, but proudly, sang "Jerusalem." Miles down this ancient canyon in the Arizona desert, his rich voice and British pride brought me to the point of tears.

While I was still living in Bath in late 1964, I was notified by my friend Eduardo Tirella that part of the movie *The Sandpiper* was to be filmed in France. Some of the outdoor scenes from that film had been shot earlier that year at Nepenthe—a great excitement for us Fassetts and the whole Big Sur community. Eduardo was coordinating the Big Sur scenes in a Paris studio and asked me to come over and help choreograph the folk dancing on the set of the restaurant's terrace. The movie was about an artist and single mom (played by Elizabeth Taylor) living in Big Sur, who takes her lover (Richard Burton playing a married Episcopalian priest) to visit Nepenthe. They watch the dancing on the terrace, one of the big-set pieces of the film. Because Taylor could only work two weeks of any one year in the States for tax reasons, they could only film her in California approaching Nepenthe and on the beach. The dancing had to be filmed in a Paris studio where they built the entire restaurant, with the huge panorama of the coast painted on a backcloth. It cost more than Dad had spent to build the actual restaurant!

I went to Paris for a week and stayed in a charming old hotel with Eduardo. We'd go to the studio every morning, and I would work on the dances with the extras. Vincente Minnelli was directing. He had a hard time trying to get me to clap off the beat for the dancers. But they caught the atmosphere so well and the dancing and music were so good that I forgot after a while that I was in Paris, not Nepenthe. It was bizarre to walk off my own property, where I'd spent most of my formative years, onto the streets of Paris.

Of the dozens of extras I taught to dance, two stood out in my memory. One was Nico, who went on to become quite a star in the music world and in Andy Warhol films. I remember this charismatic singer as a luscious German blond with a quiet coolness.

A poster for *The Sandpiper*, starring Richard Burton and Elizabeth Taylor. The scene shown on the poster was shot at Nepenthe in 1964. I helped choreograph dancing scenes shot later on a studio set of the restaurant in Paris.

Everyone at Nepenthe, including Dad and my sister Dorcas, dancing for the cameraman of *The Sandpiper* movie production in 1964. In the film Elizabeth Taylor played an artist who frequented our "bohemian" restaurant.

The other standout personality was a son of Balthus, the great Swiss painter whom I've always been inspired by. Balthus painted young girls in a way that intrigued many and upset some, but his love of pattern and texture and elegant color taught me a lot. His son was tall with dark hair and a beautiful, sensitive face. Being such a fan of his father's work, I had many talks with him between the filming and after-work parties. A crass American in the cast said loudly at one of the parties, "Why don't you two get together?" We were both so shy that it put a stop to our closeness.

Another incident on the film that amused me occurred when I went to the great costume designer Irene Sharaff to beg for different shoes for one of the dancers. This girl had complained that it was hard to dance in the gladiator-type sandals she was given with her costume. When I told Irene that, she barked, "Look, this is a very bohemian joint she's dancing at!" I was amused and shocked to hear my restaurant home called that, then I thought, "Well, I guess it is, to most people!"

Late in 1964, when Jeremy and Camilla were going through the last stages of their married life and right before Camilla would leave to set up her life with a new man, I spent their last Christmas with them at Widcombe Manor. I remember clearly making a papier-mâché angel to top off their Christmas tree. As we sat working on a jigsaw puzzle, I left the angel to dry by the open log fire. The atmosphere was a bit oppressive. There was unexpressed sadness hanging in the air, in spite of our attempts to make light conversation. Suddenly, we smelt burning and realized the paper wings of my angel had caught fire. The three of us rushed to the hearth and stamped vigorously on the angel before throwing her unceremoniously into the damp garden to cool down. Whatever Christmas spirit we had tried to dredge up was well and truly obliterated!

Once Camilla and Jeremy realized they had come to the end of their marriage, they started civilized divorce proceedings. Jeremy told Camilla, "Take anything you need or want from the house." She ordered several giant moving vans and took the lot.

Reduced to empty rooms, Jeremy did what he'd longed to do anyway. He painted all the walls white, bought some stark contemporary art pieces, and installed minimal modern furnishing. My heart sank a bit, being so in love with Camilla's decorating tastes, which had created such a warm old world. The saving grace, however, came from Julie Hodgess, a brilliant interior designer. She introduced the perfect stroke of genius by convincing Jeremy to splash out and line the new dining room with sheets of copper. Then she laid a floor of untreated leather tiles in that warm terra-cotta shade and placed a round alabaster table in the center. Candlelit dinners there were enchanting in that glowing pinkish room that reflected us all so flatteringly.

Setting up a studio in Notting Hill Gate

In all, I stayed in Bath for about six months. While there, I had visited London a few times, and eventually the vibrancy of the place was too much to resist. Bath now seemed too "small town," and I needed my own place. Although I was to remain very good friends with Jeremy and would make occasional visits to Widcombe, London was to quickly become my home.

In the early spring of 1965, a little handwritten ad in a shop window led me to a wonderful big two-room apartment in a large old Victorian house—the rent was the ridiculously affordable price of four pounds a week, about $8 at the time. Located on top of a hill, the flat was not far from Notting Hill Gate underground station. It had high ceilings, marble fireplaces, and a little balcony looking onto Lansdowne Crescent. (Next door was a small private hotel, where Jimi Hendrix was to die in 1970.)

Right after moving in, I went out late on Friday afternoon to explore the surrounding streets, which were totally new to me. I had no idea what to expect. A couple of blocks away, I suddenly stumbled on a road full of dozens of small antique stores. They were full of delectable items of china and decorative textiles that seemed perfect candidates for still lifes. Existing only on what I was earning on sales of the odd drawing or painting, I started asking shop owners if they could possibly lower their prices. They all kept mentioning a market— "Wait till the Market opens tomorrow," or "You'll find that at lower prices in the Market."

"What are they on about?" I wondered.

The next morning, I sauntered out to have breakfast at a little workingman's café called Mike's and was astounded to see that the near-empty Portobello Road I'd walked the evening before was thronged with crowds. The attraction was hundreds of stands that had been set up along the street as far as the eye could see. They were laden with vintage cloths, decorative china of all shapes and sizes, furniture, books, and old postcards, and sprinkled among them were the overflowing carts of vegetable and fruit sellers. I've always loved markets, but I'd never seen one that combined a flea market of affordable treasures with gorgeous produce and fish. What luck that I had found a place to live nearby!

Notting Hill in the 1960s was my sort of place, full of gypsy color on the terraced buildings. In those days the area was more gritty than it is now, and even slightly impoverished looking. Portobello Road itself was lined with pink, gold, rust, and sky-blue Victorian houses, many with peeling paint. Above street level, these were occupied by immigrants of modest means from the Caribbean, Africa, and Europe. At street level, Portobello Road was all antique or junk shops. Each Saturday, the narrow street would spring to life with gypsy sellers. Every nation on the globe was represented in the crowds that sauntered up and down these stalls full of eye-catching wares. It was a never-ending joyous party, whatever the weather.

Portobello was paradise for starving artists like me. We could construct our dream lives out of the cheap goods we assembled from the market. The pretty young women we called "dolly birds," art students, older artists and poets, theatrical types, and aristocrats all rubbed shoulders while drinking in the bizarre costumes and hairdos on show. I would shop like a

Opposite: My painting of colorful Notting Hill Gate. Steve Lovi's flat was in the orange section of this block of colors on Ladbroke Gardens. My first London studio was across the way in Lansdowne Crescent.

Above and right bottom: The fabulous Antoni Gaudí serpentine bench in Parc Güell in Barcelona. The joyous colors and patterns thrilled my imagination. **Right:** One of the cool Morandi still lifes that encouraged me to continue my white oil studies in the late sixties. **Below:** A white still life of mine that was inspired by Gaudí's white-on-white mosaics.

magpie and bring back to my studio treasures of decorative pottery, patterned cloths and vintage scarves, shirts, coats, and even shoes. If you didn't like your purchases or they didn't fit, you could give them away or toss them out and go back for something else exotic and cheap. In 1965, a pound was worth two dollars and eighty cents, but you often heard "That's a dollar, love." I soon learned this meant five shillings, harking back to older times.

On my first visit to Portobello, the things that caught my eye were white and cream "pudding basins," ceramic bowls with fluted interiors. I bought these along with ironstone bowls, plates, and cups in shades of white. When I got my finds home to my studio, I set up my first white-on-white still life on a white sheet. For the next few years, I painted one three-foot by four-foot still life a week. This was the size I could transport in a black London taxi. My palette was white tones. Somehow, the world of color I had been depicting in my family portraits and Bonnard-inspired still lifes seemed too rich for me. I was on a fast, seeing beauty for my paintings only in pure whites, pale celadons, taupes, and creams. As an experiment, I placed a cauliflower in one of my still lifes. It was stripped of its outer silver green leaves, but the tiny lime green ones that were left presented a streak of color in my white world that had to go!

    Part of what gave me confidence to stick with this white world was a trip I took to Spain during the beginning of my life in London. A friend from California, artist Michael Schrager, decided to seek a warmer climate and asked me to join him on a jaunt to Barcelona. There I encountered the great works of architect Antoni Gaudí. The Parc Güell blew me away, first, for the great colorful mosaic serpentine bench that crowns the park, but mostly for the surprise I got finding what's under that color-filled bench. The ceiling of the vast space under the terrace is studded with broken china—saucers and plates in every shade of pearly white. It struck me so forcibly as a fresh idea, that it came back to me as I arranged my own white crockery in my still lifes. I had also just been introduced to the work of Giorgio Morandi, an Italian painter who concentrated on a limited group of neutral objects that he painted against soft gray walls. After viewing his work at the Guggenheim Museum on my last trip through New York, I floated two feet off the ground for the rest of the day. How small canvases of three to six objects in almost no color can have that effect is magic, indeed, and spurred me on in my own neutral world.

One thing I was very confident about at the time was my line drawings. When I was at Happy Valley, my art teacher Ray Warf watched me doing the usual drawing most amateur artists produce: lots of scratch lines with the vain hope some of them would capture the face, object, or landscape I was attempting. "Why don't you try to depict your subject in one line?" he advised. "Try to keep the pen on the page as long as possible." It had a revolutionary effect on my drawings that I've tried to use ever since. When my first one-man drawing show opened at the Hazlitt Gallery in London in 1965, I found the English, who could be a little nervous with color, responded well to my monochrome lines. The profits from this exhibition afforded me a modest success, financing the next months and the purchase of paints and canvases.

    Working for Anthony Blond also helped finance my artist's life. He had a small but influential publishing firm, and seeing a use for my drawing technique, he called me into his office. I'd met him at Jeremy Fry's and enjoyed his zany humor. He was like a

My friend textile and mosaic artist Candace Bahouth at Gaudí's bench.

Dickens character to me—bushy black hair and a scrunched-up sort of face that was full of expectation as he told his stories. He'd been married, but was now finding men a lot more attractive, something I was to learn was quite common in upper-class English circles. He was developing a series of guidebooks that would help an intelligent newcomer to a city find unusual delights not on the tourist itineraries. Would I be interested in going around London drawing buildings, interiors, pubs, Turkish baths, et cetera? It was right up my alley, and it paid 150 pounds. This would keep me going for a month or two, so I jumped in.

Delighted at how quickly I completed the illustrations for his first guidebook in the series, *The New London Spy: A Discreet Guide to the City's Pleasures*, Anthony sent me to Paris. I adored this working trip, an excuse to find elegant interiors and vistas off the beaten track. Luckily, my drawings for *The Paris Spy* were as successful as the London illustrations.

The big discussion after I returned from Paris was could I do New York? "It will cost me 100 pounds to fly there and back. Can you supply the ticket?" I asked.

Anthony and his business partner scratched their heads. "Sorry, we can't run to expenses."

"But that will eat up two-thirds of my fee," I protested. They wouldn't relent, so I thought about it. I love to draw, this is a way to get published, and I had a place to stay with my American artist friend Alf Svenson. So I took the chance even though it meant losing money. "Okay, I'll do the job," I said, and off I went. I took along a small portfolio of my work with me to New York and was able to sell a couple of my drawings. Luckily, this just covered my fare.

I thought I knew New York pretty well, but the places I was sent to were new to me, like grand turn-of-the-century interiors. I realized I loved working within the limitations of a specific task like this, and supplying those missing elements that would bring the guidebooks to life.

Staying in Alf's artist loft, seeing his newest paintings, and learning how an artist survives in New York was good for me, too. Alf had a bright, attractive sister who, I remember, was swallowed up by Scientology. It was my first encounter with the group. We grieved for her as one would a sister turned nun.

Back in London, my drawings for *The New York Spy* were well received. Around the same time, I also illustrated a small booklet for the American Museum in Britain based in Bath, called *New World in the Old*. And after a few years, I did another book for Anthony, a fourth guidebook called *Venice Recorded*.

Funny to think how savvy I've become about getting remunerated for work and expenses now, but looking back, that instinct to keep working and proving myself wasn't such a bad idea. If I'd had to pay them for the privilege, it would have been the best thing I could do. How else could I find out what I was capable of?

Although I lived on my own in my studio in 1965, I was continually meeting new people and entertained visiting friends as well. Near the end of the year, Eduardo rented a house for a month in London, and I helped him give wonderful dinner parties for friends of his, like actress Sharon Tate and singer Tony Bennett. He also brought Doris Duke to see my studio one cold winter day. When she walked in to view the paintings, I had the window open to air the place. "Oh, my God! The window's open! I can't stay!" she screamed, clutching her mink to her throat as she fled back to her heated limo.

A drawing I did of artist friend Alf Svenson, whom I stayed with in New York in 1965 when I did illustrations for Anthony Blond's guidebook series there.

Above: A drawing of a Paris Métro station entrance that I did for the *Paris Spy* guidebook that I illustrated for Anthony Blond. **Right:** The grand gothic Cunard building in New York made a great subject for my illustration in the *New York Spy* guidebook. **Below:** My illustration of the fountain outside the Plaza Hotel for the *New York Spy* guidebook. The model for the sculpture was also a life-drawing model in my classes at New York's Art Students League in the early sixties.

In my explorations of London during my first year there, I also met a Glaswegian boy called Stewart Grimshaw, who was renting a room in the house of film director John Schlesinger. Having drinks at the house one day, John treated me to a private showing of his first successful documentary on London's Victoria train station. I loved it, and my response led to a showing of *Darling*, his first huge feature-film hit starring Julie Christie and Dirk Bogarde.

I was captivated by the way John told stories in his films, so a short time later I thought of him when a friend gave me a novel to read, *Midnight Cowboy* by James Leo Herlihy. The story begged to be filmed, and I took the book right over to John. About two weeks later, I rang him and asked how he liked it. "I can't get past the second page," he told me. "It's not interesting enough."

"Oh, well," I thought, "I guess it wasn't that good after all."

A year or two later, I got a call from New York; it was John telling me he was filming *Midnight Cowboy*. He had just cast Dustin Hoffman in the film. Little did any of us know that important film history was being made. *Midnight Cowboy* not only won Oscars, but it became a global sensation. In France, it was called *Macadam Cowboy*. John was so grateful that, once the film was making money, he called me into his London office to offer me 5,000 pounds as a finder's fee. This was a vast fortune for me, as I was living on less than 100 pounds a month. I was amazed and delighted, salting the money away till I needed it years later to buy a flat.

After my success with the illustrations I did for Anthony Blond's books,

I tried selling illustrations to magazines like British *House & Garden*, *Vogue*, and *Queen*. *Queen* was a very glossy up-market fashion magazine, more influential than even *Vogue* back then. Its art director, Willie Landels, was Italian and Scottish with a wicked wit. When I took him my portfolio of drawings, he looked through them with mild interest, then turned to me, saying, "We don't really need any drawings. But what is your inside leg measurement?" I thought he was being cheeky at first, but realized he was dead serious when he called two days later to hire me to model a menswear collection for *Queen*.

I was very flattered that he thought I could be a model. My very first attempt at modeling had come to nothing. In 1957, on my way back through New York after my first trip to Europe, I had actually done some test shots, but agencies thought I looked too much like an actor, lacking the requisite vacant stare.

The photographer for the *Queen* shoot was an American, Bill King, who inspired me to crack a smile and even laugh—quite daring for those days of the studied glare and mysterious, stern look. As far as I know, Bill initiated the whole leaping and laughing style in fashion photography that became most models' aim in the next few years. The pictures actually got a lot of attention, and soon I was modeling for many photographers, including David Bailey and Richard Avedon when he was on a visit to London.

Some of my subsequent modeling jobs weren't always fun, but I continued with them, as I needed the extra cash. I loved trying to feel the mood story the photographer was creating, but I didn't do that well with inarticulate photographers who would look at me and grunt and urge me to do more—but what? They would never actually say anything, just spur me on with their eyes and posture. I often left these "sittings" close to tears, fearing I wasn't what was required.

A watercolor I did of my good friend John Schlesinger in the sixties. Soon after meeting him I handed him a novel called *Midnight Cowboy* because I thought he should make it into a movie—and he did!

Meeting Billy and stepping into the world of fashion

I was constantly exploring my new exotic London between modeling jobs, painting, and doing illustrations. I'd take long walks to find old churches, markets, and charming squares. At night I'd follow the crowds of party-going British youth decked out in the latest gear from the hot fashion shop Biba or the flea markets. The aesthetic was dramatic, with dark plum nail polish and lipstick, optical-print miniskirts, flared trousers, and cheeky hairdos—shoulder length on guys, cropped Vidal Sassoon bobs on girls.

In those days, the gay scene was crowded with cute guys and lots of "dolly birds," as well. The girls felt safe hanging out with flamboyant boys eyeing each other instead of putting the make on everything in a skirt. London was definitely a more tolerant, open, relaxed place than the San Francisco I had left behind.

At a venue called the Gigolo, I met twenty-three-year-old Bill Gibb, a young fashion student going to Saint Martins College of Art. Though I was twenty-eight, Billy, like most Europeans, seemed more mature than me. He wore a shortened secondhand navy coat, flared trousers, and platform shoes. His deep Scottish voice entranced me as we left the club to get some air and have a good chat in the King's Road in Chelsea. Cautiously avoiding discussing his work, he murmured something about being interested in costumes. Actually, he was aspiring to be a fashion designer, and I guess he was afraid people would see him as effeminate. He was such a deep-voiced man, nothing about him could give me that impression. We ended up walking for miles, talking about our creative lives and dreams, ending up at his small rented room.

The next day, Billy visited my flat in the Victorian house on Lansdowne Crescent. After spending a week together, I invited him to join me in the flat, and we made plans to visit Scotland. First he gave me a little test. We were walking down a Notting Hill Gate street when he ducked into a red London pay phone booth, saying, "I've just got to make a call. Come in with me." He called his aunt Evie in Inverness and had a five-minute conversation in his native east Scottish dialect. When he put the phone down, he said, "There, do you still want to be friends?" Little did he know just how much that stole my heart. How exotic to be raised speaking a totally different language. I was smitten!

We took the sleeper from London to Aberdeen and were met in the morning by Billy's grandfather, a stout old man with a merry face, dressed in tweeds. They spoke only in dialect, so I had to guess at their conversation, but I was more curious about the landscape of Scotland's rolling hills and coast as we drove to the small fishing village of Fraserburgh.

Billy had grown up just outside the village on the family farm. When his mother, Jessie, asked permission to marry, her mother said, "You can marry, but you'll give what's in there to me," pointing to her belly. "You'll have more of your own." So Billy was raised on one farm while his parents and three brothers and three sisters lived on a farm over the fields.

When we arrived at Billy's house, his grandmother, with frizzy hair like the French writer Colette and a twinkle in her eye, said, "I suppose you are both tired and will share the same room, so up you go." Not a common reception for two men outside large city centers. Homosexuality was definitely frowned on if not pilloried in small towns. Children could

Above: With Billy Gibb in front of my shell study at our Lansdowne Crescent studio. We met when he was studying fashion at Saint Martins College of Art. **Below:** My drawing of Billy's grandfather, asleep in his farmhouse kitchen in Fraserburgh, Scotland, in 1966.

even be disowned by disapproving parents. It would be a few years till homosexuality was decriminalized and longer than that till it was freely discussed in the media and society without exciting prejudiced attacks.

When Billy opened his bedroom door, I was amazed. Here in this typical Scottish farmhouse was a room painted floor to ceiling like an Egyptian tomb. As a student, Billy had decorated the room to express his passionate longing for the romantic past.

When I later met his big, healthy, strong-armed siblings and parents, I saw how different, fine-boned, and sensitive Billy was and how his grandmother's influence had literally shaped him. She always understood him, while his longing to design frocks and have an international life was a mystery to the rest of his family. His oldest brother, then age twenty-two, had never been to London. As a world traveler who was greedy to explore the world, I found that fact shocking. London was so close, on the same little island, yet it was worlds and ages away from this protected wee corner of Scotland.

Before we left Scotland, I discovered the knitting yarns there. Realizing the colors were very unusual, I bought about twelve hanks, each in a different color, which I rolled into several large and small balls in each shade. Then I made a chart of a sequence of colors and gave the yarns and chart to one of Billy's cousins to knit a turtleneck jumper for me (see page 66). It was bold and really too strong for me, but it had started a ball rolling, so to speak.

Back in London, Billy eventually trusted me enough to show me his meticulously detailed fashion drawings. Fresh originality leapt from the pages. His kind of talent was so rare that it jolted the senses. He was longing for and deserved a place on London's fashion stage.

Having graduated first in his class from Saint Martins, famed for producing some of Britain's best dress designers, Billy got a postgraduate place at London's prestigious Royal College of Art and started there in the fall of 1966. Janey Ironside was then head of the fashion department, and she became a towering figure in Billy's and my lives—Billy was her star student. Janey dressed all in black. Since the world some years later was to wear little else for decades, it seems odd to realize how very unique she was then—with her black bob, pale skin, and dash of brilliant crimson mouth. Her outfits were always black in every detail.

Janey informed us that in the future, all embellishment in fashion would go. Clothes would be made from machines in some sort of plastic in sculptured pieces. Undeterred by this frightening pronouncement, Billy proceeded to follow his own unique vision. His plans would soon be under way for setting up a shop and having a big fashion show for his first collection.

Full of all strata of society and home to many bohemian types, Notting Hill was a great area to live in during the sixties. One young artist I met then was David Hockney. He had a studio in the area, and we used to see each other occasionally while shopping or at parties. His gallery representative was John Kasmin, whom I'd met through Jeremy. I visited David's studio just after he had discovered Los Angeles, and he showed several guests his little home movie about the Beach Boys, swimming pool culture, and palm trees.

I was amused by this blond guy with his northern England accent, gold lamé shopping bag, and relaxed attitude to his gayness at a time when it could be a dangerous thing to admit. His canvases in the Tate Gallery and his other earlier work failed to move me, but so

The stylish Janey Ironside, head of the fashion department at London's prestigious Royal College of Art. She encouraged so much British talent in fashion, including Bill Gibb.

British artist David Hockney with two of his paintings. We visited each other's studios when we both lived in Notting Hill Gate in the sixties.

much modern art left me cold that this didn't stop me from enjoying his amusing character. As the years went by, however, I came to love David's spontaneous use of color and beautiful craftsmanship. His portraits and still lifes really excite me now, and his Grand Canyon canvases echo the way I felt when I was on my ten-day trip through it. I also loved that David designed theater and opera sets and costumes. He is as theatrical as I am. We both relish the drama of life.

I also fondly remember Julie Hodgess as a particularly creative soul in those days. Her work for Jeremy Fry had really impressed me, and she influenced many other London designers from the sixties and through the eighties. She had been the inspiring decorator for the Biba fashion boutique on Kensington Church Street, not far from my studio. Loving all things art nouveau, she made wallpaper for the shop using massively wide photographer's background paper, onto which she printed huge, graceful scrolls—dark maroon on red, as I recall. She painted the same scrolls in the window, creating a black silhouette to peer through from the street. It was one of the most startling original décors in London at the time.

Barbara Hulanicki had founded Biba, which started a whole new fashion trend on the London scene in the mid-sixties. Biba girls would dress in the colors of Barbara's fashionable aunt, who favored mostly browns and shades of maroons, with dark brown (sometimes black) nail polish and deep maroon lips. She wore sassy, short hair and elegant yet boyish shoes. The look had people from all over Europe flocking to buy the affordable but highly sophisticated clothes that made Biba the byword for fashion and helped put London at the center of the fashion world.

Scene from Antonioni's film *Blow-Up*, with actor David Hemmings and supermodel Veruschka. I was an extra in a party scene in a London flat.

Julie Hodgess also decorated interiors for many of the more original and dashing aristocracy. She later opened a wonderful restaurant and wine bar in Notting Hill Gate. It was furnished with high-church items like Victorian pews, stained-glass windows, and marble tables. Julie's Bar became the bohemian eatery for artists and their patrons.

A great fan of Billy's, Julie was around at our apartment quite often, in her beaded twenties dresses with her long nose and bobbed hair, languorously dishing the latest dirt. One day in 1966 she mentioned to us that Michelangelo Antonioni was in town shooting *Blow-Up* and was looking for extras. We loved the idea of being in this famous Italian director's film, so we went along to the decorator Christopher Gibbs's house in Cheyne Walk in Chelsea. Christopher was an antique dealer and had lent his richly furnished flat for the filming. We would start at 9:30 p.m., and to stave off boredom while we waited hours to be filmed, we'd smoke a little pot and eat from a huge spread of food and wine laid out each night. I hate late nights, so I found all this waiting agony. I learned not to smoke too much or drink more than a glass of wine, or I'd just drop off to sleep.

Unfortunately, I never could spot myself in the final film. It's the scene where the German supermodel Veruschka is asked, "I thought you were in Paris?" "I am in Paris," is her enigmatic reply.

Starring David Hemmings, Sarah Miles, and a young Vanessa Redgrave, *Blow-Up* won the Cannes Grand Prix the following year. It caused quite a stir in London as well—it was the first British film with full frontal female nudity.

Billy and I continued our creative pursuits through 1966, artistically collaborating on some things and working solo on others. One day in October, we were walking down the road in Notting Hill Gate when a song came floating into my head. It was one Eduardo used to sing to me in Big Sur. I turned to Billy and said, "I've never introduced you to Eduardo. One day you'll have to meet him."

Billy replied, "Just a moment, I need a smoke," and ducked into a newsstand for cigarettes. He came out holding a newspaper. "Didn't you say Eduardo's last name was Tirella?" he asked. "There's a story about him in the paper." I grabbed the paper, shocked at the coincidence of finding it just as I was talking about him.

The story floored me—Eduardo had been run over and killed by Doris Duke outside the entrance to her mansion in Rhode Island. I called her and found out the whole story. Eduardo and Doris were just leaving her home to fly to California. He was driving, but stopped the car to get out and open the large iron gates. She slid over to drive through and accidentally hit the gas on the automatic car. It leapt forward, running over Eduardo. She was devastated, as he had become her closest friend. I felt sure Eduardo was communicating with me by sending me his song. The first line of the song that came into my head was "Nearer than my head is to my pillow . . ."

By 1967, Billy's work was starting to be noticed by those looking for the fresh new fashion talent. He was soaking up inspiration from wherever he could find it and incorporating it into his new designs. At one point we decided to travel to Paris to seek visual stimuli. We stayed in a little garret room in a hotel on the Rue du Bac.

I had been telling Billy that I wondered what he would look like without a beard. He'd had one ever since we'd met. After a long morning of walking, I took a nap and Billy entertained himself by secretly shaving the beard off. When I woke up, he was sitting at the end of the bed with a strange upside-down smile. I asked him, "What is wrong with you? You look strange." He just kept on smiling. Suddenly, it dawned on me—he had done the deed. All I could say was, "Do please grow it again! I never realized how much it suited you."

An hour later, a knock on the door informed Billy there was a call from London. When he returned from answering it, he was ash white. "You'll never guess what! I've been invited to New York to take part in the Yardley 'London Look' awards in two weeks. I have no time to grow the beard!" I knew how concerned he was about his appearance and felt terrible for him. It was scary enough being a Scottish farm boy traveling to the most professional city in the world. Before he left for New York, he tried to fake a beard with makeup. Nothing worked, and he went off with one of the earliest stubbles in men's fashion.

One of the pen drawings I did of Paloma Picasso when she sat for me in the late sixties. We met during my modeling days, work I took up to supplement my meager artist's earnings.

Participating in the Yardley awards cut short Billy's study at the Royal College of Art. He was ready to start up his professional life. An Irish woman named Alice Dunstan Russell, who had a good head for business, agreed to run a shop for his designs. They hired a brilliant Italian woman, Nives Losani, as his pattern cutter. He and his team worked round the clock for months to get those sketches from paper into three-dimensional garments. The night before his first show, we got a terrible shock. The entire collection was stolen. Lesser mortals would have given up at such a blow, but Billy and the team started from scratch to recreate the collection, and the shop—called Alice Paul, in Addison Road in Kensington—was launched a few months later. Billy's first work was similar to other designers of the time—stylish, plain little tailored dresses. But they had a highly original cut, and I knew Billy had a distinct flair that would surface in his future.

In October 1967, I did another modeling gig with Bill King. To set up a pretend party, he had gathered together some models and a few celebrities—Paloma Picasso, supermodel Twiggy, and David Mlinaric, one of the up-and-coming interior designers to the great and the good of England. A few days after the shoot, Paloma came over to my studio and sat for a series of drawings I did of her.

1968–1969
Catching the knitting bug

Although I had continued my artwork after meeting Billy, I got drawn into working with him on his collections as well. I had great interest in and admiration for his work, and the textiles he was working with intrigued and excited me—textile pattern and color was really starting to grab my attention more and more.

In the summer of 1968, Billy and I went to visit a mill he knew about in Inverness. They had a good collection of ancient tartan weaves that we thought would be perfect for his next collection. Our train to western Scotland took us through the most subtly colored landscape I had ever seen. Lichen-covered stones rested beside rushing streams of peat-stained amber water. Bracken in strawberry-blond tones, mixed with purple and lavender heather, covered the rolling hills. The air was so pure and clean that every detail could be read for miles.

When we got to the Holm Mills in Inverness, run by Bill Pringle, I was astonished to find all the colors from that breathtaking landscape on the shelves of the mill shop in their knitting yarns. I'd never seen such exquisite tones and quickly bought up twenty shades that went together gorgeously.

On the train on the way home, I began thinking about my newly acquired yarns. These subtle tones needed to be combined with great sensitivity. I couldn't rely on anyone else to knit up my vision the right way, and it would take them far too long, driving me mad with anticipation. Alice Dunstan Russell, who ran Billy's Alice Paul shop, had accompanied us on the trip and was sitting opposite me on the train. I looked at her and asked, "Do you know how to knit? I need desperately to do something with these yarns I've just bought." She did know, and because I had bought needles the right size for the yarn, I had my first lesson right there on the train. I practiced deep into the night as the train roared south to London.

By the time the train from Scotland arrived in London, I could knit! Fired up, I went straight to a yarn shop to purchase a nine-penny leaflet that had instructions for a raglan-sleeve cardigan. Back in my flat, I started to use my bag of twenty Shetland colors to create a complex striped cardigan. It looked like some ancient cloth found in a desert tomb. Since I changed colors every other row or so, there were many yarn ends, like a shag rug, running along the sleeve and side seams. I proudly showed my creation to my friend Barney Wan, who was then the art director at the British *Vogue* fashion magazine. He liked it and suggested I take it to show Judy Brittain, editor in chief of *Vogue Knitting Book*, an offshoot magazine run by the parent magazine *Vogue*.

Being so proud of my new baby, I ran to the Vogue offices the next day and presented it to Judy, a tall, sensitive Irish woman with reddish curly hair, a large nose, laughing blue eyes, and the pale skin of a Van Dyck portrait.

Judy seemed impressed. "This is where knitting is going in the future!" she proclaimed emphatically. "Could you try another design in Fair Isle?"

"What is Fair Isle?" I returned.

"You know, those intricately patterned sweaters you see from the 1920s," she said.

"Oh, yes, but how do I manage different colors in a row?" I asked in all innocence. One of the sub-editors jumped up, grabbed some yarn and needles, and showed me how to change from one color to another while knitting, using both the intarsia and Fair Isle techniques.

Before starting my design job for *Vogue Knitting Book*, I went to the British Museum reading room, where I discovered some amazing Celtic manuscripts. The graceful geometric patterns and gentle colors instantly became the inspiration for my first knitted Fair Isle vest. I bought my yarns from a London shop, so I knew knitters could find current colors to reproduce any design I came up with.

After finding a plain vest pattern I could follow for the shape, I simply cast on the recommended number of stitches and started creating rows of Celtic circles and crosses. I worked the patterns right onto the needles, with no sketches or charts or anything to follow. The yarn palette was husky fresco colors that I would like to wear myself—sea greens, soft wine tones, and golden wheat hues, all in the tweedy mixtures Shetland yarns are so famous for. What a thrill to see the pattern grow beneath the needles! As I knitted through

1, 3, 4, 7, 8: Some knitting patterns that resulted from months of experimenting with this newfound way of expressing color ideas. 2: The first design I ever knitted. The cardigan's simple stripes feature the subtle landscape colors that caught my eye when visiting Scotland. 5: My friend Judy Brittain on a turkey farm. 6: The first piece of hand knitting that I designed for publication as a pattern, a Fair Isle vest with a striped back. It was commissioned by Judy for British *Vogue Knitting Book* magazine in 1969.

that first commission, my mind was leaping ahead with excitement to all the possibilities for this lovely texture—everything around me inspired more knit designs. My creative mind was in overdrive.

After three weeks of struggle, I took the finished pieces of the Fair Isle vest to show Judy at *Vogue Knitting Book*. She loved it and said she would feature it in her next issue of the magazine. In a state of ecstasy that I'd pulled it off, I rode home to Notting Hill Gate from Hanover Square on the top of the number 15 bus. Once home, I realized with a cold shock that I'd left the knitting on the bus! There was nothing to do but start again and knit the entire thing from memory. I hadn't even made any notes of the colors or the sequence of the patterns that I'd created free-form on the needles. Determined to make the deadline for the magazine despite this, I dived in immediately and finished the new version in half the time it had taken to knit the first. I'll never know for sure, but I think it was pretty close to the original.

One thing that saved time was making the back of the vest in a repeating stripe using the same colors as those in the front patterns. I felt this intentional mixing of patterns had a very strong Eastern feel. Not everyone is as taken as I am by the juxtaposition of different patterns; when I was showing slides of this vest years later on a tour of England, a woman in my audience shouted out, "You could have got that back and front to match if you had really tried!"

Judy said to me after the vest appeared in the magazine, "One day you will be designing for the Missonis."

"Who are they?" I asked.

"Oh, just the best knit designers in the fashion world," she replied.

By this time, my father was getting very intrigued by my "highlife," as he saw it, in England. One day I got a call out of the blue: "What about renting a car and driving down to the south of France?" queried a deep voice. I couldn't believe it when it turned out to be Dad. He checked into a London hotel after he arrived, but took me and Billy and a couple of friends out to lunch at Mike's Café.

After this, I had to make a trip away for a few days, which left Dad alone in London. He somehow got hold of my address book, planned a surprise party, and invited *everyone* in the book! On my return, I was confronted with an influx of humanity into my peaceful studio. One-night stands rubbed shoulders with editors of magazines, publishers, and theater and fashion people. It was a towering success, but I shuddered every time the doorbell rang, horrified to think who might walk through the door next.

One day while Dad was still there, he said to Billy and me, "I think I'll take that Alice from Billy's shop out to lunch." Billy and I turned to each other, saying, "Alice?" Dad usually had an eye for such glamorous women. Alice was married and very involved with running Billy's shop, so she tried to hold Dad at arm's length, telling her staff not to take any more calls from Mr. Fassett. But he was very persistent, and she finally gave in. She told me some forty years later that suddenly on the way to lunch she felt "a wave of feelings for him"— feelings that led her to leave her husband some months later and follow Dad to Nepenthe.

Since my arrival in England, I had failed to convince any London gallery to show my paintings. The only show I had managed to secure was the one-man drawing show at the Hazlitt Gallery in 1965. Trying to inspire interest in my paintings was disheartening. Most London galleries, even after several invitations, would not even come to see my studio. I had finally decided to go to New York in 1967 to see if anyone there was interested. What a difference! Almost at once someone recommended a gallery just off Madison Avenue. A Norwegian Cuban American, Richard Larcada, enthusiastically offered me a show in a year's time. I skipped back to London and painted like a demon for a year, with short interruptions for my newfound knitting. How motivating it is to be wanted!

In 1968, when my work was nearly ready for my September show, I ran into Steve Lovi on a shopping trip to the center of London. I had only seen him once since our fateful meeting in Big Sur. He was visiting England and needed a place to stay. "I'm going to New York to show my work in a couple of weeks; you can stay in my flat till I return," I said. He came over and shot a very good picture of me with my canvases arranged all around me, which I used on the invite card to my New York show. He also studied each painting carefully and gave me invaluable pointers on improvements I could make. It was my first experience with his brilliant eye.

I took the Queen Elizabeth over to New York, loving the sea and remembering my first trip to Europe on the Dutch liner. All my canvases were rolled into a cardboard tube that fitted nicely under my bed in my ship's cabin.

When I got to New York, a very friendly Japanese artist mounted the canvases on bars and framed them for a price I could afford. Some of my white studies had featured broken dishes, which led to one of my admirers in New York saying, "You must have had a sad childhood if you are attracted by broken objects."

The show was surprisingly successful and sold well. I was delighted, now knowing I could survive on my own work for certain. Nevertheless, I had definite hangups about rich people and comfortable living, which I would bang on about from time to time. Richard Larcada needed to make a thousand dollars a week to keep the gallery open and therefore lived in an affluent world well beyond my small exchanges. Richard sat me down one day and blasted my inverted snobbery, saying, "You think you live so well on so little. Well, think again. You live off all the people around you who have money. You are afraid of success, so you put it down. There is something amazing about success—when you start getting it, people want to help you. They will do all they can to get you to their level if you let them."

Richard's advice made me realize I had a lot of attitudes that distorted what was actually happening, and I needed to stop putting up mental barriers to development. Opportunities were presenting themselves constantly, but I would talk myself out of them, thinking, "That's not for me," or "I'm sure they didn't really mean to help me," and so on. Despite trying to get over these ingrained attitudes, I would still fall prey to them on occasions. At a party years later, on a tip from my New York friend John Torson, the great dress designer Hardy Amies asked me to bring my knitwear to show him. "Oh, I'm not sure I really want to design for industry," I said hesitantly.

He quickly replied, "Fine, let's say no more about it," and turned on his heel, leaving me feeling distinctively disappointed. As I thought it over, I realized I definitely did want to enter that design world, and his help would have been invaluable.

During my Larcada show, I missed another opportunity, but perhaps it was for the best. I met avant-garde artist Andy Warhol at a dinner party, and he asked me to come down to his studio, called the Factory, and join in a film he was producing at the time. He looked

Playing with circular shapes in the crockery I found in Portobello flea market—a favorite painting from my white period. Pudding basins, with their ridged interiors, were particularly exciting to paint.

1, 2: Two early white and neutral still lifes—it was my fast from color. **3:** Italian film designer Nando Scarfiotti wearing a leather cape Steve Lovi made for him. **4:** Steve Lovi's photo of me in my Notting Hill Gate studio in 1968, with my white studies prepared for a show in New York. **5:** My painting of Steve Lovi in his colorful flat in the seventies.

chalky white, and his cadaverlike pallor hinted at a very unhealthy life that frightened me, so I never went. I did wonder what being in a film of his would have been like. His newest release at the time was called *Flesh* and starred a handsome Joe Dallesandro, who spent much of the film in the nude.

When I returned home from New York, I found Steve had kept my flat
in good nick and was so at home in London he had taken a large flat about one block away from me. It had a huge dividing wall down a generous-sized room that made two long, narrow ones. A week after he moved in, he hired a tiny workman to remove the wall. We all drank tea at one end and watched as this little man, with the aid of an axlike hammer and a stepladder, proceeded to chip the wall down. It only took two or three hours, and the big studio room that emerged would become the stage for the Steve Lovi Salon.

Steve painted motifs on the cupboards and hung antique Chinese lanterns, and I spent two or three days happily doing a painting of the room he had created.

Steve invited London's most creative thinkers and great lookers to hang out at his colorful studio. In the late sixties, London was *the* city in the world to be in. Mary Quant and Zandra Rhodes set the fashions, and pop groups were forming at a rate of knots. The Moody Blues, the Who, the Rolling Stones, the Animals, and the Beatles created our soundtrack and, along with Twiggy, Jean Shrimpton, and David Bailey, were reaching icon status.

Shortly after seeing my first knitted Fair Isle vest for *Vogue Knitting Book*, one of Judy Brittain's colleagues working for the British *Vogue* asked me to design a garment for a large color page she was planning. I did a long, slim-fitting coat in diagonal stripes with a rich embroidered-looking border. Working on it was just as exciting as doing my first knitted piece. At the photo shoot, my coat was styled with the Russian boots and fur hat popular at that time, and was photographed by David Bailey.

Around the same time, another delightful and surprising bit of publicity came in another issue of British *Vogue*. It was a shot of me sitting on my bed, covered in my knitted throw; I am surrounded by my latest hand-knit designs—cushions, a knitted shoulder bag, a sleeveless patterned sweater—and wearing my very first cardigan. The caption read, "Kaffe Fassett, the king of knitting." The photo was taken by Tessa Traeger, a brilliant photographer who captured my imagination in later years with her inventive collages of food, flowers, and spices arranged to form glorious pictures. She had a love for these tricky conceits that matched my own fascination for detail and witty placement. To this day I find myself spellbound by artwork created out of alien material. Jeff Koons's two-story-high dog covered in growing flowers at Bilbao's Guggenheim Museum or Ken Knowlton's fascinating portrait of a mill owner done out of 945 spools of colored sewing thread.

When Tessa's photo of me appeared, it was the first time I began to realize how powerful publicity was and how easy it was to get when you were such a bizarre creature in the world of so-called "women's work." (Years later when I produced my first book the press would beat a path to my door.) But knitting had become so obsessive for me that I hardly noticed the attention I was getting from people around me and I doubt I'd have stopped even if no one had been interested. I began to understand how those naïve artists who cover temples with pebbles, or forests with tinfoil, must feel. Driven by a vision of creative possibilities and the deep pleasure of working with your hands.

Above: Tessa Traeger took this photo of me for an article in British *Vogue* in the late sixties. The caption read, "The king of knitting." Amazing, as I had only had two designs published at that time. I'm wearing my very first sweater (see page 89).

In 1969, the day after the *Vogue* magazine featuring my diagonal stripe coat hit the newsstands, I got a call on the hall phone in my Notting Hill Gate apartment building. An Italian-accented voice said, "Hello, this is Rosita Missoni. My husband Tai and I would like to come and talk with you." It seemed Judy's prediction was coming true—but much faster than we could possibly have imagined.

An hour later, a tall, handsome man and an attractive shorter woman draped in the most beautiful machine knitting were seated at my kitchen table. "Can we see your spring knit collection?" they asked.

I blanched. "I am afraid this is all I've got to show," I said as I shoved a shoebox at them containing a few gnarled swatches of patterned knitting.

"Don't worry, your coat in *Vogue* is the most beautiful thing we've seen in knitting, and we want you to come to Milan and design for us."

As I flew over the high frozen Alps, I couldn't believe my luck. Two knit designs published, and here I was on the way to design for the best in the business. When I arrived in Milan and was shown into the factory, the first thing I noticed was the beauty of the colored yarns lying everywhere. "Who designed these colors?" I asked in astonishment.

Rosita explained, "Tai did them from a Japanese woodblock calendar he found." If a commercial house could start with such an outstandingly rich palette, I knew we could really go places.

I launched straight into my task. I saw the husky rusts, old golds, wine tones, and blacks as biblical in mood and started doing bold stripes and geometrics. I asked for taupe, aubergine, rust, and gold, and was asked, "Do you want those in cotton, wool bouclé, mohair, or silk?" How luxurious! Very few of the workers in the factory spoke English, so I had to learn my colors and the words for one line of color, two lines, et cetera, in Italian—"*due giri nero.*"

During this first week of designing for Missoni, I got so carried away seeing my combinations roll off the sample machines that I came to dread the sound of the machines shutting off at lunch break and at the end of the day. When everyone was gone, I'd always find Tai in his office working quietly on graphs for new designs. He had been a champion sportsman when young and still cut a lean, dashing figure. He spoke little English, but as he drove me to the airport, he sang "Cherry Blossom Time" in his deep Italian voice.

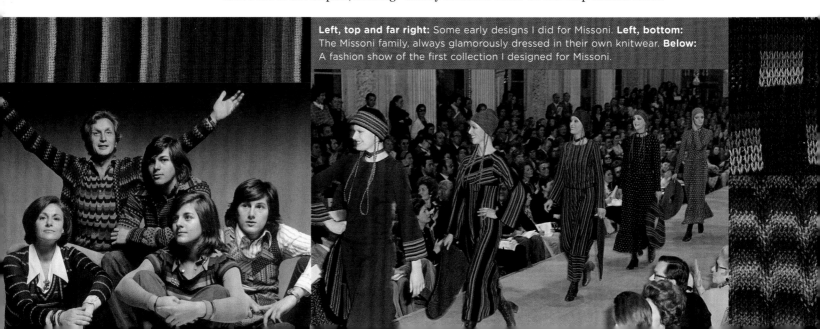

Left, top and far right: Some early designs I did for Missoni. **Left, bottom:** The Missoni family, always glamorously dressed in their own knitwear. **Below:** A fashion show of the first collection I designed for Missoni.

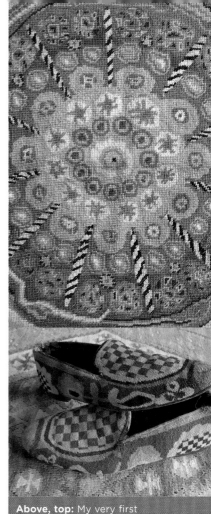

Before I left the factory, with plans to return at a future date, Tai asked me what I wanted as a fee. I actually hadn't thought about that and had to think fast. In those days, I was living on three pounds or less a day in London, and selling a painting for 100 pounds would set me up for a month or so. So I cautiously said, "Fifty pounds for a design?" Rosita and Tai put their heads together and started to argue in Italian. It got really heated, with pounding on the desk from Tai and bellows from Rosita. I sat there quaking, thinking of Mom and Dad's fights. I was about to say, "I'll take anything you want to offer, really," when Rosita turned to me and said, "Don't worry. We always talk business this way." Finally Tai looked at me and said, "Okay, twelve designs at fifty pounds each."

When I returned a few months later, the entire factory was pumping out my knitted textile designs. They were on every machine and on the cutting tables being made into gorgeous garments. I felt on top of the world.

Around the same time I met Judy Brittain at *Vogue Knitting Book*, she introduced me to her best friend, Pamela Colin, who also worked at the knitting magazine. They made quite a comic pair: Judy tall and languid, Pam short with big black hair and a sassy New York sense of humor. At the time I met Pam, she was courting Lord Harlech, a baron and a leading British politician who had been the British ambassador to the United States in the early 1960s. After seeing my hand-knit designs, she asked me to design a pair of needlepoint slippers for her to stitch for Lord Harlech. I painted a 1960s primitive flower pattern that she was very happy with.

"Do me a cushion design now," Pam begged. I had just bought an English millefiori paperweight in soft pastels in the market, so I enlarged the image of it to fit a round cushion shape. I chose colors for it, and to show Pam where the color went, I started to stitch a small amount of color around the design. (Judy's sister, Betsy, had taught me the basic stitch a few weeks prior.) Before I could stop myself, I had finished the whole cushion! This was something I'd always heard was terribly technical and time-consuming—I'd known women to struggle over an eyeglass case for months! But I could do a whole cushion in a few days and found it was mighty addictive.

My new passion for needlepoint equaled that for hand knitting. I couldn't wait to move on to other needlepoint projects. Instead of giving the cushion to Pam, I took it to Women's Home Industries, where Beatrice Bellini was running a bespoke needlepoint shop. She loved it and asked me to do more designs that she could have made up to sell. She had already knitted my long, diagonal-stripe coat design from *Vogue*.

Pam invited me down to Harlech Castle in Wales after she married Lord Harlech late in 1969. My strongest memory of the visit was waking up in her guest room covered with a quilt made of old English furnishing fabrics. The oversized cabbage roses were faded, but so memorable that they were to jump to mind more than twenty years later, when I did my first patchwork quilt design called *Rosy*.

Textile designs were starting to captivate me like this at every turn. After trying to remain a pure fine artist, I thoroughly gave in to the life of a craftsman—or, you could say, my artistic ideas transferred to the textile world. Something about creating fabric—be it knitting or needlepoint—was far too motivating for me to abandon and return exclusively to easel painting. I could express all my passion for color and form in these soft human textures and longed to create bigger and better examples.

Above, top: My very first needlepoint—a design I stitched for Pam Harlech in 1969. **Above:** The slippers I designed for Pam's husband, also in 1969. **Below:** A needlepoint chair I did in the 1990s, showing my lasting love for overblown blooms.

chapter four

1970–1979

My Design
Work
Takes Off

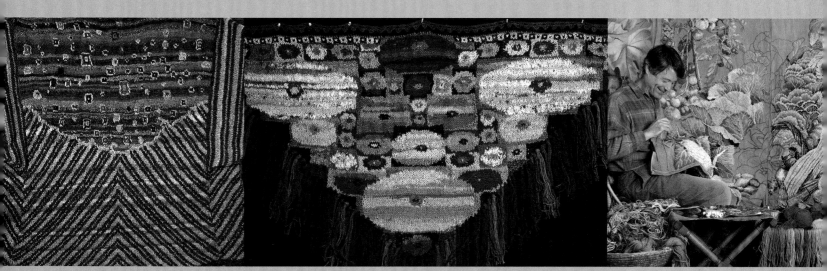

Above, left: The chenille, wool, and mohair jacket I knitted for Philippa Franses in the early seventies—my first exploration of the Roman glass (millefiori) look in knitting. **Above, center:** My first knitted shawl, made in the 1970s. I was so enthused that I knitted it in four days, winging the design as I knitted. **Above, right:** Happily stitching on a vegetable garden tapestry. The big bargello stitches make this task very much like painting with wool. **Opposite:** Zoe Hunt in my Romeo and Juliet coat. I was using a mix of yarn types and scores of colors in my one-off knits in the seventies. I used a similar color theme for the two ribbons from 2010 that flank the photo.

At the end of the sixties, I had gained an entrée into textile design—designing my first handknits for Vogue; collaborating with Bill Gibb, a budding star in British fashion; working on machine-knit fabrics for Missoni; and creating my first needlepoint designs. The seventies were to bring me more work in this field than I ever imagined I would have. I felt instinctively the moment I started hand knitting that knitting, in a new, colorful form, could change the world. Its addictive force had grabbed me and released so much creative energy, but calmed me down at the same time. Wouldn't everyone benefit from these effects? Like a religious zealot, I envisioned masses of people turning to this simple craft, but it would be some twenty-five years before that would happen. Needlepoint had similar benefits, with one exception: For this painter, it also satisfied a desire to be able to add more detail into my textiles as I created my glorious celebrations of color.

Diving into the decorative arts

Billy Gibb had been intrigued by my work for the Missonis, but felt knitting lacked "hanger appeal"—it didn't look good enough on a rack to incite impulse buying—and so had not included much knitwear in his collections. In 1969, he had begun working for the London couture house Baccarat merely to help finance his shop. The owner, Monty Black, was well into tailored Courrèges-type garments, and thought Billy's new long, flowing skirts and multi-patterns were for the birds.

I felt strongly that Billy's unique work wasn't getting the amount of attention it warranted. So soon after my success at getting my diagonal coat into *Vogue*, I decided to see what I could do to get more publicity for Billy, and I took the drawings for his next collection to show Judy Brittain. "I'll drum up a story that we will take to London's *Sunday Times*, where Ernestine Carter, London's best fashion journalist, has her column," she said. "But you must do the knitting to go with Billy's outfits—that will make a real story."

I hadn't thought of collaborating with Billy in this way, but I loved the idea, so I had a stern talk with him. "This is our big chance," I said. "We must do something really eye-catching and unusual. Forget that fashion is going with the uncluttered coats and pillbox hats worn by Jackie Kennedy. We must do something rich, with a touch of the exotic about it!" I took him to the Victoria and Albert Museum to see my beloved Persian and Indian miniatures with their layers of patterns. I also showed him the work of the French painter Édouard Vuillard with his rich mixtures of pattern—floral dresses in front of flowery wallpaper with great bunches of real flowers and patterned cloths. "That's the look we should begin with!" I said. Billy took to the idea with alacrity; he combined his ancient tartans with flower prints and geometrics, and I knitted up swatches that pulled all the colors and patterns together.

We had to find a machine knitter who could quickly do a small production for our collection, as hand knitting seemed out of the question at that time. Knitting instructor Mildred Boulton was willing to take us on and was not daunted by my complex designs.

Judy said she had to offer our story to *Vogue* out of loyalty because she worked there, but the *Sunday Times* was really her goal. Surprisingly, *Vogue*'s fashion editor, Marit Allen, jumped at the chance to showcase us and offered a full-color four-page article if we could get the clothes made. Marit went on to be a sought-after costume designer on many important films, such as the 2007 film telling Edith Piaf's story, *La Vie en Rose*, so she was well into our theatrical look.

Monty Black said even one color page in *Vogue* was worth thousands of pounds, so he was forced to make up Billy's and my designs for the amazing free publicity. "Only a few kooks at *Vogue* will buy them, so I'll only do two of each design," he exclaimed.

Opposite: My portrait of weaver Richard Womersley, who became my business partner and frequent design collaborator in the early seventies as my work in decorative arts was taking off.

99

1: A Fair Isle knit design inspired by borders on antique carpets. **2:** Twiggy bringing bewitching glamour to a Bill Gibb dress in the early 1970s. **3:** A chenille and Lurex dress I knitted with actual pearls, in front of one of my needlepoint tapestries. **4:** The Sarah Moon shot of designs Bill Gibb and I collaborated on for British *Vogue* in 1970. **5:** The exciting interplay of patterns in this canvas by the French painter Édouard Vuillard encouraged me to mix patterns with abandon. The way he placed dress prints against wallpaper prints layered with real flowers really inspired me. **6, 7:** My contemporary patchwork fabric Cogs (top) carries the pattern on, as does Floral Burst (bottom), a fabric by Philip Jacobs, who designs for the Kaffe Fassett Collective collections.

2

3

4

5

6

7

When the new collection was shown, Ernestine Carter was in the front row and said with enthusiasm, "It's such a relief to see a collection with handwriting!" She did a brilliant article for the *Sunday Times* that appeared in 1970 just after the *Vogue* piece, so we had double the publicity we expected. The new star of photography Sarah Moon, a model turned legendary photographer, did a brilliant job shooting the *Vogue* pages for us. The one omission when the article came out was a mention of Monty's fashion house, Baccarat. He was understandably furious, but took it with humor, sending a black wreath to *Vogue*, saying, "Let's bury the hatchet."

In 1970, Billy also got his first accolade, the Vogue Designer of the Year award. Most of his work by this time was highly romantic, with full, flowing lines and lots of fabric prints, some printed specially for him. Embroidery and textures like leather, lace, and knit made unique combinations, and Billy had many followers.

Despite the fact that he was now recognized as a leading young British fashion designer, Billy was very protective of and nervous about his growing reputation. When anyone would visit our flat, he would cover the drawings of new designs on his desk. Since I was always longing for people to take notice of anything I produced, it shocked me that he could be so secretive, and even at times resentful of other people's media coverage.

When his contemporary Ossie Clark started getting headlines and column inches for his new collections, it really riled Billy. Ossie had been only one year ahead of Billy at the Royal College of Art fashion school. One headline at the time proclaimed him in big letters "The Wizard of Ossie." After that, I'd often hear Billy muttering to himself, "The wizard of bloody Ossie," every time he'd spot a new article on the ever-successful Ossie Clark. He once said, "Oh, Kaffe, you'd only have to run two seams up and *you'd* make headlines!"

A few years later, when Billy was the toast of the town—with his own TV documentary and dozens of articles in magazines and papers on every collection he unveiled—his focus was always on one critical commentator who repeatedly disparaged the Bill Gibb look. Michael Roberts was a very talented fashion journalist and illustrator, but he had an uncompromising way with words when it came to fashion criticism. Billy would ignore the overwhelmingly glowing reports his work got from others and moan about Michael's latest barbed comments.

Over the following years, we watched Ossie as he became the top designer to pop stars like Mick Jagger and the Beatles, then squandered all his money on drugs and extravagant living. His diaries reveal a sad life, as he lost the will to carry on designing. Just as he was getting the courage to make a comeback and getting help to do it, he was murdered by a young Italian lover in 1996.

I continued working for the Missonis during the seventies. They had a huge launch of their own boutique at Bloomingdales in New York in 1970, one of the most popular department stores in those days. Many of the machine-knitted textiles in that launch were from that first collection I designed for them. The director of Bloomingdales asked the Missonis who the designer was, but they decided not to tell, as it was a collaboration (they had done the garment shapes), and they didn't want me to be poached. Thrilled to be working for these towering professionals and learning so much, it seemed a small price to pay.

I did more collections for Missoni later, but I had produced so many designs the first time I went to their factory that they were able to run with those for a few years. My greatest memory of my time working for them was finding a scrap of vintage knitting in a Rochelle-type stitch, where stripes of color create intricate rippled patterns. I showed this to Rosita Missoni, and she said, "We have a machine that can do it. Select some colors, and we'll add this to the collection." Before leaving I chose about fifteen colors—Old World summery tones including taupe, rust, ocher, teal, dusty pink, and pale yellow—to create a rich harmony of stripes that were just different enough not to blend into each other. When I got back, Tai took me to see the machine threaded with my colors. I was horrified to see that each color sequence had to have a separate spool per shade, so the floor was covered in dozens upon dozens of spools, as each repeat of the stripe had its separate feed. The result, though, was elegant.

Creating eye-catching color combinations has always been a very instinctive process for me. I look at a group of colors and "feel" that certain tones will distract from their neighbors while others will make a color glow or spring to life by an exciting contrast. It's very difficult to put into words, but I can arrange balls of yarn quickly for a knit class that demonstrates instantly what I'm trying to achieve—how colors are intensified or softened when they are placed next to each other. Watching colors come alive when they connect with each other and exude their innate richness is a joy I connect with every day as I work. Rosita and Tai Missoni, being sensual Italians, saw at once where my talents lay. I never had to explain myself to them.

Judy Brittain and I became inseparable friends in the early 1970s. We dined out, went for long weekend walks, and dreamed about what else life had in store for us. She often said she longed to travel, but couldn't on her meager journalist's wages unless it was for work. "If you're willing to travel in my modest style," I told her, "I will finance a trip to California and take you." I knew that the Greyhound was doing bus trips anywhere in America at ninety-nine dollars for ninety-nine days. We could fly to New York on cheap tickets and bus across to California and back for a song. She agreed, packed her jeans, sneakers, and a few blouses, and off we went.

When we got to New York in late 1970, Judy said, "I have to pay a courtesy visit to American *Vogue* as I'm here." The great figure of Diana Vreeland was at the helm, and she greeted us a bit coolly, I felt. Judy introduced me as a designer who was working with Bill Gibb. "Oh, my God!" she screamed, "You are that fabulous knit designer! The knits were the best thing about that collection!" I had been amazed that an article in British *Vogue* had pronounced me the king of knitting, so perhaps all these judges of fashion were more farsighted than I was. Though I did have my dream—that knitting could change the world— it would be twenty-five years until the masses would agree with me and hand knitting would become addictive to a substantial number of people worldwide.

As we worked our way across the vast country, Judy and I both loved looking at the unfolding landscapes and characters boarding the bus. We had a great stop in New Mexico, going up to Santa Fe for a night. Judy loved Big Sur when we got there; she even sent for her sister Betsy, who flew out from London to join us. My mother was intrigued by this exotic Irish/English import, and when Judy found a four-leaf clover in our canyon, Mother quipped, "She would!"

Above, top: A watercolor I did of my good friend Judy Brittain, who worked as an editor for British *Vogue Knitting Book* throughout the seventies. **Above:** My niece Erin Gafill's painting of the coastal view from Nepenthe. **Below:** One of my early diagonal knit designs. **Below, bottom:** My oil portrait of Judy.

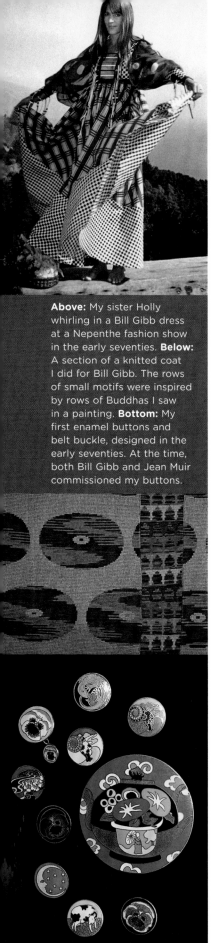

Above: My sister Holly whirling in a Bill Gibb dress at a Nepenthe fashion show in the early seventies. **Below:** A section of a knitted coat I did for Bill Gibb. The rows of small motifs were inspired by rows of Buddhas I saw in a painting. **Bottom:** My first enamel buttons and belt buckle, designed in the early seventies. At the time, both Bill Gibb and Jean Muir commissioned my buttons.

When we got home to London, Judy was so exhausted and jet-lagged that she woke up and wandered about her own flat in a daze. "Where am I?" she asked herself. She looked at the furnishings and objects on the mantel and decided that wherever she was, it was a place that she approved of. "Wasn't that good that I liked my own style?" she said to me later.

Having heard firsthand about my London life, my sisters became intrigued to visit. The first to come to the Notting Hill Gate flat was Holly. I loved showing the high life to her. We got her a red crushed velvet trouser suit that was all the rage. She later admitted that she had suffered for fashion as she hated velvet and couldn't bear to touch it. The London partygoers loved Holly, but she cut her vacation short a week because she desperately missed her kids and realized she was a mum first and foremost.

My sister Kim came next—slim and bright, but in an old pair of cowboy boots that were so worn they hurt her to walk very far in. We went to dozens of stores to try to find her new ones, but she could never, let me repeat *never*, find what she wanted. Shopping is so easy for me. I once bought an Armani suit (the most expensive thing in my wardrobe) within ten minutes of entering the store, so I have very little patience for the dithering that never seems to lead to what one wants. Kim does have a good eye and taste, but I'm still amazed by her indecisiveness whenever we shop. Later I watched from afar as she suffered great rejection but soldiered on raising five children on her own.

I seemed to spend every waking moment designing knits and needlepoints in the early 1970s and really enjoying working with colors—it was such an exciting, edgy process. I loved the fact that I could do very painterly rendering in needlepoint as opposed to the bolder simple designs in knitting. Portraits, flowers, and vegetables became favorite needlepoint subjects. I continued to design needlepoint cushions for Beatrice Bellini at Women's Home Industries to make up and sell in her shop, and private clients were starting to express interest in commissioning very large needlepoint panels from me. I kept up with my painting as well, getting enough canvases ready for my next show at the Larcada Gallery in New York, which was scheduled for 1972.

If any other design job came my way, I snapped it up if it took my fancy. I even designed some buttons back then. One day an ex-lover of Camilla Fry's, Rod Tremain, contacted me and asked if I could design a little enameled plaque for a sports trophy. I was really intrigued when I saw that he could make small, colored pictures with enamel, and I immediately thought of the exquisite buttons that could be made with this technique. After convincing Rod, I got right to work designing a series, working with the enamelers to get the colors just right. The first customers for my line of buttons were Billy and Jean Muir. Jean was a passionate, well-established British fashion designer who was drawn to Billy and his work. She came to dinner at our flat a few times, and I liked her tiny figure, deep voice, and utter belief in what she was designing. She did crisp, classic women's wear—comfortable, simple shapes in the best-quality silk jersey and often in the same plum coloring season after season.

When I first proposed to Billy and Jean that they might like to order my buttons, they both resisted. They said the two shillings and sixpence wholesale price was far too high and would bump up the garment costs astronomically. That was before Jean had seen the buttons. When the rep went around to her studio and showed the lotuses, pansies, and other designs we were doing, she rang me at once. "Why didn't you tell me they were fabulous?" she cried. She then had me do two new designs just for her. My favorite was a little black-and-white cow on a copper-colored ground. Billy had me do a bee design for him that became his symbol.

Years later, I came across some of my buttons in a flea market in London. "Those are very old English buttons!" I was told with authority by the seller. I even found some at the famous vintage button shop Tender Buttons in New York.

Throughout the seventies, I continued to meet inspirational creative types in

London—people whose energy spurred me on in my own work. I had the very good fortune to meet the great Patrick Woodcock in the late 1960s and continued to be included in his get-togethers into the early 1970s.

Patrick was a private doctor who loved the arts and made it his job to entertain the creative souls in that world. He would cook lavish meals and invite a star-studded cast. Through him, I met playwright Peter Shaffer when he was celebrating his success with *Equus* on the London stage; painter Keith Vaughan; playwright, director, and actor Nöel Coward, sharp as a tack in his early seventies; and the acid-tongued John Gielgud, as well as many others in the fashion, theater, and art worlds. At one of these dinners, I got talking to Tony Richardson, the director of many successful British films that I had enjoyed—*The Loneliness of the Long Distance Runner, Tom Jones, The Charge of the Light Brigade*. He had just traveled up the Big Sur coast, after visiting his friend Christopher Isherwood. I asked him if he had stopped at Nepenthe—at that time one of the only places of quality in Big Sur. "Oh, yes," he replied, and before I could say I grew up there, he muttered under his breath, "And I met the dreadful man who owns the place."

"That would be my father," I answered with a smile. Though this objective view of Dad was not that surprising, the fact that so many important European artists were seeking out Big Sur and Nepenthe was exciting to me.

Another interesting encounter I had in the early seventies was meeting

writer Antonia Fraser in Notting Hill Gate, a tall blond with a ravishing complexion. I totally saw how playwright Harold Pinter fell for her beauty and deep thoughts. She lived in nearby Holland Park. On a visit to her house, I spotted a pink, red, and white antique hexagon quilt and asked if I could borrow it. I really loved all the detail I could squeeze out of patchworks as subjects in my paintings. Antonia's delightful textile became a feature in a large two-panel painting I did, each panel measuring three feet by four feet. The circular table the quilt was on filled most of the canvas, giving a sensual curve to the work. This was one of my first ventures away from the white-on-white canvases I was selling with Larcada in New York. Later, my good art dealer friend in New York, John Torson, bought the painting, and it hung in his flat for many years till he sold it to one of his clients.

John was another guiding angel in my life. This Norwegian American had great taste. A collection of interesting artworks always adorned his New York apartment, from which he made his living. He always had a comprehensive view about the current shows in New York's many galleries and sale rooms and would take me out on art tours of the city whenever I arrived there. He gave me a place to stay, and our morning talks about every aspect of life were invaluable.

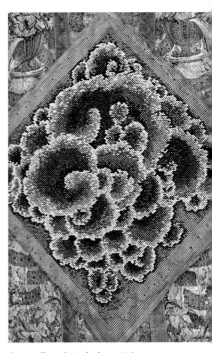

A needlepoint chair seat I stitched for my New York friend John Torson in the seventies.

By 1971, I needed to have more space for my design work and painting, so I moved out of the Notting Hill Gate flat into a flat in Kilburn. Billy was by this time hooked up with a new business partner, Kate Franklin, and they were making plans to start Bill Gibb Ltd. The first knit designs I had done for Billy were made on a domestic knitting machine by Mildred Boulton from my swatches, but in 1972, when Billy's company was under way, Harry Green of Gould's in Leicester began manufacturing the machine knitwear, and Mildred switched over to producing Billy's handknits only. I continued to produce two knitwear collections a year for Billy for the next fifteen years, while working on my own burgeoning projects as well.

By the time I moved to Kilburn, I was having to occasionally employ knitters and stitchers who could help me keep up with all the work I was getting. There were knit swatches to complete for designs I was doing for companies, and one-off knits and needlepoints to prepare for private clients. In the fall of 1972, Richard Womersley joined my small design studio. He was a sensitive, private fellow with a fine head straight out of a Piero della Francesca painting. Richard was also very musical, but was working in a technical examinations office. I asked him to help me on some needlepoint I was stitching, and he proved to be brilliant at it. He quickly learned to knit as well and designed some intricate Fair Isle pieces, then collaborated with me on Missoni and Bill Gibb knits in the following years.

Richard had such natural talent for stitching that I put him to work helping me on a commission from George Harrison. I had gone down to George's gothic Victorian house in Henley to see what he wanted. His wife, Pattie, had visited and invited me to make a very large needlepoint piece for the music room. When I got to the house, I was asked to wait in the kitchen. Some adolescent kids were knocking around the big kitchen and then left me alone till a fellow with a perm came in, grabbed a guitar, and started picking away absentmindedly. I had never seen George with a perm, so I didn't recognize him. Finally he looked up and asked, "Who are you?"

"I'm Kaffe, here about the needlepoint hanging."

"Oh, my God, I thought you were just a friend of the kids! Come on, we'll go look at the music room."

Since the Harrison's house was high gothic, I went straight for antique instruments for the two planned panels. For my source material, I found a wonderful collection of decorated instruments with inlaid ivory and marquetry at the Victoria and Albert Museum.

When I presented the finished panels to George in his house, he looked quite taken aback. "I thought they would be modern instruments," he declared.

"Oh well, you can't win them all," I thought.

One of the great characters I met soon after I moved to Kilburn was the carpet dealer and textile expert Jack Franses, an Englishman of Greek Jewish descent. He had a handsome, manly face and wild black hair that suited his active mind and quick wit. His huge shop on Piccadilly, near Fortnum & Mason and the Royal Academy in the heart of London, was painted a rich teal blue and was always hung with stunning old carpets or tapestries. It became a regular haunt for us young textile makers. Jack would always delight in our interest, taking time to show his latest finds or enthusiastically educate us about different countries and their typical kinds of weaving and motifs.

1: One of the needlepoint panels of instruments Richard Womersley and I stitched for George Harrison's music room in 1972. 2: Pattie and George Harrison stepping out in the latest gear in the early seventies. 3, 7: The one-off vest I made for textile expert Jack Franses, and a watercolor I did in his carpet shop in the center of London. 4, 5, 6: Early machine knits I designed for Bill Gibb. After the extravagant use of color in my hand knits, it was difficult to limit myself to six shades.

Jack had a deep love of the textile arts. When I wanted to buy an old carpet from the market, he would come have a look and tell me if it was worth the price. His eye for exquisite textiles was unerring. Since the world of carpets fed me so many ideas, I couldn't get enough of Jack's great treasure trove of a shop. I painted a watercolor of it one day and often did sketches of details from his carpets to use in my knits.

One of the first private one-off knitting commissions I did was for Jack, a vest of large primitive circles outlined in bright, contrasting colors. On the back I knitted a two-color design I'd seen on an Islamic arch—this became one of the most famous early motifs in my repertoire and was known as Jack's Back. My second important commission was for his beautiful wife, Philippa. She had red hair and large green eyes. I knitted a drapey chenille jacket for her—dove gray with intricate Roman glass-like (millefiori) details at the yoke and diagonal stripes in shades of steel. I have shown it since in many exhibitions and at lectures.

Establishing a name for myself as a designer

Despite my burgeoning career as a decorative artist, I made a big push to give Richard Larcada another painting show in 1974. I'd gotten over the flush of excitement of showing my paintings twice in New York at his gallery, and for a time, I felt both he and I were both going on to other things. I was so absorbed in my knitting that I wasn't producing enough new work for a third show there.

About a year after my second New York show, my friend Charles Heim in California informed me he had a contact who wanted to show my paintings in his gallery in Seattle, about as far away from New York as you can get in America. Charles rounded up old work of mine he had in San Francisco, and I got enough paintings sent to him from Nepenthe to patch a show together. I didn't bother to inform Larcada about this minor event.

Out of the blue, Larcada had to deliver a valuable painting to a client in Alaska and just happened to have a stopover in Seattle. He wandered around the art section of town and stumbled onto my show. He was irate, feeling he should be my sole agent in the United States. He wrote me at once stating that we should freeze all my prices on any work no matter how old, and I should prepare a new show for him. I was shocked he had caught me out, but thrilled at his renewed interest in me as an artist.

After the first two shows of white-on-white studies for his gallery, I started to branch out into a bit of color. I was frequently visiting the Victoria and Albert Museum, where the Persian and Indian miniatures were still fascinating and influencing me. I loved all those layers of pattern—flower prints on stripes on geometrics in joyous colors—all working so well to create a harmonious arrangement. I started collecting everything with bold patterning that I could find—paisley and embroidered cloth on which I would place strong floral china or stripes and dots. The table in the studio started to hum with patterns. Some were delicate and faded, some theatrical with bold color. Intricately colored still lifes became my obsession now, replacing my white chinascapes. Patchwork quilts that I'd find in the flea markets or borrow from friends became the perfect bases for the pattern world I was creating.

When I took these new paintings to Larcada to show him, he was delighted, but the real enthusiasm came from a powerful, outspoken interior decorator named Sister Parish, who clutched her bosom and gasped as she entered the gallery. She was a force in interior décor in the United States, the originator of the American country style, and an influential designer in the restoration of the Kennedy White House.

Sister Parish got right on the phone and beckoned her clients and decorator colleagues. The designer Mario Buatta (the Prince of Chintz) and others headed to the gallery to start buying up this new guy in town. At one point Sister Parish broke off a call to whisper across the gallery, "How does it feel to become famous?" I was taken aback, as I certainly didn't think about myself or my work in those terms—I was just ecstatic whenever I was able to earn enough money to pursue my art and design work at full throttle.

As a result of this show in 1974 and my newfound "fame," the well-known agent and fashion publicist Eleanor Lambert came to see the work and had me visit her fabulous antique-encrusted apartment on the Upper East Side so she could interview me. Eleanor was a great promoter of U.S. style and fashion and had started the International Best-Dressed List for this purpose in 1940. She sat on a low banquette in front of me wearing a chic New York short skirt that afforded me a "tunnel view." Well-preserved sixty-two-year-old as she was, I didn't know where to look—as the English say. She lived to 100 and claimed her longevity was due partly to heredity, but mostly to hard work. When people at the Larcada Gallery heard that Eleanor was writing about me for a New York newspaper, they felt I had made it indeed. One assistant said to me as he looked around the gallery at my show, "What does it feel like to own *all* these *paintings*?" Strange thought for me.

Left: The painting show I had at the Larcada Gallery in New York in 1974 ended my white-on-white period—from then on, my painting would be infused with color and pattern. This pattern-on-pattern still life features china, paperweights, and swatches of Designers Guild fabric prints. It is one of the works bought by an Iranian couple for their shop in Tehran in 1977, right before the Ayatollah overthrew the Shah. **Overleaf:** One of the Indian paintings that lead me to combine colorful patterns in my painting and textiles.

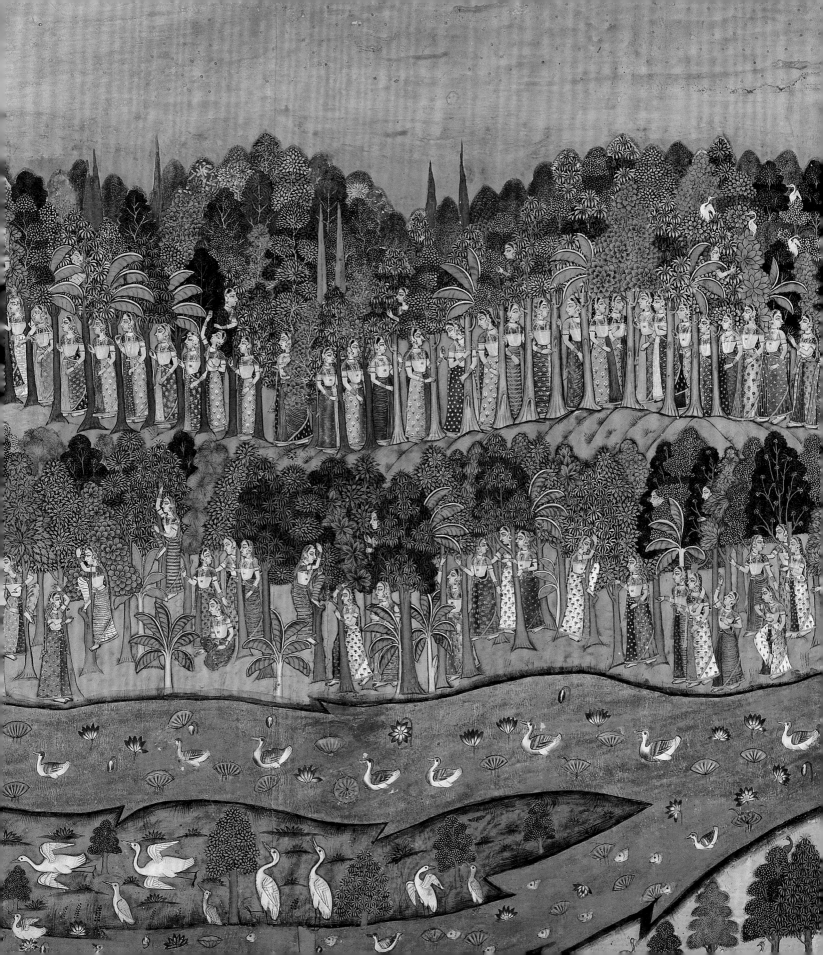

Although my heart was in London, where my creative life was unfolding, I always returned regularly to visit my family for glimpses of that colorful, vital California life. By the mid-seventies, Dad was very involved with Billy Gibb's shop manager Alice Dunstan Russell. He had convinced Alice to join him in California. She arrived with one of her sisters, and when Dad took these two Irish women to Nepenthe, he told Mom that they were "just some friends of Kaffe's." But Dad and Alice's relationship got serious quite quickly, and Dad rented a house down the road so he could move in with her.

When I visited Big Sur, I noticed how happy Alice was living in America and running our fabulous Phoenix Shop at Nepenthe, which sold unusual antiques along with books, pottery, jewelry, and garments. This was a double blow to Mom, who had dreamed all her life of setting up this shop and now was practically barred from any decisions about its management. There was her husband, having a very public affair with someone who was taking over her dream.

I don't think I was quite aware how difficult it was for my mother; after all, it was the swinging seventies, and everyone I knew seemed to be bed-hopping. Back in England, when I ran into Alice's husband at a party, he pinned me to a wall with questions about Alice. "Oh, she is so happy," I heard myself saying, then realized I was talking to the other spurned party. Before I could apologize, he said, "I'm so glad. I want her to be happy," and he looked genuinely relieved.

Fortunately, Mom's creative spirit and energy were never dampened by her personal troubles. On one visit to Nepenthe in the mid-1970s, I saw she had acquired a peacock. At sunset the peacock would find its way to a large framed window on the roof of the restaurant where everyone inside could see it clearly. Because of the growing dark inside, the sunset was reflecting in the window, and the peacock would see itself and display its huge, glorious tail, making the equivalent of a stained-glass window in the restaurant below. I heard one customer shout, "Nepenthe was always fabulous, but this is too much!"

Sometime later, when the bird was hit by a car on our driveway, Mom rushed out with a shovel and buried it at once. "I don't want anyone fighting over the feathers," she pronounced.

By 1974, Alice had had a child. Dad called my fourth sister Havrah, which amazed us all, as this was his and my middle name. My mother sometimes took care of Havrah when Alice was in the shop. It was a very loaded, interesting arrangement, but somehow very Big Sur.

My oldest sister, Dorcas, a tall, elegant mover, took up flamenco and belly dancing. She gave amazing performances on the restaurant terrace until she found religion with a church in Seaside.

Dad lost interest in running the restaurant after he got together with Alice, but he did come back after a while and got more involved again. This meant Alice had time on her hands, so a visiting Irish poet caught her eye and wooed her. She asked Dad if he minded having an open relationship, and his definite "No!" had everyone on the coast laughing their heads off. When she eventually got more involved with the poet, Dad cut her off from the shop and hired someone else to run it. Alice then announced she needed a settlement or she would take him to court for palimony. She said the best years of her life had been dedicated to developing the shop. I was surprised when Dad called me to try to find out anything I knew that could besmirch her name. It was like mafia stuff.

Dad and Alice finally agreed to settle out of court for $10,000. Because Dad was known to be good at operating the stock market, Alice gave him the money back so he could invest it to give her an income. All the investments shockingly failed, and they lost every penny—another very Big Sur drama. Dad eventually bought a house near Carmel for Alice, her sister Gina, and Havrah. Years later, they took care of Dad as he aged and had a stroke. I even heard him saying to someone, "I have two Irish nurses at home!"

By the mid-1970s, Holly was running the restaurant, and my shy little sister proved to be amazingly organized at all of it, though she did worry a lot. Once Dad was established in his new town residence, she often checked in on him. As was true for all of us, her relationship with him was often less than ideal. One day she was feeling very vulnerable and wanted a hug from her old dad. He was abstractly rattling on, criticizing the running of Nepenthe, so she left disgruntled, got a mile down the road, and thought, "Damn it, I'm going back." She rang his bell, and Dad came to the door very puzzled and concerned. She blurted out, "I came here for a hug and I want one!" It was such a shock to him that he just threw his arms around her and gave her the most heartfelt hug she could ever remember.

My pen drawing of my sister Holly in the seventies. I went to see my family in Big Sur annually throughout the decade, where I would find Holly painting, knitting, and running Nepenthe.

With my creative life unfolding in London and my knitting design developing at a rapid pace, I was doing some serious thinking about where to focus my energy. On a visit to New York, I met up with Drue Heinz, a philanthropist of the arts and the publisher of the *Paris Review*, and she ventured to give me some words of advice that embedded themselves in my memory. After putting up a still life of mine she'd just bought, she turned to me and said, "Don't dabble in the crafts if you want to be a serious painter." She saw I was wearing a sweater I'd knitted and thought she should warn me. She had hung my large still life, measuring four feet by six feet, on the main living-room wall with a Morandi and a Renoir, not bad company for a novice in his mid-thirties.

But as I returned to London, an overpowering urge to go on knitting seized me. I suddenly realized that when I was painting, I was filled with doubts and often procrastinated, doing anything to avoid having to go to the studio and finish a painting. Once I got painting, it drew me in and I'd have a return of enthusiasm and confidence for a while, but the next day the same reluctance to get started would overcome me.

A knitting project, on the other hand, had me leaping out of bed. I'd often get sucked in before I even bothered to dress or have breakfast. Each new project pulled me along with great excitement as I wondered how it would turn out. Designing on the needles as I knit meant living dangerously, and each piece was breaking new ground in a never-ending flow of ideas. As I sat knitting, I'd dream of all the exciting variations I could go on to when this one was done. Each time I'd shop for new colors, I could hardly wait to see the combinations unfold. Finding a new layout as a vehicle for my colors was pure gold. After a while, the painting studio gathered dust as I sat in my knitting chair, spinning out one colorful web after another. Cocktail parties and even my beloved English country house weekends became a bore if I couldn't take my knitting along.

The distinction some purists draw between art and craft doesn't exist for me. So many artists today seem to be able to use textile making in their work that the barriers are softened. I always try to make my textiles as beautiful as I can manage, imbuing them with all the efforts of a work of art. It's up to others to describe, if they have to, what it ends up being.

Some of my favorite commissions in the early days after Richard Womersley had joined the studio were from a Hungarian American named Muriel Latow. She was a very talented interior designer who had an elegant flat in central London. Muriel was larger than life in every way—huge, expressive, rolling eyes and colorful dyed hair, usually red with a bold streak of blond. Being tall with a very ample figure, she wore sacklike dresses of stunning color and texture, often styled with enormous amber beads or something equally dramatic.

Muriel told me she had had an art gallery in New York in the early sixties, and had been friends with Andy Warhol and had given him many of his most famous ideas. Even though I could plainly see she had very creative concepts and certainly inspired me, I couldn't quite believe she had hung out with Andy and told him to paint everyday objects, like soup cans and money. I'm sure now it was true; she evidently made him pay her fifty dollars whenever she gave him an idea.

Muriel had a way of cutting to the essence of a situation very much like my friend Steve Lovi. She once said to me when I was resisting going to a big party, "Kaffe, your work is breathing for you. Social life is bullshit!" When my artist and designer friend Lillian Delevoryas showed her a lamp base she was planning to put into production using appliqué fabrics, Muriel exclaimed, "It's horrible!" I can't remember if Lillian took this criticism to heart—she went on to win many awards for her work, so it certainly didn't stop her flow of creativity. We were used to Muriel shooting from the hip.

Muriel had definite taste, but was usually open to my suggestions when she asked me to paint or stitch for her. She designed houses for a very wealthy clientele, and my first commissions from her were two elaborate needlepoint chairs—one of undersea coral and another of oriental trees. When these were done to her satisfaction, she commissioned me to paint murals. In 1974, she asked me to do a mural in a bathroom in a lovely old house in Hampstead, north London. I got Richard Womersley and a new recruit to our studio, Jill Gordon, to help me paint the background bits. Muriel had to take a trip to America and left me with a letter to give the owner of the house if he interfered with our painting.

The owner did stick his head in the room a couple of days later and said, "Okay, you can admit it. Have you guys ever actually painted before this job?" I swiftly handed him Muriel's letter. He was amused and read it to us: "Listen, don't worry. These people know what they are doing. Eat another of my special brownies and chill out!" After that he left us alone. When the exotic oriental flower painting was done, Muriel had cloud-shaped mirrors cut and placed over it in the strategic gaps left for them.

A little while after completing the mural, I called the owner's wife to ask if I could possibly come to photograph it. "Sorry, I am too busy," she would always reply. I finally said, "I must get a record of the mural. Couldn't I come over on a day you can't be there?"

"No, this is one job that will have to go unrecorded," she answered. My heart sank. I sensed that another mural of mine had been painted over. My angels were definitely telling me to take another path in life. I was grateful I had thought to do a watercolor of the painting in progress.

Yet this experience somehow didn't deter me when Muriel asked for another commission in 1975. She wanted a mural throughout the hallways in a big house she was decorating in the English Cotswolds. I suggested that we do botanical themes similar to tapestries with borders. She loved the idea, and big tulips were first, then a massive hall done as a plant-filled jungle scene.

Left: A knitted coat I made for interior designer Muriel Latow in a fashion show at Sudbury Hall in Derbyshire in the late seventies. **Above, top:** A close-up of Muriel's coat. **Above:** Muriel inspecting the mural she commissioned me to paint in a Cotswolds mansion. **Below:** Another part of the mural I painted for the mansion. **Below, left:** A needlepoint called Oriental Forest that Richard Womersley and I stitched for Muriel.

I moved to a cottage near the house that summer and was joined for the months of painting by Californian artist Craig Biondi, a very handsome young fellow whom Muriel found devastatingly attractive. Craig and I painted away happily, always thrilled when Muriel would roll up from London to view and react to our efforts. She would fall heavily against the wall in a passionate swoon on seeing our latest detailed painting.

When the Cotswolds murals were done, the owner of the mansion sold it and moved to a new residence, taking the murals with him. With foresight, I had painted them on canvas glued to the walls. It was another sadness for me in the mural department, as the paintings were designed to work within that house, and I couldn't imagine them somewhere else. They've probably been stored all this time, and I was never paid for the last two I completed.

I had also stitched a needlepoint bedcover for the master bedroom of the same house. It had an oval of shells resting on frosty winter leaves, the whole composition depicted in thousands of colors. Because I had had a falling out with the owner when he refused to pay for the last of the murals, I borrowed the bedcover for an exhibition and decided not to give it back. He pursued me for it, sending threatening letters. I hired a lawyer, then spent every waking hour thinking how I'd defend my actions in court. "There is no way he can win, is there?" I asked my lawyer. After all, he owed me more than the bedcover was worth.

"Oh, yes, he could win," she answered.

I thought to myself, "It's not worth it, to lose peace of mind over money." I returned the bedcover that afternoon, which was hard for me as I had another buyer with money in hand.

But aside from these experiences, I loved working on commissions for Muriel. I also knitted two very strong garments for her. One was a triangle motif kimono jacket, and another was a floor-length coat in magenta and black, bold zigzags moving up the body. She sold it back to me years later when she needed the money.

Muriel always made a big show of loving what I did, praise that every artist craves to receive. She also had a sideline, writing soft-porn romantic novels, under the name Roberta Latow, that I enjoyed reading. They were all about slim, sexy, glamorous women, but I could see they were Muriel. They always had her garments, shoes, hair, and objects. This huge woman lived a rich fantasy life that was, one could surmise from the details in her stories, not completely fantasy.

I'll always be grateful to the women in my life who inspired me to create beyond what I felt I could produce. This is the best gift to any artist, to be stretched and appreciated. Women's liberation was a huge topic at this time, but as I looked at my life, I was amazed there was a need for it. So many doers and leaders that I worked with and for, like Judy Brittain and Muriel Latow, were capable, artistic women. Brigid Keenan was another one. A vivacious blonde full of mirth and cracking ideas, she was an editor for the London *Sunday Times* newspaper. She loved the needlepoint paperweight design I'd done for Women's Home Industries that was featured in *Vogue* in 1969 (see page 95). In 1975, she asked me to do a cushion design that could be sold as a kit through the *Sunday Times*. I did a bold carpet-inspired design in navy and cream with a center of primitive flowers and a contrast dot design bordering them. It was a runaway success, far outselling any previous offer. Brigid's early encouragement of my needlepoint cemented a friendship between this delightfully funny woman and me to this day. She married a British ambassador and later wrote a hilarious, best-selling book on her role as his wife called *Diplomatic Baggage*.

The wonderful Brigid Keenan, back-combing in Damascus. She commissioned my first needlepoint kit for the London *Sunday Times* and was one of the many creative, strong women in my life.

Another strong woman who inspired years of design from me was Tricia Guild, who headed a rising soft furnishings business called Designers Guild. She started her company in 1970, but we met some time later, probably 1973, and by the mid-seventies I was doing designs for her. She and her partner, Simon Burstein, a very dashing dark-haired fellow who ran his family's prestigious London fashion boutique, Browns, came to the studio to meet with Richard Womersley and me. The first pieces Tricia commissioned from us were a few needlepoint cushions for Browns Living shop, which she was running at the time. Richard was by then a weaver producing gorgeous woven throws, and she ordered some work from him as well; this was the start of a long working relationship for them.

My wash drawing of Tricia Guild. She was responsible for me becoming a fabric designer. We loved collaborating on the collections that followed.

Tricia was so inspired by my sketchbooks that she saw me clearly as a fabric designer and gave me the encouragement I sorely needed to pursue that. I had the feeling designing fabric-print repeats was a very specialized job that needed a precision I didn't aspire to. She said people could help me with that. Tricia saw that I loved geraniums and had me use them on fabric designs, pottery, and needlepoint cushions. The second furnishing-fabric collection I did for her was stripy daisies and rows of beans creating decorative patterns. For the bean pattern, I had gotten a bag of mixed dried beans for making soup from the grocery store, spilled them onto a tray, and studied their colors and patterns. The first big design I painted on a flattened cardboard box because I liked the brown background. The printers handed it back like a dirty diaper. "Please put this on paper. We can't work from this board!" So I started again (shades of my first knitted vest for *Vogue Knitting Book*, left on a London bus).

Tricia and I worked together brilliantly. She was a stunning woman, with olive skin, fabulous curly black hair, and dancing eyes. She loved my fabric design and used it in just the exciting combinations that turned the press and her customers on. She would often hang my paintings in her Designers Guild showrooms and encouraged me to do knits for cushions and throws to accompany them.

One day near the beginning of our working relationship, Tricia informed me she was looking for a unique birthday present for Simon Burstein. She wanted one of my watercolors for him, but wondered if I could customize the frame by painting colors and patterns on it. As I was working on it, I got a call from Simon asking if he could pay me a visit. I said, "Fine," and hid the frame before he arrived. He informed me he wanted a special Christmas gift for Tricia. As she loved my paintings, could I paint something medium-size that she would like?

"Okay, but bring over some of her favorite china so the still life will really be to her liking," I told him. The next day he came back with a set of her favorite Clarice Cliff antique china, carefully wrapped. He told me he had had to get it out of the house while she was at work so it would be a surprise.

When Tricia got home that night, she noticed at once her cherished pieces were gone and demanded an explanation of Simon. He made up a tale of being so cross at her over a disagreement that he broke the china in a fit of pique. "Well, I can understand that passion, and I'm flattered you feel that way, but just give me the pieces so I can glue them together."

"Uh, I buried them in the garden and I don't want them retrieved," he said.

Simon had his birthday just before Christmas and was amazed at his gift. When I popped in to see how the painting Tricia had given him was received, he met me at the door saying, "You must be the richest artist in London!" When Christmas rolled around and Tricia opened her gift, it paled next to the ecstasy of getting her Clarice Cliff china back in one piece.

1, 3: The rose and fruit chair back panel I designed and stitched for Tricia Guild, and the needlepoint in progress. **2:** Working on my Jar Tapestry. **4, 5, 6:** My Geranium print and two needlepoint cushion centers I designed for Designers Guild. **7:** Working in the studio on a bargello needlepoint bench cover, wearing my pearly king knitted top. **8:** A portrait I painted of Tricia Guild and her daughter. **9:** The watercolor that inspired the Geranium print above. **10:** The Bean fabric collection I did for Designers Guild, painted on cardboard.

I continued to do fabric print designs for Tricia throughout the mid- and late 1970s. At one stage during this time, she traveled across America and suddenly understood my buzz of color even better. She called me up to exclaim how the strong color in the landscape of America had gotten to her. After this, she painted every room in her vacation home in Tuscany different tones of a deep new color. I was able to really pull out the stops on my next fabrics for her. Gone were the milky shell tones and pastel pinks of my first collections. Judy Brittain once said, "I feel everything you do for Designers Guild is painted in milk." But once Tricia and I were into intense color together, fruit and bright flowers figured in the fabrics and her room sets, which were often photographed for publicity and her beautiful books. She also commissioned several needlepoint designs from me for her own home. My favorite was a rose and fruit panel for a chair back that inspired a luscious gold palette.

I was constantly impressed by Tricia's passion for her work and for life in general. I remember vividly one day when I had dinner with her, and she asked what I was doing. I told her that my friend Steve Lovi was staying with me and what an inspiration he was for every aspect of my life. As I described him, she became more and more agitated. "Oh, my God, I love this type of man!" she cried. "I have to meet him." So I arranged a meeting and she did, indeed, fall for him with enthusiasm, to put it mildly. She hired him to photograph a series of advertisements for her. They were black and white with only the fabric in color in the shots. He had to keep reminding her that his proclivities lay elsewhere, but it didn't dampen her enthusiasm for him. It's what I love about this passionate woman. She is nothing if not wide open to her current craze, so unlike most reticent English people, who don't act on their enthusiasms till they are absolutely sure.

Tricia would go from mood to mood in styling her look for the Designers Guild interiors over the years. But she did it with such bravado that we all followed along, dying to see where she would go next. Soon the bright color gave way to stern neutrals, and the minimal look was embraced. She did it so well, but I'd been there myself with my white-on-white paintings. Through those minimal days, I was the designer for her more romantic side. I had painted big bunches of roses on my living-room walls on a washy yellow background. She liked that and had me do a fabric of it for her. I'd just paint some roses, and she would have her amazing team beautifully reproduce them in dozens of colors that felt so painterly you could hardly tell print from painting.

By the nineties, when Tricia went into her next color phase, her team was so good under her direction that she didn't really need my input, and a working relationship that had lasted more than twenty years gradually phased out. It had been a rich, rewarding time that helped me a lot in developing my patchwork fabrics.

When I was growing up in Big Sur, Dad would occasionally quote Gurdjieff, a Greek-Russian spiritual teacher who had had a profound influence on generations of followers and who had made a big impression on Dad. My brother Griff had joined a group back East near the house he built, and he and his wife, Roz, were well versed in Gurdjieff teaching and exercise routines.

In the early 1970s, I'd learned a meditation technique and practiced regularly at first, but like a lot of good things our better self is drawn to, it started to be less important to me as life's excitements distracted me. Then in the mid-1970s, my friend Lillian Delevoryas introduced me to a meditation group in London that followed the writings of Gurdjieff's main disciple Ouspensky, who had broken away to form his own splinter school. Lillian, having found this source of vitality and centering for herself, reawakened that enthusiasm in me. I realized I could gain energy and clarity in my perception of life by sitting down and repeating a mantra for half an hour every morning and evening. Also, discussing it with a group helped me to value it and keep to the routine. When I was tired or depressed by some setback, the stillness of sitting would put my life's events into perspective.

Lillian's group met in a big London house that had been bought by current followers of Ouspensky headed by Dr. Roles. Richard and I joined together, were initiated into Maharishi's transcendental meditation, and learned the Dervish turning that had been brought in from Turkey.

Learning the turning was a long and arduous training, starting each morning at 6:30. A board was placed on the floor with a smooth, protruding metal "nail." You placed your bare toes around this nail to help center you as you learned the solitary motion and posture of the Dervishes. The hardest thing was to hold your arms up straight and outstretched to the sides of the body at shoulder height—one hand open to the heavens receiving blessing and power, the other hand angled down giving to the earth. Some days I tried so intensely to get the turning motion that the space between my toes would be bleeding at the end of the session.

When the group finally got it sufficiently to wear the costume and do the turning in a large circle with music, we all felt a thrill—though we had a very long way to go. The costume was a huge white circular skirt weighted at the hem to help it whirl, a little white jacket, supple leather dance shoes, a black cape, and a tall brown felt fezlike hat. We learned that each part of our gear had significance. The white part was our shroud, the black cape our coffin, and the hat our tombstone. When we threw off the black capes and emerged in our whites with tall hats, we would spin out onto the dance floor and whirl around a still figure in the center, called the sheikh. The sheikh would move slowly in his black robe while we orbited around him, representing the planets. The music was tragically sad, but with a beat and ongoing momentum that kept us flowing. Enduring the agony of holding your arms up at the shoulders and parallel to the floor was only possible if you could manage to enter the moment and be present. The minute your mind wandered, it became totally exhausting. "I know about those weights pulling your arms down," my teacher would tell me sympathetically. But on the few good days when I was rested and centered, I experienced a real high from the ceremony, and it all seemed worth the efforts.

One day in 1975, when I was working away in the studio with Richard, I got a call from a visiting knitwear manufacturer who wanted to buy designs. Because I had never been able to find a manufacturer willing to create the complex type of colorwork I was designing, I was quite blasé on the phone, saying I wasn't really interested. Maurice Bretzfield, a Californian who got knits made up in South Korea, was persistent. "If you don't sell me designs, I'll just buy some hand-knit samples and knock you off. It's your choice!"

"Come right up," I said, knowing he could, and most likely would, do as he threatened. Richard was looking at cars to buy at that point, and the first collection we did for Maurice paid for the down payment. During that period I favored bold designs with clear outlines. One of the sweaters I designed for Maurice depicted a row of overlapping geese I'd seen on an early Egyptian painting, worked in rusts, browns, creams, and ochers.

Maurice came back several times for more designs. "Where do you sell these?" I asked.

"Oh, they don't sell really, customers want much safer designs of plain colors, maybe a few stripes," he explained. "But when I put one of your samples at the front of my stand at trade shows, it attracts buyers in." A couple of years later, he bought one of my favorite still lifes from a show I had at the Hazlitt Gallery in London. That was the show where one of the gallery owners said, "If you were eighteenth century, we could sell you easily."

What shocked me about the pace at which these American entrepreneurs lived was a story Maurice told us one day. He had poured his best efforts and ideas into a house for himself and his family in Beverley Hills. Just as he was about to move in, a guy offered him so much money for the house that he sold it—before even moving in! Somehow that shocked and sickened me—it was like an emotional earthquake. It made me realize again that I'm not motivated by money.

With both Richard and me working madly on all the design

commissions that came to the studio, we were able to take on more and more work in the mid-seventies. We had also started hiring more helpers to knit swatches and to participate in stitching needlepoint designs. This sampling of some of the work taken on in 1976, the same year I started lecturing about my work on tours organized by the British Crafts Council, gives an idea of what was coming out of the studio: a one-off sweater for Jack Franses; a large needlepoint hanging and two big needlepoint panels for private clients; a needlepoint kit offer for British *Good Housekeeping* magazine; two knitwear collections for Bill Gibb and one for Missoni; knits, woven fabrics, and fabric prints for the New York fashion house Sportwhirl; fabric prints for Designers Guild; and knitted garments for Women's Home Industries to sell in their shop. I never took on work solely to make more money (although supporting myself was always a necessity), but because I was so excited by the idea of a new project and my mind was buzzing with color compositions. Never one to follow color forecasts, I would just see what yarns were available and follow my gut feelings about which ones would make a good combination. Since I was visiting museums rich in decorative history, my imagination was full of medieval and Renaissance references—deep rich palettes of lapis lazuli, husky reds and rusts, mossy greens and earthy ochers. I never lacked ideas.

Richard was by this time also heavily involved in weaving, which he had started in 1973. In 1975, he had received a grant from the British Crafts Council to buy a new loom for himself. Up until then, he had been borrowing a loom in a weaving school. Although I have taken up the challenge of many crafts, learning weaving was something I had no patience for—too many technical issues to deal with. It was amazing how from the start Richard brought color and bold pattern into his designs when most British weavers, it seemed to me, were quite monochromatic and technique bound.

With so much on our hands, we decided to officially form a design company in 1976, and Richard took over the ground floor flat in the same Victorian brick house to have plenty of space for himself and his loom. (Over the years, I was to slowly expand my work and living space into the whole house, as other tenants moved out or sold up.)

The buzz of color and pattern Richard and I produced in so many forms caught the attention of ambitious entrepreneurs over the years. We were offered backing to create a large design company that could supply an entire department store with just Kaffe Fassett products—sheets, towels, wallpaper, china, and more. After talking it over, we'd decline each

One of Richard Womersley's early woven blankets photographed on Hampstead Heath in London. It was designed around the time we had a joint exhibition of our textiles at the British Crafts Centre in 1977.

offer, as the thought of running such a big enterprise would surely mean loss of control of our design processes. Perhaps we were too cautious, but there is great satisfaction in being able to design and guide each work, keeping closely to my original intention rather than giving in to the inevitable compromises you'd have to make under pressure of big business. The hands-on making gives me immense energy and fulfillment.

In the seventies I was always on the hunt for yarn because I was trying to get as much texture and color as possible into each piece I knitted—silk, mohair, and many types of wool and cotton gave my work a visceral, almost animal-like surface that enhanced the colors. One day around 1976, Richard thought he found the perfect place for us—it was a company selling off ends of weaving yarn collections in Bradford in the north of England, called Texere. At the mill-end shop, we spent hours gathering scores of colors on one-half or one-quarter used cones of yarn. As we spread our finds out before the tired shop salesman at the end of his day, he started to weigh each of our cones, looking puzzled as to why any craftsman would want so many shades. Suddenly, he stopped, shoved all the cones into a huge plastic bag, and said, "Just get out of here!" We grabbed the bag and ran down the stairs to our car, laughing all the way home. I thanked my angels over and over as I knitted up huge experimental coats and shawls in the next year and Richard wove his gorgeous blankets out of that free material.

My first big knitting show and getting into needlepoint kits

My knitting was developing quickly, and in the late 1970s, the British Crafts Centre asked if Richard and I would like a show in their gallery. Wow, in the heart of London we could show what we really loved to do—make textiles! The two of us grabbed the chance. We filled this big space top to bottom with layers and layers of pattern and color, making it resemble a bazaar in India. I quipped to a yarn shop owner that I thought we'd get a full house at the opening, and she laughed, remarking how full of myself I was.

Knitting and weaving didn't attract that much attention in the seventies. Wanting to get involved with the publicity for the show, I asked the publicist which magazines she was approaching, and if she was explaining to them that this work was done by two men? "Kaffe could be thought to be a woman's name," I explained. She looked at me with big English eyes, "Do you think that's ethical?" This was Britain in the seventies, shy of juicing up a story for a little extra publicity. How times have changed with spin doctors galore.

Male knitters were still an oddity at that time. Though knitting is overwhelmingly considered a female activity, I never saw it as exclusively so. I loved doing it and had so much to explore in the field that it never occurred to me to be put off doing it. After all, I had grown up at Nepenthe in the presence of a male knitter, Lewis Perkins, who knit up such exciting color.

Richard and my show opened in April 1977, and in spite of the English reticence, the event was a smash. We had so many at the opening that the lure of the textiles was undeniable and journalists began to take note.

Around the time of our British Crafts Centre exhibition, Richard was beginning to produce gorgeous woven throws for Designers Guild that were to become a highlight of Tricia Guild's showroom. And I was starting to do slide shows that would eventually take me all over Britain, talking about my work and about the excitement of working with color. David Cripps, the foremost craft photographer of the time, had photographed pieces of my own work for me, plus decorative art from my personal collection. I also took along a few selected samples of my own one-off knits and needlepoints full of intricate color compositions.

On my lecture tours, I learned a lot about many areas of the country I'd not had a chance to explore, and I quickly became a reaction junkie—what I had to show was so different from the usual knits and needlepoints that gasps and sighs would be heard from most audiences. One Women's Institute group—WI being the largest women's organization in Great Britain—went mad after my talk. Most of the audience rushed home to start knitting, leaving a nearly empty hall for the second half of the meeting. This was a great reaction from a group usually categorized as staid in the British media.

In Edinburgh, Scotland, I was picked up at the train station by the worried organizer of my slide talk. "I could only get thirty or so interested, so it will be a small talk in a large hall," she apologized. But when we entered the venue, it was bursting at the seams with more than 350 attending. People had come from far-flung islands as well as Edinburgh and Glasgow. It was a brilliant night!

But by far, the best thing to come out of these events was meeting with Zoe Hunt at the British Crafts Centre exhibition. A young woman who worked for the gallery, Zoe came up to me saying, "I'm a knitter who wants to get established. Could you let me work for you for a year to find out to how to run a design studio and promote myself?" I told her I didn't know how good a knitter she was. Could she follow my nonexistent instructions? I didn't put things on paper, just cast on and winged it—no graphs, no dimensions, no yarn quantities.

Undeterred, Zoe came to the studio soon after our first meeting, and I handed her one of my knitted garments, full of color changes, using at least 150 different yarns. "Here is a garment, here is my yarn stash. See if you can gather the colors and go off and make a copy of this. And then we will see."

Zoe spent three hours tracking down the yarns for her project in my stash, then disappeared and came back in two weeks with two garments. I looked with utter amazement. I could not tell which was mine colorwise, but hers was neater. "You are hired!" I cried. And we settled down to years of stimulating collaboration. Zoe was tall and stunningly beautiful, with long black hair cascading down her back. In short, everyone thought we were the perfect couple. She had a very Dickensian boyfriend with the delectable name of Edwin Belchamber. He was a tall broomstick with long hair and hands. He was also a very fine artist, designing wonderful cakes and a range of needlepoint kits, among other things. For a while during the time Zoe worked with me, she lived at my place while she and Edwin were working on a house together in a down-market part of London, which brought back memories of my Boston studio Daimon's Lair.

Zoe had the sort of creative mind that could tackle any design problem, but she also had the patience to technically work out garment shapes and fine finishings without compromising the color and richness. She made so many things possible that I would have struggled to do half as well on my own.

Left: My great friend Zoe Hunt, looking gorgeous in a chenille and Lurex top she had just knitted for me. We collaborated beautifully for many years. **Above, top:** My niece Winona in Cross Patch Coat. **Above:** Rory Mitchel in Floating Circle crewneck. **Below:** The famous Carpet Coat shot in Malta.

Despite my consuming passion for my design work, I didn't give up my artwork. In the late seventies, I illustrated a cookbook by my friend Pam Harlech (*Feast Without Fuss*), and again sold paintings through the Hazlitt Gallery in London. For the cookbook cover, I did a large, sprawling still life of vegetables, pots, and dishcloths that was used as a wrap-around dust jacket. I was sure either the publishers or Pam herself would want to buy the painting, but that didn't happen. So one day, when I needed a canvas for a large screen with oriental pots in my studio, I painted over the unwanted cookbook still life. A year later, a couple visited the studio looking for a painting to hang in their newly decorated kitchen. They loved the screen painting and, after buying it, invited me to their house to view it in situ. We loved the way it looked, and I asked them what had brought them to my studio. "We saw a cookbook with a great painting on the cover and wanted that for our kitchen."

"Well," I thought, "you have the painting, but heavily disguised."

In 1977, a Persian couple made an appointment to come to the studio. They knew about me because they carried Designers Guild fabrics in a shop they had opened in Tehran. Before they arrived, I recalled traveling through Tehran in the early seventies and hearing students talking about overthrowing the Shah. Since he was pictured in every shop and stall in the markets, I felt he was too omnipresent a force to possibly be removed.

The couple looked at my work and picked out eight canvases that were influenced by the Victoria and Albert Museum's Persian miniatures. "We'd like to have these in our shop," they told me. "Sorry, I can't really lend work to go so far away," I said.

"Oh we intend to buy them!" they said, and promptly wrote out a check. When they left with eight canvases, I felt as if I had lost my family, a really hollow feeling. Then I took it as a huge vote of confidence and got busy painting more.

Only about a year after that visit, history started unfolding. Ayatollah Khomeini, in Paris, was sending tapes to his followers, who were growing stronger by the day and, indeed,

The acrylic of china pots that I painted on top of the still life I had done for the cover of Pam Harlech's cookbook.

did overthrow the Shah and welcome that old man in as a hero and leader. I have no idea what became of my paintings, but a pretty little furnishing shop would have definitely met a sticky end in a society about which the Ayatollah said, "There is no humor in Islam."

I continued doing commissions for Muriel Latow in the late seventies, one of which made my train journeys interesting. In 1977, I was working on three sets of knitted drapes for an apartment in London she was decorating. Muriel loved the Map Coat I had knitted, which was later sold to the Aberdeen Art Gallery in Scotland, so the drapes design was huge fantasy maps on striped seas. I was winging the design, creating it on the needles as I knit, and these pieces were each seven feet long—a lot of knitting to get through for the six panels required. Once I start on a project like this, I keep going on it so the creative flow isn't interrupted, with breaks only for the requisite sleeping and eating. When any necessary train trips presented themselves during the making of the Map Curtains, I carried everything along with me—an assortment of colors and textures of yarn in a large cardboard box with the knitting on a circular needle sitting on top. I'd pull this huge monster out of the box and start knitting. I never once had trouble getting a table to myself, sometimes even half a carriage, as people tried not to look at the mad knitter. And it was a man!

In September 1978, a fellow named Hugh Ehrman opened a shop at 123 Fulham Road in London. He and his brother had decided to promote and sell the best of British craft—jewelry, textiles, and so on. I had first met Hugh briefly in 1976 when he was working as Judy Brittain's assistant at *Vogue* when she was the Living Editor at the magazine; we were both at a *Vogue* photo shoot in Bill Gibb's flat. A year later, Hugh took over Judy's job, and a year after that he opened his shop.

I remember a visit I had from Hugh while he was concentrating on setting up the shop. In those days, I lived on one floor in a drafty Victorian house and often worked in my bedroom because it was a tiny room heated easily with a small electric heater. Hugh came up and sat politely asking questions. He and his brother Richard wanted to commission a needlepoint hanging from me to hang on the shop wall. When I told him the price, he was taken aback. Because I had to pay several other people to work with me on large pieces like this, which could take weeks, the cost was more than they could afford.

My subsequent advice to Hugh was to have a bread-and-butter item that could sell while he waited for the few well-heeled customers to court his expensive handmade craft. "A needlepoint kit or three would fit the bill well, and I'm the man to design them," I told him.

"What is a needlepoint kit?" he asked.

Convinced by my suggestion, Hugh soon found a canvas printer, and I designed a needlepoint of flowers in a vase inspired by a carpet. The design sold so well that he packed up the rarefied crafts shop and became a needlepoint business. This business made big waves when it started, as the designs he sold were a breath of fresh air in the cutesy world of embroidery kits then available. I still thoroughly enjoy designing for Hugh to this day.

In the last year of the seventies, I took a memorable trip to California. My niece Erin, my sister Holly's daughter, was a teenager and was growing into a beautiful woman. She had large eyes and a strong face like her father, whom she had never really known, because he had left Big Sur when she was a toddler. She often fantasized about what

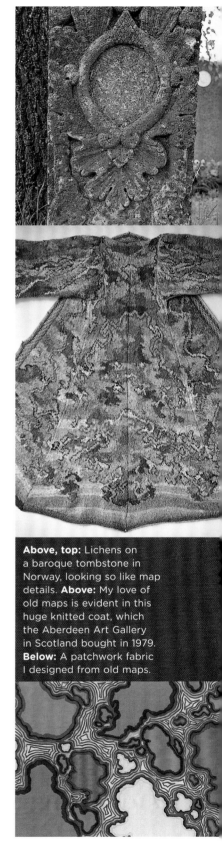

Above, top: Lichens on a baroque tombstone in Norway, looking so like map details. **Above:** My love of old maps is evident in this huge knitted coat, which the Aberdeen Art Gallery in Scotland bought in 1979. **Below:** A patchwork fabric I designed from old maps.

he would be like and decided she wanted to find him. Tony had last been heard of in New York, and Erin had a possible address for him there. As I would be stopping in New York on my way back to London, we flew there together.

My brother Griff, who had settled on the East Coast, met us at the airport with his wife, Roz, and their three kids. We drove in their big family car straight into Manhattan's Chinatown to have dinner. The atmosphere in the car was partylike as we chatted and laughed with each other. As the car pulled up into the only available parking place across from our restaurant, I saw an old figure bent over, examining something in the gutter. "That looks like Tony!" I exclaimed, looking at Roz, who confirmed with an astonished knowing look, "That's him." I turned to Erin, who was busy with the kids, and said, "If you want to meet your father, I can introduce you."

She looked at the shabby old figure and said, "I think I'll take a rain check on that." I was tempted to just jump out and grab him, feeling we'd not have the chance again. But what if he was really crazy or drugged? It could have scarred the teenage Erin for life. So I sat watching Tony shuffle away down the street. Later, we heard he had been put into a mental hospital and was in and out several times.

As Roz and I sat over that dinner, we looked at each other again, saying, "Did that really just happen?" Erin and I had just flown from Big Sur into such a large city, and at our first parking spot, we'd found the one person—out of several million—Erin was looking for. Erin did eventually meet up with her father later on a few trips East, and they corresponded, so she was able to connect with him. When he died in 2010, she was more moved than anyone else in the family, who hadn't been in contact with him for more than forty years.

The most powerful impression for me of that trip to the States in 1979 was seeing Judy Chicago's *Dinner Party* sculpture at the San Francisco Museum of Modern Art—a huge banquet for the pivotal women of history. Each place setting on a massive triangular table was set with a hand-glazed plate on a decorated cloth personalized to suit each character from Boudica to Georgia O'Keeffe. It was the cloth—painted, embroidered, highly worked—that got my imagination soaring. The fact that these so-called feminine crafts were celebrated with this traveling exhibition that had people lined up through the museum to get in told me that I was on the right track concentrating on these needlecrafts.

I fantasized that I could have exhibitions of my own work in museums one day, but I realized that it was quite rare to see big shows of humble crafts that the average person could do. Quilting was only just beginning to grab the attention of the art world after a great show of American quilts at the Whitney in New York in 1971 (*Abstract Design in American Quilts*), but knitting had no such profile or public interest in the seventies. After seeing the Judy Chicago show, I knew it was only a matter of time before the fertile flood of design now being poured into knitting in Britain, by me and other young designers, would be recognized.

Opposite: The first needlepoint kit I designed for Hugh Ehrman's shop in 1978. I love the way Steve Lovi so sensitively styled this shot.

chapter five

1980–1989

The Glorious Eighties

Above, left: Zoe Hunt modeling Geometric Star Jacket for *Glorious Color*, which came out in 1988; and her husband, James Dewe Mathews, wearing Star Vest from *Glorious Knits*, my very first book, published in 1985. **Above, center:** A mural I did for a client in London in the eighties. It was sadly painted over after all my months of work. **Above, right:** My niece Winona in my Carpet Coat. **Opposite:** In front of the Jars Tapestry, with a couple of my knits from the 1980s.

Since the day I began designing knitting, needlepoint, and fabric prints, the process has never been less than absolute bliss, and my enthusiasm for textile arts only grew through this decade. Having gained some recognition by the beginning of the eighties, I was able to see that people were responding to what I produced, and this really egged me on to try to take the joy of working with color and textiles to an even wider audience. It might have been the buzz of my first lecturing engagements that encouraged me to move eventually into books, where I would be able to give even more people a glimpse into how to create exciting textiles. Of course, having my work in museum exhibitions and on TV in the eighties spread my enthusiasm to even wider circles. But one of the key elements in all this "evangelistic" activity was working with the people at the yarn company Rowan, who started manufacturing yarns in the colors I needed to produce kits of my knit designs, and who featured me in their many publications.

Knitting and needlepoint galore

The British were doing a lot of hand knitting by the beginning of the early eighties. Knitting and women's magazines were rediscovering the classic Fair Isle knits that had been popular in the twenties and thirties, but the yarns being used were fairly conventional, and Shetland yarn, with its multicolored tweedy effects, was the most exotic. My quest for enlivening smooth wool knits by mixing in textured yarns like mohair and chenille was quite a new thing.

In 1980, I met Stephen Sheard at a workshop I was doing at Roehampton Institute. He told me about his yarn company, Rowan, and showed me some white chenille he was about to produce.

"If I had some ideas for colors for your chenille, would you listen?" I asked.

His response was positive. I rushed back home and laid out twenty colors from my vast yarn stash. Stephen used all of them to dye his yarn and then asked me to do designs using these yarns. This led to our first boxed kits. Finally I could make my designs available to more knitters and get them excited about color knitting.

By the early eighties, I was doing many designs as knitting instruction offers in magazines. One stands out as the most successful. I went to Britain's popular *Woman & Home* magazine and chatted with the craft editor, who loved the idea of doing a knit jacket. I told her Rowan had given me the okay to do a design for a kit that used twenty colors of yarn. Till then, the maximum for a knitting project was five to six colors, and even that was thought extravagant.

I designed an easy-to-knit jacket featuring rows of triangles that used only two colors in a row—a simple Fair Isle technique. Yet with twenty colors in the concoction, the finished knitting looked much more complex. I chose a quiet palette of dusty pastels because those popped out of the yarn range offered by Rowan at the time. I knitted different scales of triangles giving the design more movement. The chalky tones all went together so it was only a matter of picking pairs of colors that contrasted enough for my triangle shapes to show up in this two-color per row design. The simple little scoop-neck jacket over a soft gray blouse on a beautiful, calm model appealed to the middle-aged knitters who were the core readership of British women's magazines back then. They were also becoming my main fans at my lectures. I was featured on the cover, and the magazine sold 7,000 kits in two weeks. In those days, 100 kits would have been hailed as a big success. Amazingly, *Woman & Home* didn't keep any of the money for themselves, so Rowan and I were put on the map and handsomely financed for further projects. I was bursting with pride, as was Stephen.

After the success with my Super Triangles jacket in *Woman & Home*, Rowan started to become a lot more adventurous. They used designers like Sasha Kagan, Jessi and Jamie

Above: My Super Triangles Jacket, which generated a lot of excitement for Rowan yarns when it hit the cover of Britain's *Woman & Home* magazine in 1981. **Opposite:** A pen drawing of a fountain in Brighton, done during one of my extensive tours of Britain in the eighties.

Seaton (who went on to found the upmarket *Toast* catalog), and my favorite knit designer, Susan Duckworth. Susan was the poet of pattern knitting, using butterflies, pansies, and motifs from Gustav Klimt in a ravishing palette. Colorwork hand knitting was experiencing a huge revival, and it suited me just fine.

Another mural commission came my way in 1980. A couple wanted their house in Ireland to feature in their London dining room and asked me to copy the mural I'd done in the Cotswolds for Muriel Latow. "I'm afraid I can't copy what I've done for someone else," I explained to them. "But I'll do a tapestry-like theme that has your house and landscape in it." I hate doing elaborate sketches for murals, so I had only myself to blame when I did the work and the lady of the house told me her nine-year-old daughter didn't like it. I soldiered on, and when it was done I could see she was still a little disgruntled. I got Steve Lovi to come and photograph it with me wearing one of my knitted jackets in front of it. My client then informed me that she needed to know how soon I could pack up my stuff and be out. "Why?" I asked. "Because I need to have the wall treated before we can do the floor. I'm afraid it's not what I ordered." I hoped I wasn't right in thinking she was going to paint it over but I covered it with three or four more layers of varnish, just in case.

A month later, Lucinda Lambton, a great enthusiast of the arts in England, rang to say she was doing a TV show about murals in London. "I've just done one!" I said. "Ring this number and go and see it." She rang back ten minutes later to say, "I hate to tell you, but . . ."

"Don't worry, I know," I told her. Lucinda made wonderful eccentric shows about architecturally quirky English places so it would have made quite a program.

The picture of me in front of my mural came out in *Vogue* the next month. My arms were spread out as though I was saying, "Don't touch my painting!" It was all a good experience, but it really was the last nail in the coffin of my mural painting.

Steve Lovi took this picture of me defending my mural for British *Vogue* magazine. The client had it painted over even before the picture appeared in the magazine.

My needlepoint design was burgeoning in the early eighties, and aside from designing for Hugh Ehrman's needlepoint kit business, more needlepoint hanging one-off commissions were flowing in. Hugh's mother loved what we were doing and was one of my most enthusiastic clients. When I went down to her country house to see what she wanted in the way of design, she said, "I've cooked a cabbage in gin—new recipe. Hope you like it!" I did, and painted a sketch of a large oriental bowl she had, which I wanted to put in the tapestry. I surrounded the bowl with grasses at the edge of a lake with a cat creeping up, seen through the foliage.

Creating large works appeals to my sense of drama. The technique I use is to first trawl through my vast book library to find appropriate images, in old paintings or photographs. Then I draw an outline sketch, placing my chosen subjects in a pleasing arrangement. Next, I divide the sketch into inch-square sections and transfer the design outlines onto my needlepoint canvas with waterproof pens. The prepared canvas is hung on the wall in the studio or just held across the lap for stitching. If the canvas is really big, I divide it in half so two stitchers can work at either end of each section. The stitcher fills in the outlines while consulting the source pictures for the right color and shade. Every so often, I stand back to see if it is all reading as it should and make color changes where needed. With a good play or interview on BBC Radio 4 to listen to, the quiet, industrious hours of communal work on these kinds of pieces are some of the happiest I've known. It is so much more fulfilling for me than my lonely time in the painting studio.

When we were almost finished with Hugh's mother's piece, she called in a flap one day. "I've just heard a terrible rumor," she cried, "that there is a cat in my tapestry!"

I said, "Yes, there is."

To which she replied, "I can't hang it in my house if it has a cat. I can't bear cats!" So I dutifully took out the offending article. In the end, she loved the tapestry and I did, too, borrowing it to hang in a few of the exhibitions I had around England.

Someone who used to help me on big tapestry commissions in the early eighties and who would lend a critical eye on whatever we were doing was Rory Mitchell, a set designer from the BBC. I had met him in August 1979, and he lived nearby. His place became a wonderful refuge for me to get away to in the evenings to share a meal, watch TV, and chat. A small, beautiful Irishman, he had the physique of a jockey. Although he had trained as an architect, he really loved his work at the TV studio doing sets. One of his most memorable sets used columns of oversized film canisters and was the backdrop for the Barry Norman film program, on which the host critiqued the latest movies. He also painted a backdrop of Rothko-like canvases for a discussion program on the nuclear war threat.

Rory was a good photographer as well and traveled to America with me a few times, where he took wonderful shots of decaying surfaces and big American cars. He loved to dance and do mime and was spotted by someone working on the Tarzan film *Greystoke*. Next thing I knew, he was training to be an ape and came home wearing dark brown contact lenses that made his eyes look like a monkey's. Scary! He went off to Africa to film and could not wait to get me to the premiere to see his performance. Unfortunately, I could not tell one ape from another and never had a sense of him in that hairy suit in the dim African light.

When this acting role was over, Rory wondered what to do with his life. He had left the BBC and didn't know where to turn. I tried to encourage him. "You are very talented and

The needlepoint hanging I designed and stitched for Hugh Ehrman's mother, after the offending cat was removed from the design.

1, 2: The Oriental Jars needlepoint, showing my newly acquired ornamental pots; collecting porcelain has been a passion since I arrived in England. **3:** Years later a teapot pattern featured in my fabric Frilly. **4:** Coffee bowls I found in Morocco made a good subject. **5, 6:** Porcelains in the V&A, like this Buddha, have also inspired my textiles.

good with your hands. Why don't you make furniture as you've always wanted?" He could not entertain the idea of working on his own with no regular pay. One day he burst into tears and showed me his empty pockets. The next day, he went back to the BBC. They rehired him but made him start at the bottom and work his way up like a novice. It was humiliating for him and made me realize how courageous an artist has to be to make a start in his dream field. And Rory didn't have much support from his family. His mother was always a harsh judge of him, so he didn't feel he could ever talk with her about any fear or weakness.

Working on my first book

On a roll with my knitting in 1983, I had a few commissions for one-off knitted garments from celebrities, including stage and screen actress Irene Worth, artist Helen Frankenthaler, and Barbra Streisand. In town working on the film *Yentl*, Streisand asked if she could come and see our work. She came to the door one day looking like a quiet, plain housewife—not at all the fierce, handsome face you see on screen. She said, "Hello, I'm Barbra," in a little wispy voice. She proceeded to go though my big trunk of samples, trying on a few, and settled on a deep blue smock-like blouse with rich patterns around the yoke. "I like this but never wear blue," she said. "Can you knit it in black?"

"Okay," I said. Zoe did a smashing job knitting up the multicolored garment, replacing the royal blue stripes with black chenille.

Then Barbra asked me to do a fine knitted dress for an antique glass brooch she had. I loved the idea but was worried about it being drapey enough unless done in very fine yarns. Hand knitting like that I feared would take forever and it would cost the earth. I decided it was too much for us to take on and turned the commission down. Nowadays, there are many gorgeous fine yarns, and I wouldn't be daunted by a larger project, even by hand.

Steve Lovi was back in California in 1983, struggling to make ends meet as a photographer. His restaurant-owning father in Chicago had gone bust and could no longer send the monthly checks that Steve used to live on. At the time, I was trying to design a special sweater for him, so I called him and said, "If I send you a ticket, would you come over and advise me on what you'd like as a sweater?"

He said, "Perfect timing, I was just needing to get away."

When he got to London, he stayed in my flat in Kilburn, looked at all the things I was knitting, and said, "There's a book in this. Let's create one!" This sounded like a perfect idea to me, as I was keen to convey my love of color and knitting to as many people as possible so that they could share in the excitement of it all. The satisfaction I was getting from this simple craft was never-ending, and I wanted to broadcast my message to the world.

Steve and I lost no time, and we started approaching publishers to see if any would respond to the prospect of a book on all this unusual knitting. Finally, after four publishers said we were asking too much or that the designs would not appeal to enough people, we landed in Gail Rebuck's office at Century Publishing. She had heard of us from someone who told her to take notice. She offered the £25,000 advance we were asking for and decided on an autumn 1985 launch.

Zoe Hunt modeling the chenille smock that Barbra Streisand had me reknit with black instead of blue yarn. In the early eighties I got quite a few commissions for one-off knitted garments that Zoe knitted me.

1, 2: Rory Mitchell and actress Indra Ové modeling for my first book, *Glorious Knits*. **3, 4, 6, 7, 10, 13:** More knit designs from *Glorious Knits*. **5, 8, 12:** Jeremy Fry's castellated house in Malta, where photographer Steve Lovi and I stayed when we were shooting knits for the book; years later, we draped it with quilts from my book *Kaleidoscope of Quilts*. **9:** The beautiful Marsha Hunt and her daughter, Karis, modeling for *Glorious Knits*; Marsha has been a friend since the early days in Notting Hill Gate. **11:** Steve Lovi in one of the English gardens he was so passionate about. That day he told me how happy photography made him. Steve masterminded our shoots for *Glorious Knits* so they coincided with colors in the gardens by season.

I rushed home and began calling yarn companies whom I knew had rich palettes of colors and who might give us sample yarns. After a few had turned us down, I turned to Rowan and said, "Because you are always willing, I'm giving you the whole book. All the designs with knitting instructions will be in Rowan yarns."

Steve and I started huge plans for garments in certain colors to be completed in time to catch the spring display of blossoms at Kew Gardens, or to catch other outdoor displays. Steve was highly aware of gardening, and good at envisioning garments coupled with colors of certain flowering trees and shrubs. He knew when and where they would be at their best. We also planned trips to Malta and Holland to find different color, light, and ambience.

In Malta, Steve and I, and the model we brought with us, stayed at Jeremy Fry's wonderful tower built for the Knights Templar. We drove all over the island finding boats and old houses to shoot against. Coming home to London, we shot in gardens like Kew, Regents Park, and Hampstead Heath and used mostly friends and acquaintances as our models.

Then we were off to Holland to do shots of the lush tulip fields. We decided the Keukenhof Gardens with their showy tulip displays would be best for intense, localized color and asked if we could have a day shoot there. "That's fine—anywhere you like," the managers of the gardens said in a welcoming manner. The next day, we turned up at the gardens with models we had hired from a Dutch agency, two girls and a boy. Steve and I gasped as we saw nothing but green shoots on black earth where color-filled, lush gardens had been the day before. The previous night they had cut all the flowers off, to strengthen the bulbs, I guess. We ended up photographing the girls against huge dumpsters full of cut flowerheads.

Working on my first book meant having to work with a bigger team than I was used to in my little studio. I had an editor assigned by Century who rewrote all my words so they became formal and most unlike me. "I want to have a casual chat with my readers," I told them. Most books on craft at that time sent me to sleep with their formal writing, but the knitter Elizabeth Zimmermann had demonstrated in her book *Knitting Without Tears* how personal and funny you could be in a craft book.

We disagreed, too, about the layout of the book. Steve and I wanted a lush, colorful approach. The art editor said, "This is not the way to lay out a knitting book." We were asking for double-page photos and pictures as large as possible, if not bled to the edge of the page. "You are designing a coffee-table book," the editors cried. But in the end, we were able to convince them of our vision.

I totally relied on Steve to orchestrate this book. He had such a strong vision—planning which outfits I should make in which palettes and planning for certain times of year when gardens would be strong in the appropriate colors. When it came to laying the book out, he guided the cropping and placement of each of his photographs on each page. That taught me a lot about what it takes to realize a vision only you have.

Luckily, working with Steve ran fairly smoothly. One of the qualities about people that brings them into a harmonious working relationship, I've observed, is similar rhythms. If you have a sense of urgency about getting tasks done, and the person you are working with has all the time in the world and doesn't see it as a big deal if things don't get done, unbearable tensions can arise. I'm an early riser. No matter how late I retire, when the light dawns in the sky, I feel the urge to be up doing things. When I'm staying somewhere new, as we often were when we went on location to shoot the first book, I'll wait to hear the first stirring of the household and leap up if I hear any little rustle.

A table setting commissioned by British *Vogue*. I placed all my flea-market finds, odd plates, a silk tablecloth, and fruits and flowers against a borrowed oriental carpet.

Coming down to the kitchen of the places we stayed on that shoot, I'd always find Steve already up, usually sitting outside smoking and doing the crossword puzzle. He is the only person I know who is always up before me, often rising at 5 a.m. When he started working for magazines, an editor who wanted him to do a still life of objects for her pages agreed to come set up the shot at 10:30 the next morning. Steve rose at 5 a.m., had his cigarette and coffee, set up the shot the minute the light dawned, shot the picture, sent the film to the lab by motorbike, and had the results back as the editor arrived to start work. Steve could be quite sharp with people who turned up after an agreed-upon time.

When both of us were getting a little stressed about our first book, Steve said to me one morning, "You haven't given me my little pat on the back lately, Kaffe." I was astonished. He was so brilliant I got tired of always saying how amazed I was at his quick, sure eye and great flow of ideas. It never occurred to me that the great Steve Lovi, the brightest genius I knew, would need reassurance. It was a revelation, and I realized at once that I needed the same. But I got it so often from those around me that I forgot how lost we creative-flow people can get if we don't have constant reassurance. Mind you, we can work against someone else's doubts, and often have to, but the team of believers is a very necessary part of what makes us able to produce as much and as quickly as we do.

Traveling around Britain and its great houses over the years, I kept coming across postcards of charming needlepoints done by Bess of Hardwick and Mary, Queen of Scots, in the late sixteenth century. These two powerful and creative women had stitched quite simple subjects, like snakes and spiders, into small panels for a large needlepoint tapestry to hang in the great Hardwick Hall in Derbyshire. The gold, silver, and silk tent-stitch renditions are little masterpieces of needlework.

I began to dream of doing the same sort of hanging—made up of small panels pieced together—with the help of the British public. Finally, in 1984, while Steve and I were finishing my first book, BBC television's *Pebble Mill at One*, a daytime magazine program, agreed to feature the launch of this project.

I took a large needlepoint tapestry of mine to hang in the studio while I explained my dream to the nation on TV. I also took along my six-inch-square needlepoint picture of a flowery bowl on an old book as an example demonstrating that anything the viewers wanted to celebrate they could stitch up. I told them I didn't mind how primitive or simplified the image was—they should just send me their offerings and I'd include them in a large needlepoint called "Count Your Blessings." The program wanted to call it "The Heritage Tapestry," for more gravitas, I suppose.

In the next six months, more than 2,000 six-inch needlepoints arrived through my letterbox. The response was amazing. The needlepoints were so full of imagination and pure joy that they had me regularly in tears as I opened one surprising package after another. I was so moved because it was a clear demonstration that with a little encouragement, untapped talent and creativity can flow from most people. The sheer variety and poetic statements that were sent with them were deeply satisfying for me.

A group of students and guilds came to help me sew the small squares together and add borders, creating a large paneled screen. When it was done, I called up the National Trust of Britain to find out if they'd give the screen a home in one of the multitude of grand houses they owned and ran for the nation. They made it apparent it was so complicated

Left: Appearing on BBC television's *Pebble Mill at One* program in 1984 to launch the Count Your Blessings Heritage Tapestry project. **Above:** Some of the needlepoint squares from the more than 2,000 contributors to the project. As I opened the packages, I was often moved to tears by the inventiveness of the stitchers. **Right:** My small bowl on an old book that I made for the tapestry. **Below:** The needlepoints being assembled in my bedroom.

for them to arrange that I decided to try to find a home for it myself. I called the Duchess of Devonshire and asked her if her family seat, the great Chatsworth House in North Derbyshire, would be interested in displaying it to their many visitors. She gracefully agreed, and I went down to install it the next week, followed by cameras from *Pebble Mill*.

As I sat waiting to be filmed, I gazed around the grand rooms at Chatsworth and remarked to the Duchess how much I loved her oriental brocade curtains in a rich shade of antique crimson. They were a little shredded.

"They cost a fortune to replace!" she cried.

"Oh I like them as they are," I said.

"So do I!" she replied.

That is one of the most endearing things about the English for me—this enjoyment for disheveled opulence.

The needlepoint Heritage Tapestry screen drew many admirers while it was at Chatsworth and has now moved to another grand setting open to the public, Harewood House in West Yorkshire, where it has a permanent home.

Glorious Knitting
hits the bookstores

When my book *Glorious Knitting* was about to be printed, Gail Rebuck said, "I think we will print 5,000 copies."

"Oh, please go with more," Steve and I pleaded. I felt that, at first, few would get what we were offering, and by the time they started to get it, in half a year or so, there would be very few copies left for them to purchase. In the end, Gail decided to print 40,000 copies for the United States and the United Kingdom—an enormous number in those days, especially for a knitting book. Looking back, I have no idea what convinced Gail to order such a large print run. There was nothing on the market remotely like *Glorious Knitting*—a fact that could have put her off as easily as enthuse her. We were lucky that such a personal and committed collection was allowed to emerge without being dumbed down, as so many craft books seem to be.

Even Stephen Sheard at Rowan, who really supported the project of promoting knitting, told me sadly as we were finalizing the book, "What a pity that knitting has hit its peak and is on the wane."

Since I was such a freak—a six-foot-three Californian man who was knitting—I got a lot of attention from the press when the book finally came out in the fall of 1985. Steve's photos were luxuriant, and the knitted coats and jackets were very unusual with their use of color and pattern, so we appealed to our hippie generation, and the publishers sold our 40,000 copies in two weeks. There were no copies left by Christmas.

The heady excitement of touring all over America to promote my book (called *Glorious Knits* in the United States), mounted as I flew from major city to major city. None of us could have predicted how much coverage we would get from the press, TV, and radio.

I'd do workshops in large yarn stores that stocked only so much Rowan yarn, as they found it a bit rarefied and expensive compared to other brands. This made me fear that

Rowan would always be a niche market, even though the people who discovered us and liked challenging designs were ardent fans. One of the first people in America to get my point and help spread the word like a true missionary was Liza Prior Lucy. She was a yarn rep for the New York and Pennsylvania areas. The day she came upon *Glorious Knits*, she enthusiastically bought six copies to give to her mother and several close friends. That very night, when she got home with the books, she got a call from Ken Bridgewater at Westminster Fibers (Rowan's distributor in the United States), asking if she would rep the Rowan line.

"Sorry, I've got too many lines, no time to take on more," she said, and was about to hang up when Ken said, "We also sell *Glorious Knits*."

"Darn! I could have had those books at wholesale," she thought and gladly accepted, becoming our strongest rep.

When I was told about her, someone said, "Liza will guide you for part of your tour. She will probably talk your right leg off." When I joined her to fly together, I discovered she was as excited as I was about my tour, and that she loved and really got my work—we sang a duet from day one. When I spent a night at her house, meeting her two children and her husband, Drew, I asked the next morning if she wanted me to change the sheets for her. "Are you kidding!" she cried. "I'm going to cut them up to share with friends, talk about the Turin Shroud!" It was that spicy humor that appealed to me so much in Liza.

Liza Lucy, who dragged me kicking and screaming into the world of patchwork, for which I will be forever grateful.

When shops would call me every weird version of "Kaffe" except how it is really pronounced, she would say, "Look, you have a 'safe asset' with Kaffe Fassett." Some people called me Mr. Asset after that. But the funniest thing was people thinking the new knit designer everyone was talking about was named Gloria Snits.

The audiences for my book signings got more and more enthused as I worked my way west. What became apparent, however, was the lack of enthusiasm from bookshops. I would find journalists and TV presenters gushing with excitement, giving me airtime and pages of print and photos, while the bookshops would see my book as just another knitting book. Some yarn stores didn't get it, either, or were downright hostile to all the color and pattern. "Too complicated for my customers."

When I got to St. Louis, I was told a man who was mostly into sports would be interviewing me for the radio, and he wouldn't be interested in me. He turned out to be an old sailor who knitted in the Navy and who loved the book! The print media were equally enthused, so I rushed to the biggest bookstore in town and said, "I've just done tons of important media on *Glorious Knits*, would you like me to sign your copies?"

"Oh, *that* book. We only ordered two copies, and they are gone. Knitting books never sell very much, so we don't bother ordering them." What a downer. I went around town looking for yarn stores to see if they might be a bit more with it. I found one called Maddie's and went in to inquire if they knew of my book. I was wearing one of my sweaters, so when the rather depressed-looking shop attendant asked if she could help, she suddenly snapped to life before I could say more than, "Do you carry *Glorious Knits*?" She yelled "Maddie, get out here! It's him!" The shop owner appeared at the back room door. "My God, I've collected everything I could find on you for years. You have to sign these books!" When I got to know this extraordinary woman, I learned that she had long ago been a heroin user with her lover, and they had stumbled into Nepenthe while driving the coast road. When they climbed the hill to our restaurant and saw the view of the coast one clear summer morning, she was inspired to give up drugs. It was shops like Maddie's that helped make *Glorious Knits* a bestseller and eventually convinced bookstores they should take notice.

Another highlight on my publicity tour was discovering Canada. My sidetrip to Toronto was a revelation. I discovered the Canadians to be witty, well read, and really into knitting! Sarah MacLachlan was the publicity person for Little, Brown who was co-publishing *Glorious Knits*. She was bright and had the respect of most good people in the media world, so was able to get me on choice TV slots, long radio interviews that I loved doing, and endless newspaper and magazine coverage. Sarah and her husband, Noah, have since become good friends and she now heads the Anansi Press publishing house.

In Dallas, I was able to do a TV morning show before my signing in a big department store, so I tipped the audience off on what time I'd be where. My first customer at that next signing was a wiry little mountain woman who had driven down from her farm after she saw the TV program. "I'd rather meet you than Jesus!" she yelped in her husky voice.

When I got to Houston, I was glowing with all the attention and really poured my heart out to a young woman journalist doing her first interview. She looked at me with big eyes after hearing my story. "It sounds like you found your *thing*!" I loved her response.

Even our models got acclaim from our enthused audience. A handsome blond American man living in London had turned out to be a natural at modeling. In an opening group shot, he is seen wearing striped blue and white tights. He was a waiter for a health restaurant, and one of his customers kept squinting at him with a puzzled look. Suddenly she cried, "I know who you are. You're that ass!" Obviously, she had been studying his derriere in the book.

The opening page of *Glorious Knits* (called *Glorious Knitting* in Britain) with a symphony of stripes. Steve set up this shot, stringing up the knitting on clotheslines, and Zoe and professional dancers were our models.

I went home to Big Sur as well on this trip, to celebrate with Mom, who rejoiced in the success of the book. While I was there, I heard that one of the founders of the Esalen Institute, Dick Price, had gone up his canyon to meditate, and a rock loosened by rain and wind tumbled down the canyon wall, striking him a death blow. My sister Holly and I went to a moving ceremony for him, sixty or so people making a circle in a meadow celebrating his life. I turned to Holly and said, "One day they will be doing this for Mom."

Two weeks later, back in London, I got a call informing me that Mom was diagnosed with colon cancer and was in the hospital. I rang her room, where I found her in quite an upbeat mood. "If you get bored, give me a ring," I told her. "BORED! Are you mad? They are giving me every test known to man," she said with laughing exasperation. It was tough for her as a follower of Christian Science to put her trust in a hospital and modern medicine. As I thought about it, I wondered how she would cope with radiation therapy and constant visits to doctors. She would have to move to town, and she would hate giving up her beloved coastal home.

I woke up in the middle of the night two days later with these words in my head: "You've had a great life. You don't have to hang around. Why don't you just go?" Half an hour later, Dad called to say she had died. "Thank God!" I said.

"Funny reaction—just like your sister Dorcas," he said. Everyone I knew said I would be hit by grieving soon, but all I could feel was admiration for a splendid life, well lived, that the curtain had come down on. I did dream of my mother often over the next few years. In these dreams, she was always a peaceful presence, radiant with health.

After my first book, I was able to start to introduce my work around the world. Outside of Britain and the United States, the first country to show interest in displaying my knitted garments was Japan. The organizers of an exhibition of my knits offered to fly me in for the opening at the prestigious Keio Department Store in Tokyo. I was to tour New Zealand before going on to Japan.

The New Zealand tour came about because the head of the knitters' guild in New Zealand, Ann Hayman, wrote to me asking if she could bring thirty knitters to do a workshop with me. I wrote back saying, "For a thirtieth of the price, I'll fly out to work with you." On my first stop in the country, a couple in Dunedin put me up in their attractive house and invited a TV crew to film an interview with me. That piece was played across the country and guaranteed large audiences for my many lectures up the islands.

I found New Zealanders immensely lovable—a healthy, hardworking populous who adored walking their intensely beautiful landscapes. They made me think of the Big Sur pioneers I'd grown up among. The audiences were full of enthusiasm, and I got to know and love Ann Hayman, who was one of the few people I've met who shared my birthday.

When I hit Tokyo, Zoe Hunt joined me. We were met by an elegant older man named Mr. Suzuki. He translated for us when we were interviewed or when we were greeted at our exhibition of knitted garments in the department store. They made us sit from 10 a.m. to 5 p.m. at the exhibition with short breaks for lunch and tea.

I soon realized how formal and stylized the Japanese could be when I asked, "Do you think we could have a cup of tea as we sit greeting people at the show?"

"But it is not 3:30!" they protested, "3:30 is teatime." When the appointed time came, they closed our desk at the show and ushered us to an office where tea was presented almost

as formally as a tea ceremony. When I commented that the buyers at the show rarely ever had a reaction that I could detect, Mr. Suzuki just looked puzzled. I asked him what the box with a slit in it was that I saw people placing paper in after viewing the show. He lit up with a big smile. "Viewers vote for each garment in order of preference—Japanese reaction!"

At a press conference the next day, I noticed the male journalists called Zoe, "Joey." One of them asked, "What if Mr. Fassett ask Miss Joey to do something and she does not do it?" Exasperated by the long questions and ever-longer translated answers, I playfully said, "I beat Miss Joey round the head with a bat." This drew huge laughter from all the guys in the room.

I asked Mr. Suzuki why he took so long to translate my short answers. "I put your answers in formal Japanese," came his reply. The poor man hardly knew what to make of us rather laid-back creatures in the formal, stiff world of the big department store. But I realized it was no way to judge Japan, as we rarely encounter the department store inner politics in the West.

It was a pleasant surprise to see how art and craft were valued in Japanese culture, and it was a thrill to see our show advertised on subway trains—I got to recognize my name in Japanese characters. Our translator did a good job, so I was able to converse to an extent with the visitors to my exhibition, but I didn't need to "evangelize" knitting. The well-respected Japanese craft world had already decided the Japanese should take up knitting. By the time I returned some years later, a huge exhibition was mounted of colorful Japanese knits; public workshops had drawn many people into the craft.

The biggest shock to my romantic view of Japan on my first visit there was the crudeness of a good percentage of the modern cities. It was the worst of 1950s American concrete jungles with the occasional beautiful modern building or old temple and, of course, always beautifully planted parks. One of the richest sights for me was the banks of tower blocks seen from the elevated highway in the apricot morning light as we entered Tokyo from the airport. Most apartments had colorful duvets airing on their balconies, making each block into a patchwork tapestry. "You notice everything," said the patient Mr. Suzuki after a string of observations erupted from me. My eye is always painfully alert when arriving in a new place.

Zoe and I went on to Kyoto after Tokyo. I was still a bit thrown by the restrictions placed on us and all the bowing. I told the head of the department at Keio Department Store that I was thrilled to see that the Kabuki theater was on while we were there. It started at 4 p.m., so I knew we'd have to leave the exhibition a half hour early. The department head said sadly, "What a pity." Meaning, no way can you see the theater if there are people to greet at your exhibition.

But Kyoto was so amazing with old temples and gentle village streets to explore that I forgot any regrets. It was the detailed jam-packedness of it all that appealed to me. My most memorable visit was a side tour to Imari, where we climbed the hill of the temple dedicated to foxes. Large gates painted shades of red and orange were placed one after another, creating a tunnel that extended for two and a half miles up the hills. We were so spellbound by the mind-boggling feat of placing all these huge gates in place that we almost got caught up the highest hill at sundown and had to run down before it got pitch dark.

The greatest gift I got from the Japanese was their playfulness with patterns. Before leaving their country, I stuffed my bags with textile fragments, full of wonderful ideas to try out when I got home.

1: A float with huge fans in Tokyo Disneyland, where I took Brandon for his birthday. **2:** My watercolor of a kimono at an exhibition at the V&A Museum. **3:** I take photos on all my trips, shooting whatever catches my eye and delights me. I thought the brilliant blue plastic buckets in this graveyard in Japan looked like jewels among all the gray tombstones. **4:** The Kabuki costumes make a powerful impression. **5, 7:** The endless red gates at Imari that progress two and a half miles up the hills. **6:** Origami birds hanging outside a shrine in Japan. **8:** My Fan fabric, which draws inspiration from Japan.

Over the years, some of the most satisfying moments on my travels happened when I bumped into my knitting designs by chance. I'd had one encounter when I was passing through the center of London and saw my Tapestry Leaf Jacket on a woman cyclist. I rolled down my taxi window and shouted, "Bravo, Tapestry Leaf!" The poor lady nearly fell off her bike.

On one trip to New York, I was thinking how rarely I saw anything I designed knitted up and worn by someone. Then I took in a show at the Guggenheim Museum. My eyes practically fell out of my head when I saw that the young woman selling tickets was wearing a version of my vest that had appeared in *Vogue*. It was in strange colors but beautifully knitted. I said to the girl, "You might like to know that I designed that vest you are wearing."

She looked at me with genuine pity. "I am so sorry, this was made in England."

"I live in England, did it for *Vogue*. Who knitted it?" Her sister had, and had also started a business knitting for customers on the strength of it. Suddenly, she believed me and said, "You *really* designed this?"

As I am either knitting or doing needlepoint whenever I travel, it occasionally initiates conversations. Once I was knitting on a long flight next to a rather tough-looking man. I felt a little self-conscious but wanted something to do in the long hours of the flight. "You really know what you are doing," he said after several hours.

"Yes, I'd better, I do this for a living," I answered.

"I should learn how to knit," he said. "It would be perfect to do in my job."

"What is your job?"

"I drive trains."

Another time, I was knitting away and wondering why so few people ever commented or took notice of my work even when I'd be doing something amazingly colorful and intricately patterned. A woman suddenly approached me and said, "Can I see what you are doing?" At last, I thought, and gladly handed her the swatch I was knitting. She turned it over, saw my untidy yarn ends, and shook her head sadly, saying, "No, no, no, that's not how it is done. Now, there is a very famous man who knits beautifully in London, why don't you look him up? His name is Kaffe Fassett."

"Oh, I shall," I answered, hoping she wouldn't realize who I was.

On another occasion, I was wearing one of my sweaters while shopping in a yarn store in Washington State. As I paid for some buttons, the woman at the till looked admiringly at my sweater, saying, "Is that a Kaffe Fassett?"

"Yes," I said proudly.

"He is such a talented man!" she said, and even when I paid with my credit card stating my name, she didn't really notice—the encounter gave me the strange feeling of being a ghost, but it was delicious to feel her admiration.

Right around the time *Glorious Knits* came out, Richard Womersley and I were talking about how much more publicity the book would give us. Commissions for one-offs were increasing, as were offers to do knit and needlepoint designs for magazines and newspapers. Richard was hinting that he couldn't take the pace if he were me. I just said, "I can take it, but I need help!" From that stage on, I started gathering teams to assist with tours, commissions, further books, and so on. Learning how to work with others has been one of the most rewarding aspects of forming this public persona.

Several talented craftsmen and craftswomen became regular needlepoint stitchers and knitters for me when I was originating designs, including Jill Gordon, Elian McCready, Kay Kettles, David Forrest, and, by the late 1980s, Juliana Yeo. Juliana and Elian both loved telling stories, so while they stitched or knitted for me, they would entertain. All my stitchers were good at reproducing vegetables, flowers, or fruits from sources—such as old paintings of seed packets—that I'd give them as references. Jill Gordon was a self-taught painter and one of the most talented and intuitive stitchers I have met. Her painting always delighted me, and she later produced her own needlepoint books with great flair. At present, she is also designing patchwork fabrics for Free Spirit.

At one stage, we were joined by a young North Yorkshire lass named Maria Brannan. When she came to be interviewed for the job, she was chaperoned by her aunt, who was a nun. I guess I didn't appear too scary, as she stayed on, and was a brilliant knitter and needlepointer.

The only trouble was that since we all worked a bit on each piece, I couldn't really set a price per project, so I paid by the hour. Unfortunately, as they all got to know each other and relaxed into their work routine, the stories got more vivid and the work slower and slower.

Flush with the success of *Glorious Knits*, my publishers urged me to write a follow-up book right away. Needlepoint was my strongest obsession at that time, and I knew it should be the subject. Steve Lovi agreed and started filling my head with ideas and projects. The first thing I tackled was a big Victorian-style rug of flowers on a lattice of sticks. I used black as a ground against which to throw the brilliant flower tones. It was exciting to work on a big, ambitious piece at the start. I used every flower painting and garden illustration I could find to capture bold, open blooms with distinct profiles. After working on this big scale of a rug, I had a woman sidle up to me a year after the book's publication with a version of the design in miniature cross-stitch. I have a very real prejudice against cross-stitch because the rules and designs for it are usually so precious, but I must admit her version with those jewel colors in neat little crosses on black cotton was charming and suddenly reminded me of embroidering my dance costume at Happy Valley School.

I next looked at Victorian faces to make head-shaped cushions in fine detail. I used an unlimited number of colors with subtle shading, so I didn't even attempt to make a chart. At a book signing, a young mother, there with her young boy and girl, asked me why there were no charts for these. She wanted to stitch those heads. "Look, why don't you make it up?" I said. "For instance, stitch your beautiful children." I throw these suggestions out all the time and am usually rewarded with bafflement or hostility. She found me at another event a year later and produced two gorgeous heads of her children from her bag. Bravo! We were both proud.

The book went on developing, Steve orchestrating the projects with as much passion as I had doing them. Needlepoint is wonderful for taking on the road when a long project is needed. When I went on my New Zealand trip in 1986, I was stitching a table rug, and many train rides and subway journeys went flying by with color in my hands. During a trip to the north of England for a lecture, I was stitching away as usual with my yarns lined up on my train table. An Indian businessman was rushing through the carriage when he suddenly stopped, came back, and asked with interest, "Are you selling these yarns?" I suppose on an Indian train, you could visualize someone selling little items at any opportunity.

Above: The brilliant self-taught artist Jill Gordon visiting the studio, and her calendula still life. **Below:** Juliana (Jules) Yeo working on the Marks & Spencer needlepoint tapestry.

1, 8: I designed two needlepoints for Marks & Spencer, a British chain store, to use on Christmas packaging. The one above featured fruits and leaves and the one on the opposite page, flowers. The large-scale flowers that appear in my work are inspired by artists like Severin Roesen. **2, 3:** A fruit-themed chair I did for Caroline Collis, and my watercolor study for it. **4:** Camp chairs I covered with needlepoint florals—I call them the Gibson Girls. **5:** My Palm Fan ribbon. **6:** Bold roses were a great subject for a hooked rug. **7:** The Flower Trellis Carpet, which was the first project I designed for *Glorious Needlepoint*, which came out in 1987.

The needlepoint cockerel tea cozy I designed for *Glorious Needlepoint*.

Glorious Needlepoint came out in 1987, just two years after my first book, and the making of it went much more smoothly. Steve and I now had experience with book production, and I understood how important it was to be surrounded by a good team I liked working with—photographer, publisher, editor, knitters, and stitchers. Because I now know how to make it all a pleasurable experience, I have had at least one book on the go at all times—if not two or even three.

When it came time to launch *Glorious Needlepoint*, I was invited onto *Woman's Hour* on BBC Radio 4, so I rushed around the studio to find a small item from the book to show the host, Jenni Murray, as she was interviewing me. I settled on my needlepoint Rooster Teapot Cozy and plunked it on the chair beside me in the studio as I waited to be interviewed. As Jenni started to introduce me to the listeners, I suddenly heard her purr in her silky English voice, "And today we have with us Kaffe Fassett and his lovely cock." I gulped, realizing it was live radio. The young women who were behind a glass window operating the microphone and sound levels fell against the glass in hysterics. I blurted out, "My needlepoint rooster tea cozy, yes!" I met Jenni at a party years later and she informed me she had dined out on the story ever since. I just said, "*You* have?"

The news of the success of *Glorious Knitting* reached Naomi Sargant

at British television's Channel 4 shortly after it came out. I'd been to see her a year before, feeling there must be a good TV opportunity in what we were doing, but felt she hadn't shown much interest. When I went to ask again, she said, "Where have you been? You are in my 'yes' file!"

Naomi told me to pick a filmmaker to work with. I thought of all the TV I'd seen, and recalled a series on painters that really stayed in my head. I described it to my agent, and she went off to find out who made it. A week later she came back saying it was made by someone called Anne James, and added, "I think she is retired and certainly not very cutting edge."

Sounds good to me, I thought, and called her up. "Hello, is this Anne James?"

"Yes," said a rather cool English voice.

"Your series on painters is the most beautiful and sensual TV I've ever seen," I said.

"Balm to the ears," came the reply.

We met two days later, when I encountered a short, no-nonsense woman with keys on her belt. She had worked for the BBC for years and knew what she was about, and I told her roughly what I did and what I wanted to present in the film. My aim was to celebrate color— to show the viewer how to see, look, and delve into color and enjoy it. I asked Anne how she would go about planning such a film. She made big maps of the elements of my life. Then she put me in her car, and we drove to places in England I liked visually, and on the way we talked. I told her, for example, that I loved English shell grottos. She then barked into a tape recorder, "shell grotto," and on we spun, sometimes sailing round and round one of Britain's many traffic circles two or three times till we decided where to go next. It was great fun.

I loved Anne's attitude. She told me, "I prepare a script for the producers at Channel 4, but on day one I jump in and swim for my life." She was serious, and was always totally focused on what she was doing. On the first day of filming, she said, "The temptation will be great, but don't tidy up too much in your studio. We want a real atmosphere."

The filming was thrilling. It took a week to film each half-hour episode of a five-part series. Anne organized the episodes, which covered my needlepoint, knitting, and painting along with arts and crafts that stimulated my imagination. She wanted to capture how I saw the world and used it in design, so she would film me stitching, knitting, or painting, or visiting places that inspired me, like lichen-covered gravestones, and she would ask me questions about color along the way. The last episode I shot was down in Arundel and Brighton the week the 1987 hurricane struck, knocking down whole orchards and uprooting fifteen million trees in England. It was so unusual in Britain, no one saw it coming. The sea had been very rough the day before in Brighton, and we returned home to shoot the next day in the studio. I thought the roof and windows would blow in that night, the wind was that strong. Next day, all the lights in North London were out. We had to rent a generator for the shoot, so my house was the only one in our area blasting with light and coffee grinders as the crew filmed.

Left: Shooting the five-episode TV documentary called *Glorious Colour*, produced and directed by my friend Anne James for Britain's Channel 4. **Right:** A still from the series *Glorious Colour*. From left to right, British composer Sir Richard Rodney Bennett, musician Cynthia Millar, and Richard Womersley. **Below:** Knitting on my bed with my needlepoint panel and fruit cushions beside me, as I pontificate on the joys of color for the documentary.

My salvation—the mixed swimming pool on Hampstead Heath that Anne James introduced to me after making our TV series *Glorious Colour*.

Anne told me that she often went swimming in the outdoor ponds on Hampstead Heath right though the year. I was fascinated that she and an eighty-three-year-old friend would dip in even when they had to break a hole in the ice-covered ponds in the winter. She said, "Of course, one dunks like a biscuit," referring to the quaint British habit of dipping cookies in their cups of tea. Then she got me started on it in high summer, and two years later, I was doing the winter dips as well. On our daily morning visits to the ponds, we would park quite far away and stroll through the woods of Hampstead Heath, deep in stimulating conversation about TV, radio, films, and books. After a refreshing dip, we'd walk back to my flat, where we would have hot coffee and buttered toast.

I still find my way there to refresh my spirit in the life-enhancing waters. Anne has now stopped her winter swims, but we walk and chatter from time to time. One day a few years ago, I thought it was time to thank this amazing woman for bringing me to this restorative Heath. Noticing that there were many benches scattered across the park with dedications to past lives, I decided to have one dedicated to my very alive Anne. After a lot of bureaucratic delays, I got it placed near a bandstand, with a plaque saying "FOR ANNE JAMES for life-enhancing swims." She was thrilled and told all her friends, "Some people are rewarded with a knighthood on the Queen's birthday—I got a bench!"

The start of my museum exhibitions

The TV series *Glorious Colour* went out in a 5:30 p.m. slot at the beginning of 1988, and I got a lot of reaction. Some people recorded the series and watched it over and over, sharing it with friends, slowing it down to try to figure out how I knitted with color.

By this time, I was heavily involved preparing for a big exhibition. One day in 1986, I had gotten a call from the office of Princess Michael of Kent to inform me she had been to the Phoenix Shop in Big Sur and seen my work, and she wanted to pay me a visit and see more. She arrived the next day striding alone up the front path to ring the bell, her Bentley and driver waiting outside. Richard was there to witness the meeting. We both sat spellbound as this tall, swanlike woman strode up and down the studio telling us she, too, had written a book.

"What's the subject?" we asked.

"Princesses, of course! What else do I know about?" She tried on several knits and ordered a dark-toned peplum jacket, in which she looked fabulous. She then asked, "Is there anything I can I do for you?"

"What's on offer?" I asked.

"I am a trustee at the Victoria and Albert Museum. Would you like a show there?"

"Well, that would be interesting," I ventured.

I had asked the director of the museum, Roy Strong, a year earlier if we could have a fashion show there, and he had turned me down. But two weeks after Princess Michael requested it, we had a meeting in his museum office and set a date for the show. "Of course, we will need funding," he said. "Can you help with contacts, Kaffe?" I flew home on wings and phoned around, contacting my publisher Century, Rowan Yarns, and

Princess Michael of Kent and British dress designer Zandra Rhodes. Princess Michael helped arrange the exhibition of my work at the V&A Museum in 1988.

Ehrman Needlepoints. From each I got an agreement of £10,000. It took me just fifteen minutes. Boy, did I feel powerful! The museum had said £25,000 would do for the show, so we had enough left for a poster to appear in the Underground stations. We could get going right away.

When we started preparing for the V&A show, Steve, Richard, and I set about selecting from my mountain of knitting and needlepoint to make up an exhibition. We also selected gorgeous items from the china department of the V&A to show with my work. At the same time, Steve and I started working on a book called *Kaffe Fassett at the V&A*, which was to come out in time for the show in November 1988—a sort of grand catalog for the exhibition. But when a Scandinavian critic said, "What is Wee & A?" we changed the title to *Glorious Color* for the foreign editions.

At our first meeting at the V&A, I was asked what I wanted to use in the pictures for my book, and I said, "Oh, things with dots and spots for one." The museum representatives just threw their eyes to the ceiling, asking, "What period? Or country of origin?" Somehow, after a lot of pointing and peering at the collections on two floors of the treasure house, Steve and I made our selections. I commented enthusiastically how much I loved the V&A. One of the department heads said, "It would be okay except for the people coming here!"

Steve was later allowed to bring my work into the V&A top studio, where he photographed my cushion and knit designs along with the museum objects that inspired them. The trouble was that we weren't allowed to touch the items from the museum. So to make the photo still lifes, Steve would have to say, "Could the representative of the Oriental Department please move the Chinese figure two inches left, and could the English China Department representative please move the cabbage tureen one half inch to the right? And quickly!" The reps from the various departments stood around bored, not really into us or our type of pictures.

The book came out shortly before the exhibition opened and was a triumph. The people at Channel 4 were so impressed they added a sixth part to the TV series and presented the series again that fall. The new episode was shot in the V&A and in my favorite English garden, Hidcote, in the Cotswolds, which was designed by an American. The garden managers had taken the very English stance that they actually didn't want any more visitors, as it was hard on the gardens, but they let us film anyway, after some persuasion.

With the book coming out and the Channel 4 series repeated, my exhibition at the V&A was the second most successful show of their history. I shivered with delight when I saw my name on enamel road signs all around that part of London pointing the way to my show.

It was opened by Princess Michael, dressed in black with oversized white lace cuffs and collar. There was a little fuss over the size and manning of a shop in the exhibition. We had postcards, calendar books, my previous books, and knit and needlepoint kits. "How many people will run the shop?" I asked.

"Oh, one is fine," they answered.

"I think at least two will be required," I ventured. They just smiled. But when we sold £15,000 worth of postcards alone, and the lines of people waiting to be served in the shop were twelve to twenty long all day, every day, they changed their tune.

It was said they doubled the people coming to the V&A during my show. As a result,

16 November 1988 - 29 January 1989
Exhibition sponsored by Century Hutchinson, Ehrman and Rowan Yarns

V&A

VICTORIA AND ALBERT MUSEUM HENRY COLE WING
SOUTH KENSINGTON, LONDON SW7 2RL NEAREST TUBE: SOUTH KENSINGTON RECORDED INFORMATION: 01-938 8349

Above: The exquisite, fanciful porcelains from the V&A Museum and my needlepoint rendition for *Glorious Color* (called *Kaffe Fassett at the V&A* in the UK). **Left:** The poster that appeared in the subway system in London to announce my textile show at the V&A in 1988. It features the Cauliflower and Cabbage cushions from *Glorious Color*, which came out in time for the opening of the exhibition.

I was featured on the most prestigious arts program on BBC Radio 4, which I listened to often. The critic attacked my work, which was one of the few negative reviews I've had in years of books and exhibitions. She said I created a cacophony of color and pattern, and, anyway, why was an American allowed to show at the V&A when so many British craftspeople weren't? After that, a big article appeared in a leading paper saying, "Why is the great V&A stooping to having an exhibition of knitting patterns?" But most of the reaction was enthusiastic, as I was the first living textile artist to have a one-man show at the museum.

One upshot of the Anne James TV series was that I got many calls from men wanting to learn how to knit. And I've had several memorable encounters with male knitters since. Once, in an airport, a young musician rushed up to me, saying, "Aren't you the knitter? I have to show you my knitting," and proceeded to unpack his half-knitted sleeve. It was a plain beige sleeve, but he was as proud as a puppy dog.

I did an interview on Irish TV one night, and on the way back to London the next morning, the attendant processing my ticket said, "Oh, it's the sweater man," in his rich accent.

I was also asked to do an interview on an English radio program that featured mostly young music trends. When I asked why, they told me, "Our director is a male knitter."

Another memorable episode was when a group of Australian policemen shared expenses on a trip to England. They all wanted to meet their football heroes, except one. He was a knitter and wanted to meet yours truly. We had him over to the studio, where he spent the day helping us on various projects and chatting away in his Aussie accent. I admired his courage to tell his big sporting mates he was going to meet his "knitting" hero.

Denmark was the first country outside of England to request my V&A show for themselves, and setting it up there was a pure joy. I loved the Danish, who were a bit reserved and elegant like the English, but with style and taste for color and design. Raiding the archives of the great decorative arts museum in Copenhagen for extra items to add into the exhibition of my work was great fun.

The New York Craft Museum also wanted the exhibition, but said they would only take it if we could get the V&A items from the original show. "Fine," said the V&A staff member. "You will need a courier for each item to fly to New York along with it." (First class, no doubt!) That put a kibosh on that, so I didn't show in America for years. Meanwhile, the exhibition went on a world tour including Sweden, Finland, Norway, Holland, Iceland, Australia, and Canada. At each of these museums, I would be allowed to rummage in the archives and pick decorative art items to group with my textiles. It gave a chance for each show to sport items not seen recently in the museums, and it made each exhibition unique. The TV series *Glorious Colour* played nine repeats in Toronto. On my visit there, I'd switch on the TV on Sunday mornings to hear my voice droning on—amazing!

Eva Vincent, who had a shop selling my yarns and needlepoint in Stockholm, urged me to bring the show to Sweden. I spent a weekend looking around exhibition spaces in Stockholm. We finally got to the rather gothic Nordiska Museet, Sweden's largest museum of cultural history, which I took to at once. It was run by two lovely women who liked the idea of a show and gave us a large space at the top of the museum.

When the show opened, Eva found a troupe of dancers to stage a dramatic presentation of my knits. I remember particularly a tall dark fellow with flowing oriental trousers, bare-chested and wearing one of my long, flowery knit coats. He struck a pose at the top of the entranceway stairs and danced down them to powerful music. Six hundred and fifty people attended the opening. So many people were put out that they couldn't get tickets that we had a second opening just as packed. TV covered the exhibition several times, as did magazines, newspapers, and radio.

Knitting is very tactile, so I told the museum guards that anyone could touch if they wanted to. The first day, I saw a little beady-eyed woman in a hat clutching at our hanging coats and shawls to get at the backs to see how they were constructed. She and other eager viewers threatened to rip apart our display, so the "Do not touch" signs went up tout de suite! After that, I have always tried to have a sample people can handle in my shows.

One hundred and seven thousand people attended the Nordiska Museet exhibition, with lines down the block in front of the museum, which of course, attracted more viewers. People would ask, "What could be in there to attract such crowds?" Eva set up a little shop inside the museum, selling cards and kits and books, as well as yarn from her shop. She went home each night with a paper bag full of money, praying she would not get mugged.

In Norway, the soon-to-be queen attended a private view of our next museum show in Oslo and asked me to her home for tea. Once there, she showed me her collection of needlepoint chairs and cushions. At one point, I said I was surprised a fabulous old tapestry had a dining-room table in front of it. "Oh, shall we move it?" she asked, and we set to shoving the big table aside. Her husband came in at that moment. "Rearranging furniture? I am *out* of here," and he rushed from the room.

I am definitely a missionary—my work brings me such joy achieved with such simple techniques that I want everyone to experience this way of expressing their own creative ideas. This handwork is therapeutic, relieving the angst some people are prone to. These museum shows running to packed audiences were a great way to demonstrate this message.

While all my museum shows were happening, and even before the V&A show opened, I was already deeply immersed in another major book. On our trip to Tokyo in 1986, Zoe confided in me about wanting to collaborate on a book of children's knits. Our minds went into orbit as we planned what it could be like. We'd have to have adult garments, too.

Steve grabbed the idea when we arrived back in London. Once we got going on it, he suggested we call it *Family Album*. We wouldn't hire the usual models, but would travel all around finding new places and actual families to model the garments. After many months of knitting, with Zoe and me spurring each other on to do colorways and themes that intrigued us, Steve and I hit the road to take pictures in 1988.

We first went to Morocco, where we used kids in villages and students at the American school in Tangier as models. I also had an introduction from my friend John Torson to artist Marguerite McBey, who had lived in Tangier much of her life in a gorgeous house there. She was still a beauty in her eighties, and we photographed her wearing the Red Diamond sweater with a child model in her wild and wonderful garden.

Another shot was taken in a tiny Moroccan hill village full of screaming kids. They got so overexcited we almost were devoured as we fled for the car after the shoot. The colors on the walls and in the children's clothes were worth it.

Steve and I then went on to Key West in Florida, where we found children and their parents who were living on boats, and other local families for models. One old grandfather in large shorts was taking care of his grandkids in a park. He was very agreeable that we should photograph his little ones in the sweaters I was hauling around in a suitcase. We did charming pictures of the happy old man with his grandchildren climbing around him. Unfortunately, every single shot revealed that his testicles were hanging out of the shorts— neither Steve nor I had noticed because we were so focused on the knitting and all the rich color around us! This was before Photoshop, so these photos had to be eliminated.

When the book came out in 1989, the English cover showed a small blond boy sucking his thumb in one of our sweaters. I wanted the same shot on the American edition, but was told the American Orthodontic Society would disapprove of it. It is bad for your teeth to suck your thumb, they said, but I insisted and it was used.

Unfortunately, the American publisher's publicity department thought I didn't really need any specific marketing, and our gorgeous book faded with hardly a trace—proving the vital importance of marketing. I've always felt that in this frenetic world, any project needs to be spotlighted if it is to find its audience. Years later, *Family Album* was considered a rare treasure and copies were changing hands at quadruple the original sale price.

Photos from the 1989 book *Family Album*, which Zoe Hunt and I worked on together. Shooting the knits for the book was always adventurous as Steve Lovi and I found our models on the road, starting in Morocco and then in Key West. In Morocco, artist Marguerite McBey (above center) modeled the Red Diamond Sweater in her enchanting garden. I modeled as well, in the chaos of a hill village in Morocco (below).

A drawing I did of Billy Gibb, wearing one of my early knitted vests.

The same year Steve, Zoe, and I were finishing work on *Family Album*, my friend Billy Gibb passed away. It was a shocking loss to the fashion world and his large Scottish family I'd gotten to know so well. In the days before he died of cancer, I sat by his bed knitting a baby blanket and chatting to Billy's mother as he passed in and out of consciousness. Each time I experience the departure of someone close, I am filled with renewed wonder at the life force that keeps us on this earth or deserts us to go elsewhere, and I resolve to use what time I have as productively as I can.

My needlepoint stitching studio was busy with commissions in the late eighties. One was from Sally, Duchess of Westminster. I had met her originally through Jeremy Fry, and she really impressed me. She was a tall, slender figure and had been written about in *My Father and Myself* by J. R. Ackerley.

Sally had a huge house in Wickwar, where she had created her pride and joy of a garden. The garden was the size of two football fields and was like a botanic sample book. It was a delight to wander its borders and woodland walk, and I went to visit it when my stitching studio was going full swing. My favorite things in the house were the panels of Chinese hand-painted wallpaper in the dining room. The delicate colors with big peony trees, a red lacquer birdcage suspended by a blue-and-white scarf, and all the flower forms cried out to be stitched. At that point, I noticed she had a dark brown sheepskin rug on the floor, striking a horrible contrast with the lyrical wallpaper. "You really need a carpet that reflects these stunning wallpaper panels," I told Sally. "Instead of a dead sheep," I thought. When she heard of the needlepoint carpet I could make her with my studio of stitchers, she agreed at once and gave me the commission.

1, 4: Studies from my sketchbook of the hand-painted Chinese wallpaper in the dining room of Sally, Duchess of Westminster. **2:** The wallpaper itself; it inspired the needlepoint carpet I made for Sally in 1989. I followed my sketches while stitching the motifs freehand onto my canvas. **3:** The finished carpet.

I did many watercolor sketches of the Chinese wallpaper panels and couldn't wait to get started. Sally wanted a coloring that wouldn't show the dust and dirt too much, so we agreed on a taupe background, which I broke up into shaded diamonds so the stitchers could easily reproduce it. We all enjoyed working on it. David did wonderful flower forms, and his early frustrated interest in art shone through. Juliana and Maria also worked well on it and were thrilled when the Duchess came to visit halfway through. She asked me what it would cost. Since I'd talked her into it, I tried to keep the price low so only took into account our stitching time with no allowance for sketches and design. When I told her, she muttered under her breath, "C'est rien!"—it is nothing. Realizing I could have made more didn't matter, as it was such a joy to make. Unfortunately, Sally died a year later, but we went to an auction of her effects and bought the carpet back at the same price I had charged her.

The eighties were to end with great sadness for me. In the summer of 1989, Rory and I went to the beach for three days to get away from it all. After a lazy day in the sun, we started back to our bed-and-breakfast. Rory looked a bit worried as he felt around for his keys. "I've lost the car keys," he said with growing concern. We went through all his pockets, then spent an hour poking around the sand where we had spread our blanket. Nothing. We went back to the car and called the Automobile Association to rescue us. As we sat waiting, I asked him to play a game that I had loved when young. "What would you like to do if you could do anything in the world? No limitations. Just have your dream job."

He looked off into space through the car window for a long time, then said the saddest thing I've ever heard: "I can't see anything." I shudder when I think of what followed.

One day not long after, I noticed that Rory was really off-color and seemed to get annoyed at every little thing. Two days later, I got a call asking me if I knew a Rory Mitchell. He was in a hospital, having been found collapsed in a doorway on the street. He seemed fine mentally when I visited him later that day, but was definitely not well and was being made to submit to a series of tests. It turned out he had a rare strain of meningitis.

I sat with him for the next three days. On the third day, he suddenly went from rather weak to bright and funny when Zoe and another friend visited. He sat bolt upright in bed, cracking very funny jokes. He also recounted a letter he had gotten from his mother stating how glad she was that he was with a loving friend. He almost cried when he said, "Why couldn't she have said that years ago?"

The next morning, Rory was very tired but in a good mood. "I think you overdid it a bit last night," I told him. "Yes," he sighed. I told him I was going to lunch and would be back in an hour. He whispered with a little smile, "I love you." As I went to lunch, I asked Richard what we could do about Rory when I went on my six-week promotional tour of the United States for my next book. We were thinking he might suddenly get better or he may need looking after, which we would have to arrange. When I returned to Rory's room an hour later, a nurse met me at the door. "We did everything we could, but he just slipped away. He was one of our favorite patients, and we so wanted him to pull through."

Rory was definitely not there when I viewed his husk. I felt bad that he had died so young, but saw that a timid soul had found real freedom and confidence in his last days. I think he knew, as I am sure my mother did, that he was going. We had a big funeral in an old church near Regents Park. Lots of his colleagues from the BBC attended, as well as his sisters and mother, shocked he had died so young.

My greatly missed friend Rory Mitchell.

Looking back on a decade and reflecting on where creativity has taken me, I see how basic humble elements in life can lead to the highest flights of fantasy. This excerpt is from a diary I kept in 1988, written when Steve and I were on a trip to the United States. I remember thinking how deadening consumerism had become by then:

> Steve and I have both been depressed by the consumerism of unattractive goods. The soulless, clean plasticness of houses and shops, et cetera, out here in middle-class America. The phony New England look. Walking through shopping malls, supermarkets, America does stagger me with its fanfare kaleidoscope of choices. It makes me look back to England and its limited resources with affection, like something I can deal with, find my way through, and that is somehow ultimately healthier for my soul. Perhaps it harks back to my childhood of slender resources. Mom spending our clothes allowance on building materials while sending us to the Goodwill shop with a dollar to outfit ourselves for school. The adventures of seeing what we could find in the piles of secondhand clothes to make ourselves ready for the world. Clothes were approached like elements of a patchwork quilt (Holly was later to make one out of Mom's smock tops when she died).
>
> Putting a plaid shirt with striped trousers, finding shoes and a belt to make it work, embroidering on a shirt or sweater, dyeing and overdyeing to get rich color schemes—all this makes a good grounding for my approach to knitting. Also, the lack of endless choices, making something exciting with what one could afford, was the name of the game. So going to England and finding only standard items in stores was quite normal to me, as it wouldn't be for kids lavished with every conceivable variation of style, foods from around the world, tools, recording equipment, computers, and more.
>
> Now England has much more choice than ever before (my twenty-two years here have witnessed many changes), but there are only four channels on TV and a finite amount of foods and clothes. Somehow there seems more knitting, working with hands making, and certainly a lot of interesting design in handmade items.

I had found a flow of ever-renewing inspiration from the markets, museums, and media of London in the eighties that kept my imagination fizzing. The popularity of my museum shows and books made me realize that the world was hungry for colorful, detailed textiles and was rising to the challenge of following my hints at how to make them. Whatever I could come up with was taken up, so I was encouraged to give my imagination full rein.

Above and opposite: Loving complex jumbles of pattern, I was fascinated by this Moroccan pottery stall and this scrappy tile panel. Watercolor is such a good medium to catch these travel impressions.

chapter six

1990 and Beyond

Finding Color in a Gray World

Above, left: A needlepoint hanging of shells that I designed for a Norwegian cruise ship in the nineties. **Above, center left:** A mosaic I did at the Highland Stoneware pottery in Scotland. **Above, center right:** Painting a still life commission for Kim McLean (see finished painting on page 210). **Above, right:** One of the many chairs I have covered with needlepoint. My subjects for this one were a large cabbage and other vegetables. **Opposite:** The wintertime shoot for my book *Quilt Road* was going badly, with quilts blowing onto the ground around us. I shouted, "Take *me* in a quilt for the damn shot!" I have nicknamed this image "Old Monk."

I entered the nineties with optimism. My exhibition at the Victoria and Albert Museum had given me a lot of publicity, and there was increased interest in my design work. More and more invitations came for workshops, lectures, TV and radio appearances, and even charity involvement— opportunities that took me to countries such as India, Vietnam, and South Africa, and exposed me to global influences in color and pattern, leading me into quilt fabric design. In the nineties, writing books became an integral part of my life, and with the help of Liza Prior Lucy, I discovered my passion for patchwork quilts. The *Abstract Design in American Quilts* show at the Whitney in New York in 1971 was still buzzing in my head as I launched into quilt making. Large quilts would give a grand sense of scale to dramatize my use of color, which my knitted garments could only hint at. In the twenty-first century, my travels and contact with needlecraft enthusiasts also expanded. I realized that textiles, with their texture and rich depths of color, gave me a motivation far beyond my painting. In turn, my enthusiasm for them brought me a larger following than my fine-art work had.

1990–1994
Inspiration from around the world

In 1990 I was, among other things, working madly on my next book, *Glorious Inspirations*. It was to be a selection of paintings and historical decorative art that designers (including myself) could use as source material for fabric designs, needlepoint, and knitting. I was always looking for stimulating source books, and because I couldn't find a comprehensive one, I decided to create it myself. Luckily, my publisher took up the challenge to finance this tome, which included masses of expensive photos. Going through hundreds of good design examples with my photo researcher, Mary Jane Gibson, charged up my imagination. We found transparencies of tantalizing mosaics, paintings, tapestries, ceramics, embroidery, and even tattoos! The final choices would, of course, reflect my own love of rich coloring and intricate detail. But I felt sure there would be many that would rejoice in the bold impact of my selection of strong graphic shapes in dramatic colorings.

Interspersed throughout my book would be some of my own one-off needlepoints with their source. One such example was a needlepoint chair I did as a commission. My introduction to the client came from Simon Burstein, who had gone on from his relationship with Tricia Guild to marry Nathalie Rykiel, the daughter of the French fashion designer Sonia Rykiel. Sonia was one of those creatures who became more beautiful as she aged, with pale skin, a flaming halo of red hair, and a sharp but appreciating eye.

Simon wanted me to design and stitch a needlepoint covering for a chair to take center stage in Sonia's newly opened Paris shop. It was a thirties-looking, deep amber bentwood chair with a black leather seat and back. My design featured roses, pansies, and fruit set against a graphic black polka-dot ground that echoed the carpet—a composition that would counteract the modern lines of the chair. The fruit and flower colors sang out on the black dotted stitching.

By 1990, my newfound "fame" made me a candidate for BBC Radio 4's *Desert Island Discs*. This popular radio program asks its guests to choose eight records they would take with them if they were stranded on a desert island. The presenter winkles out the guest's life story, illustrated with excerpts from the chosen records. The show is a British institution. (My friend Anne James said being invited onto it is the equivalent of receiving a knighthood.)

I was in Hawaii in 1990, visiting a yarn shop housed in a flight attendant's bedroom in a tiny town, when I got the call from my business partner Richard Womersley to start compiling my records. I was to be on the show when I got back to Britain. My mind went ballistic. Was it true? It must be the V&A show that brought it about.

A Radio 4 addict, I had listened to this weekly program for more than twenty-five years as I knit and stitched. Like many listeners, I had already contemplated what I would choose

Above: A needlepoint chair I designed in 1990 for Sonia Rykiel's shop in Paris. I used the dotted carpet motif in my stitching of flowers and fruits.
Opposite: A jug I hand-painted on blue-and-white tile at the Highland Stoneware Potteries in Scotland.

if it were me on the show. I had racked my brain to recall what music was significant to me at various points in my life. I remembered Dad playing "Symphony on a French Mountain Air," a great rolling orchestral piece with a little tune that had worked its way into my child's mind. Joan Baez was a must, as her music was such a part of Big Sur life. Then the Beatles' "Hard Day's Night" burst on me as I entered life in New York, and it set me up for moving to Britain. Bulgarian folk songs that Charles Heim had introduced me to meant so much to me as well. "I Just Called to Say I Love You" was for Rory. The high voice of a choirboy in Allegri's "Miserere" was my first choice to take to my desert island if I could only have one.

1, 3, 5: Brandon Mably at his desk, the nerve center of the Kaffe Fassett Studio, painting, and giving a color knitting workshop. **2:** Sweater from Brandon's first knitting book, *Brilliant Knits*. **4:** Brandon's most popular fabric, called Fish Lips. **6, 8, 9:** More of Brandon's prints. **7:** A button vest I made for Brandon. **10:** Sheila Healey's portrait of Brandon.

One of the events in 1990 that marked a clear dividing point in my life was meeting Brandon Mably. He was living in a studio flat nearby and holding down two jobs, cooking for post office workers and working at the fish counter at the local supermarket. We got talking at a bus stop, and he expressed interest in the work I was doing. When he visited the studio, he was so observant and spot-on about what worked and what didn't that I thought he must have trained as a designer. In reality, he had no art training of any kind; he just had a natural, very keen eye. I asked him back and did a portrait of him in the little round glasses he wore in those days.

Brandon then started visiting the studio every day. I encouraged him to draw and even start painting. Learning to knit took much longer, but he got there in the end and was quite a whiz at needlepoint. Finding himself so at home with creative work, Brandon begged for a job. He had noticed the disorganization in the studio office and was dying to sort out a more efficient way to run things. I was hesitant, as my life was going at such a pace that I couldn't imagine how I would find time to train someone to manage my office. Finally I said, "Okay, you can have a job, but you'll have to train yourself. Start Monday."

Brandon was quickly able to help me with communications—dealing with the press and arranging workshops, exhibitions, and lectures—and to assist me on teaching workshops. The office became more efficient overnight, and the slow-working staff were let go, leaving the two of us to make most of the samples much faster; we would use occasional help or students when we had larger, urgent commissions. With Brandon running the nuts and bolts of the office and cooking, I was free to concentrate on designing.

At the beginning, I took Brandon to visit the great art collections London is famous for. He knew nothing of the Impressionists, or any art movements or great painters. His discerning eye and lightning brain took it all in, and on further visits to shows and collections, he recognized painting styles at a glance. It was a joy to see him learning and appreciating so much. His drawings and watercolors started to really catch the essence of his subjects and led to excellent designs in knitting, needlepoint, rag rugs, and fabric prints.

My first portrait of Brandon Mably when he still wore little round glasses, painted in 1990, the year he joined the studio.

I was working on at least two books a year and doing an increasing number of interviews, so traveling to teach was put on hold. In the early fall of 1990, a call came from Ron Mendelsohn asking me to go to Australia for a tour of workshops and lectures later that year. Ron was the Rowan distributor there, and he had a yarn shop called Sunspun in Melbourne.

I had vivid memories of my first trip to Australia, after *Glorious Knits* had just come out in 1985. Although I enjoyed it, I remembered how world weary I felt then, being on my own, so I said coolly to Ron, "If I can bring an assistant this time, I'll come."

"Fine," was the reply. I knew Brandon would love Australia and the Australians, and they him. How exciting to travel with someone so appreciative of life's riches.

This started my worldwide travels with Brandon. He got the flavor of that amazing continent straight away. I was able to show him the colorful Ayers Rock—or Uluru, as it is now called. They wouldn't allow us to climb it, as I had on the first visit, but I will never forget the vastness of its rolling top plain. During sunrises and sunsets, the whole rock turns to liquid copper.

We explored the landscape, loving the rocky outcroppings, and got loads of inspiration from the galleries of aboriginal paintings in Alice Springs.

The best thing we did was take a balloon ride across the desert at Alice Springs. The view from above of the little round plants on the desert floor at five in the morning is so like the dot-filled Aboriginal paintings. When we came down, the big, hairy Aussie guys who flew the balloon in little shorts and boots had us sit in a circle as the sun rose and eat chocolate cake and sip champagne—total bliss.

Our trip ended in Perth, where we heard about an eccentric house. It was in a fairly well-to-do suburb, and was absolutely covered in wacky mosaic. Every home in the neighborhood looked similar, except Evi Ferrier's amazing abode. Wanting to see more, we rang the bell. A tall, handsome woman with a prematurely gray bob answered and broke into a huge smile when she recognized me, and we were invited in to see this creative, mad woman's house. She was working her way around the property smothering every available wall in broken china. We hung our coats on teapot spouts in the hall.

On subsequent trips to Perth, we stayed with Evi in that house, and I helped continue the outside wall coverings from her boxes of shards and broken plates. She told me she sent out her dinner invitations saying, "Bring a plate, cracked, chipped, or broken, and leave it here." One of her favorite techniques was cementing a whole plate to the wall and then hitting it with her hammer. Wanting to spread her mosaic color magic, she worked with prisoners, making delightfully chunky benches and wall plaques to lighten the gray prison world. "I'm not going to stop till I cover all of Australia," she crooned one day.

Brandon and I joined Evi for refreshing winter sea dips in the early mornings while we were in Australia. Meeting free spirits who share so dynamically their inner imaginings is one of life's greatest gifts as we travel the wide world. Evi reminded me so much of the

Left: The amazing mosaic walls by Evi Ferrier in her house in Perth. Right and opposite far right: My fabrics that draw inspiration from Aboriginal dot paintings and the bold colors of Australia. Below and opposite: Deflating the red balloon after the dawn ride Brandon and I took over the Australian landscape in 1990.

friends my creative mother cultivated during my childhood in California. She joins my strong creative women friends like Muriel Latow, Tricia Guild, and Candace Bahouth (see page 198), all laws unto themselves and giving us all a blast of fresh air.

Evi introduced us to her friend Tootsie Buckeridge, who was married to a wealthy property developer. In 2000, she ordered a large needlepoint hanging for her very modern dining room facing the sea. It was a mostly gray interior with a dark stone table. Brandon suggested I do a stitched piece from a painting of stones I'd done. Tootsie agreed, so we produced a large fifteen-by-six-foot tapestry for her. It was exciting to work on that scale, but so hard to resist color. I had to maintain that neutral palette of gray tones, but I heightened a bit of ocher and rust that I found in the stones. David Forrest, Brandon, and visiting students helped on it, making it go quite fast. In three months, it was done and sent off to Perth.

Sometime in 1991, I was running around my studio organizing a dozen things and trying to meet looming deadlines when a call came to the studio from an organization that advised charities. When Brandon said I was too busy, the caller said, "Tell Kaffe I want to take him to India." I rushed to the phone and heard her say, "I knew that would get your attention."

The trip was scheduled for early 1992. I was to be part of a team of visual people, all invited as advisers, to see what handcraft pieces we thought could be produced in India for a group of charities to sell in shops in Britain to raise money. Buying these crafts would also help the Indian communities directly. Our remit was to travel around and look at a fabulous cross-section of textiles, jewelry, embroidery, pottery, and other crafts and offer our advice.

The excitement of going to an exotic country I had dreamed about for so long was intense. It was also a luxury to travel with this group, which included a journalist from the *Financial Times*, a professor from London's Royal College of Art, and most intriguing to me, Jonathan Glancey, an articulate, sharp writer for *The Independent* newspaper, whose interest was architecture and style. As we toured the country, Jonathan would rise each morning before any of us and go see whatever architectural gem of the past was featured in that area, often stopping at the flower market to buy us all bouquets or fragrant leis of blossom. I shared a room with him, so we had some good talks on the way.

India burst upon my senses as I felt it would, but more intensely than I had imagined. The first deep impression was standing transfixed at the flood of humanity flowing unendingly down Delhi's streets—there was so much color in that river of people. Many were on motorbikes or bicycles, so saris and scarves of magenta, gold, scarlet, lime, and orange fluttered in the rush of traffic, making it feel that a dozen circuses had come to town. The soft mint green of many mopeds added to the color rush.

As we explored markets, textile shops, and palaces, the intensity of color made me feel permanently stoned. Soon I began to enjoy the smaller villages where craftsmen and women worked, and we could see their humble abodes and workshops and the simpler country shops and decorated walls. I loved the way life was lived for all to see. Laundry became a fascination—long clotheslines of garments like party bunting in parks or on beaches, or more often spread on bushes or the sand to dry. The most spectacular vision was a scene in front of Delhi's Red Fort, the great red stone walls of this ancient fort becoming a backdrop for a row of deep magenta and red saris hung on an impromptu clothesline. I made our taxi driver stop so I could take a photo. It was too good to miss.

1, 7: My Sprays fabric inspired by Moghul carpets, in two colorways. **2:** Red Fort in Delhi, the day they washed every red sari in the country! **3:** A stall selling brilliant colored powders in India. **4:** Jonathan Glancey entertaining orphans in India during a trip we made to advise charities on decorative crafts to buy for their shops in Britain. **5:** A Christian cemetery in India. showing what color can do. **6:** This glorious arrangement of laundry lines on an Indian beach delighted me. It's so Christo! Sometimes I believe I travel the world looking for great laundry.

Above all, India proved to me that color was a vital ingredient in life, a fact that so much of Western fashion and décor seems oblivious to. As we wandered through market stalls and huge indoor textile emporiums, I saw a feast of rich, unapologetic color that had my senses buzzing. I bought beautiful bits of cloth in the form of scarves, small towels, shirts, and more, to inspire me at home. But the real treasures that are still in my head were the poor people in the fields and towns wearing stunning combinations of color, often faded to a gorgeous level of subdued vibrancy. The rich upper echelon wore black or beige, for the most part, and never really turned my head. But to see a hardworking woman, carrying bricks or a pile of straw or fruit on her head, in a deep orange sari with purple edges, was food for my hungry eyes.

When I saw that even cemeteries—the ultimate gray experience in America and England—could be a symphony of cool blues and chalky greens, I knew I was in a land where color was a definite life-enhancing element. It confirmed for me once more that I was right to pursue this magic in my work.

A lot of people have introduced themselves to me after being inspired by my books and TV interviews. Some have become woven into the fabric of my life, others pleasantly confided their feelings and passed on into the stream of life. One who really made an impression was Bich Tyler, a delicate waif of a Vietnamese woman whose powerful will I would discover later on. She made herself known to me at a knitting festival and invited herself to the studio. "I'm leading a tour of Vietnam, now that it's opened up, and I want you and Brandon to come and see what can be done in the way of encouraging industries like embroidery and pottery," she said. We jumped at the chance and had the trip of a lifetime to Vietnam in the early nineties.

At the outset, I felt really shy about being an American in a country I thought couldn't help but hate what we had done to them in the name of peacekeeping. I need not have worried. We got the friendliest reception I've had anywhere in the world. The spirit of these people building up their country as fast and hard as they could was an inspiration. I loved the old, crumbling past, the colorful oriental details on the buildings, and the streams of people everywhere in bright prints.

When we got to the middle of the country, it was raining, which created one of the most unique street ballets I have ever beheld. Vietnamese rain gear consisted of a big poncho of waterproof material that came in lavender, powder blue, pink, and yellow. Many people were on bikes, so they looked like huge flowers whirling down the roads, topped with conical straw hats. Often, there would be stalls selling bright fruit and flowers on the roads, adding to this dance of color. Even plastic flowers and kitchenware had a twinkly charm here. Since my lifelong quest is to find color in a gray world, I loved the soft pinks, yellow, and blues of the old Vietnamese buildings.

My most deeply satisfying impression on the trip was an encounter with the market streets of Hanoi. I felt I was walking into one of those Chinese paintings of booths of different crafts in minute detail. Each trade had a section of shops specializing in their tools or materials. Fabric shops, of course, got me going, with their bolts of patterned cotton and silk stacked in wonderful patterns. Pottery and porcelain shops were near layers of beaded curtains in twinkling colors, some hanging from trees. My favorite was the hardware section with boxes of screws and nails, layers of saw blades, and all manner of carpentry tools.

Our Vietnamese friend Bich Tyler, who took Brandon and me on a tour of her country.

1, 4: A beaded curtain market in Hanoi, one of the many stimulating color treats I saw during a trip to Vietnam in the early nineties. **2:** A Vietnamese river in the early morning mist. **3:** A lost-looking boy in a covered fruit market with bananas creating an interesting pattern behind him. **5:** A stall selling nails. **6:** Plastic flower stalls, with one of the rain ponchos that so entranced me during this trip. **7:** Dyed papers drying in a field; they are used to wrap candied ginger. **8:** Even the plastic ropes at this stall became an exciting color happening for me.

The lumberyards with stacks of wooden planks and bamboo poles were equally enthralling. All of this was viewed against the backdrop of the flow of traffic, rickshaw bells, and impromptu street restaurants.

We went to several potteries and got a little embroidery done in Hanoi that should have led to a production of napkins and tablecloths, but I'm sad to say very little in the way of practical projects came out of the trip. My experience in Vietnam was so haunting, however, that I went back to film a documentary called *Kaffe's Colour Quest* in 1995, and that was an equally satisfying trip. In the film, I showed a scarf I had knitted that was inspired by the layered rice terraces I'd seen in the countryside during my first visit. Other influences to my work, such as the bright fabric and plastic in the market, were also explored in the film.

A travel-inspired knit I designed for *Rowan* magazine in 1992 became one of my all-time favorites. On a trip to Istanbul the year before, I had spotted in the bazaar a worn, faded kilim carpet that I simply could not walk away from. I asked the stall owner how much it cost. "Five hundred pounds," was his quick answer, "but do come in and have a cup of tea with us."

"Oh, I only have forty pounds to spend," I said, "so it's not worth your time."

"Sit and enjoy," he answered. So I sat down and let him show me many other carpets and embroideries. I only really liked that one carpet, so I kept saying, "But I only have forty pounds."

After we looked through everything and sipped a few cups of tea, he said, "Okay, what is your last price?"

"Forty pounds is all I have," I repeated.

"Okay, the *last last* price?" This went on for half an hour longer. Suddenly, he grabbed the carpet off the wall and handed it to me. "Okay, forty pounds and it's yours."

Delighted because I always value worn pieces of history, I came home and hung the carpet over my mantel for a year, till I couldn't resist using its wonderful patterns and faded palette for a knitted jacket. It was one of the most complicated and ambitious knits I ever attempted for *Rowan* magazine. Using different types and thicknesses of Rowan yarns in many shades for the jacket, as well as combining two different yarns of thin strands to create some of the hues, made it a challenging knitting pattern, but it turned out to be a very popular design. When it was photographed for Rowan, they used an unknown model, doing her last job in England before being discovered in America.

Soon after Kilim Jacket came out in *Rowan* magazine, Steve Lovi visited me from America, where he was busy setting up a new base. He was always interested in my new knit designs and how they were being modeled, styled, and photographed, so I showed him the pictures from the shoot. I had thought the theme was interesting, the setting nice, and the models okay. Steve, however, looked at the magazine and instantly picked out the main girl, saying, "Now *there's* a face. Who is she?" Steve's eagle eye was in action once again, recognizing Kate Moss as the star that would become the world's archetypical model.

Stephen Sheard once asked me, "Couldn't you design another knit like the Kilim Jacket? It was one of the biggest hits." Song writers must be asked this type of question all the time. If only we all knew how to predict which of our creative output would be hits—we never can really tell.

Above: The carpet that inspired the Kilim Jacket, one of my favorite knit designs. **Left:** Kate Moss before she became a famous supermodel, modeling the Kilim Jacket in a Rowan knitting magazine that came out in 1992. **Below:** The famous Tricia Guild modeling the back of the Kilim Jacket.

By 1992, I was involved in designing costumes and the set for a ballet.
Jeremy Fry was sponsoring the Northern Ballet Theatre, and it was he who approached
me about working on it. The ballet, *D'Ensemble*, was set to a piece by Dvořák, and because
the choreographer, Graham Lustig, had the same passion I had for the flower paintings of
Odilon Redon, I jumped at the chance. I had nurtured a passion for the jewel-like colors of
that mystical painter ever since I had seen his show in Paris in the fifties.

When I presented a small model of the stage set I had designed to the theater for
the dancers and directors to have a first look, I got total stunned silence. Afterward, I
complained to someone working in the theater about the lack of reaction, and he said, "Just
come and look at the set they are dancing on in the present production of *Sleeping Beauty*."
He took me into the theater and turned on the lights to reveal a black, silver, and gray set.
"And most of the costumes are dark versions of these, too," he told me. "They are shocked at
your bright colors!"

But they went ahead with my design. The backdrop was that complex colored mist of
Redon's with floating flower forms, and the dancers' costumes reflected those brilliant flower
tones. I made the women's clothes as colorful as big blooms—chartreuse with magenta,
purple with deep turquoise, scarlet with fuchsia, and so on. Using that sharp contrast of
colors that my mother had encouraged me to acknowledge as legitimate, I put the ballerinas
in flared skirts of these rich colors, with gores of a contrasting hue that would be revealed as
they spun around or were lifted. For the men, I designed silk shirts, tights, and vests of rich
tones like peacock blue and emerald green, or deep red and magenta.

The floor was painted so viewers in "the gods" (as the British charmingly call the
cheapest seats in the upper balcony) could see the dancers against the colorful texture of
impressionistic flowers. The set was beautifully painted by a strong female scene painter
who caught the atmosphere perfectly from my tiny sketch. Brandon and I were properly
gobsmacked as we entered the gigantic studio and saw the twelve-inch-square painting I had
done for the set expanded to fill the entire back wall. The painter was on a huge scaffolding
painting our flowers.

Left: The sketch I painted
for the backdrop of the
D'Ensemble ballet, produced
by the Northern Ballet Theatre
in 1992—heavily influenced by
Redon. **Opposite:** Standing on
the set of *D'Ensemble* as it was
being painted in a huge studio.

My niece Nani, Kim's daughter and my mother's favorite grandchild, grew into a handsome woman with a distinct talent for cooking and presenting food. In 1992, she opened a café on top of the Phoenix shop at Nepenthe called Café Kevah, after my father's mother. Two days before the opening, Dad announced he didn't want any dinner, lay down to nap, and slipped peacefully away with a smile on his face. The opening was combined with his wake.

Even after Dad was gone, he had the power to shock me to the core. We all gathered to hear his will, with Alice joining us. He had written in it, "Alice gets nothing. If she says she does, she is a liar!" He actually did leave Alice the house they shared, which was to go to Alice's daughter, Havrah, if Alice died. But to hear those words written out officially in a will was a bombshell!

I've had a lot of heartfelt gripes about Dad all my life, but now looking back, I feel much more appreciative of the struggle he must have gone through to keep a dream like Nepenthe alive while raising all of us kids. Most importantly, I see what a motivator his reluctance to support me was. He inspired my inner resourcefulness. His doubts forced me to prove I could do whatever I dreamed.

Brandon's father found more comfort in the pub than in his family home, so in the summer of 1992, Brandon decided to buy a house for his twin sister, Belinda, and their mother, Yvonne, in the little town of Rye near England's south coast. He and I had stopped our busy schedule to house hunt for weeks, and were thrilled when we found an 1840 house with a big kitchen and a little glass-walled room leading to a long, narrow garden at the back.

We all threw ourselves into fixing it up. I painted a mural, did mosaics in the bathroom, and donated my large collection of tiles to cover the kitchen and the floor of the garden room. Brandon and Belinda painted great colors everywhere—bright poppy red in the living room and pinks and blues on stairways and in bedrooms. We were always finding carpets, dishes, and furniture for the house, so the ongoing project became a very creative time. Yvonne would cook delicious meals, and we'd eat in the glass room or in the garden on summer evenings.

I also knitted a big throw for the red living room of every shade of red I could find in my yarn stash. A few years later Belinda decided to paint the room lime green—amazingly, the red throw worked in that coloring just as well.

This venture into interior design fit right into the efforts I was making at the time on my upcoming tome called *Glorious Interiors*, which would be published in 1995. I was creating lush room sets and filling them with specially designed needlepoint, knitting, rag rugs, and mosaic. Painting murals for other people in the past had only whet my appetite for conjuring up whole fantasy interiors of dramatic colors and textures.

Some of the decorated rooms of the Rye house are featured in the book. One shows the sunroom covered with Rupert Spira's stunning tiles. I had met Rupert in the late seventies when I started practicing Dervish turning techniques. I was amazed to see a very young public school boy (sixteen or so) doing the turning effortlessly. He had a mop of black curls, olive skin, and shining eyes. He was at the prestigious boarding school Eton at the time, and his teachers let him off classes to attend, as his stepfather was our sheikh. Rupert's mother was also in the Dervish group, and Richard and I had quickly made friends with this enthusiastic woman who taught art and had us visit her charming house in East Sussex.

When he graduated, Rupert took up pottery and utilized some barns on the property to start a serious business. He was making colorful pots until a potential customer dropped by one day and casually inquired if Rupert made tiles. "Of course," was the reply. Having never made a tile before, he took the sample the fellow wanted to copy into his office and tried to figure out how to make it and how much to charge. After a few trials and errors, he became a glorious tile maker, doing huge architectural commissions in London and Paris. His tiles had the elegant palette of the ancient medieval mosques I'd seen on my travels through the Middle East.

I started collecting Rupert's reject tiles that had fascinating flaws in the glazes, making them more desirable to me. Once I had enough, I had a tile floor made in the bathroom of my London house. To this day, it is the only room that is finished to my ideal vision.

The best time I had with Rupert was traveling all through Spain looking for interesting uses of old tiles, and we were far from disappointed. We went to Seville, which was rich in tiled murals, stairs, and wall plaques. Cordoba was a fabulous cultural shock with a gothic church inside a huge mosque.

Left: A voluptuous set of tiles that Rupert Spira and I found in a Seville park when traveling through Spain in the early nineties. **Below:** A tropical mural I painted in the garden room in our house in Rye, with Rupert Spira tiles. **Right:** Rupert Spira tiles in my London bathroom, glazed in magnificent colors. **Right, bottom:** Blue-and-white tile inspiration from Oporto, Portugal.

Above: The living room in our home in Rye, on the south coast of England, after Brandon's sister, Belinda, painted it green. **Left:** The original red living room in the Rye house with a knitted blanket, for which I used every shade of red I had. **Below:** The mural I painted in the garden room in Rye. **Right:** My dining room in London all dressed up to illustrate ways of using leaves, including in needlepoint, rag rugs, and knitting, for *Glorious Interiors*.

In 1993, as Steve was now settled in San Francisco, I needed a photographer for my book *Glorious Interiors*. I was nervous as hell. Many photographers at that time seemed to want a clean, hard look in their work, while I luxuriate in lush complexity of detail and visual texture. First and foremost, I needed someone who understood and loved color. Going through dozens of portfolios of work sent to me by my publisher, I suddenly spotted a little sack of garlic, left in its lavender mesh bag sitting against some blue pots in a still life. "That shot was done by Debbie Patterson, a food photographer," I was told. Her acute sense of color was in all her work, and when I heard she had assisted the great Linda Burgess, whose work was very much like Steve's, I knew I'd found my photographer.

We got along so easily that the photo sessions didn't seem like work. I do get highly stressed on shoots and tend to rush on to the next shot before the current one is done, so I need a lot of calming down. Having the same sense of humor, Brandon and Debbie got along so well that it tended to make our shoots too playful. The horsing around made me fearful of wasting time and losing the plot at first. Once I saw that Debbie could play and still work really brilliantly at my fast pace, I started to relax, and to trust more.

Debbie is a mother of three active boys, and I'm sure she is quite a strong leader in her house, but she has a gentle, feminine way with me, always checking to see if I am happy with a shot and its styling, but having many good ideas of her own. She is visually educated and often has good location suggestions, understanding the sort of colorful places I am drawn to. Even when I get tense and nervous, she will walk around the vicinity of an outdoor location I've found and stumble on an even better place to shoot our quilt or cushion. She knows quickly what will read in the camera. Brandon and I often take our own shots at the same location and are amazed how difficult it is to get the right balance of color, light, and composition that makes an object come to life—something Debbie achieves every time.

Learning to relax and collaborate has become one of the most satisfying aspects of my creative life now. Being able to trust another's ability to understand and carry out what is required is very necessary when you take on as much as Brandon and I do.

On my trip to India in 1992, our advisory group had visited the Oxfam offices in Delhi—Oxfam is a large charity that works with developing countries and has a network of thrift stores all over Britain. A fellow there had said, "Oh, you are just the sort of designer we need here." Sure enough, a couple years later, the London office of Oxfam called me up and arranged for me to go there again. This led to the beginning of a new venture for me into woven fabric design, and from there to quilt fabric design.

Oxfam had a scattergun approach planned for my 1994 visit. Brandon and I were scheduled to go to several weaving communities and see what we could do. When we got to the first one, miles into the countryside in Andhra Pradesh, we remembered how unfruitful our trip to Vietnam had been, trying to get too many projects going and arriving at nothing definite. So we decided to stay in one village and see if we could develop something solid.

The weavers had already written to me in London, sending a quaint book of yarn colors to choose palettes for my woven fabric designs. As I didn't weave and always arranged color best with yarn on a knitting needle, I knitted a long sample scarf of stripes in different moods and scales. First off, they were upset because "knitting's not weaving."

"Oh, I know that," I told them, "just make a weave that looks similar to my knit." Then, much more difficult, they didn't have the colors we needed. I offered to go buy them, but the nearest source would not sell less than one hundred kilos per color. That was a dilemma, as we needed over twenty-five colors! The place that could sell sample amounts was two hours away, which meant four hours out of one of our precious few days. And it was afternoon, so I'd be picking colors in the dark with awful strip lighting. "Okay, needs must!" I said, and off we went.

In a dark back room, I sweated over hanks of cotton threads. Guessing their true values in that ghastly light, I just picked a lot that seemed to go together, and we returned to the village. The next day, the weavers stretched the threads down the dirt streets to create their warps, all the while brushing them with rice starch to prepare them for weaving. Then they put these warps onto little stick looms in their dirt-floored houses and sat in a dugout pit in the floor to weave. Thank God an articulate man from Kerala had been sent to translate and advise on the weaving. He was bright and spoke several dialects and beautiful English.

Our translator quickly saw how limited my knowledge of weaving techniques was and suggested the wefts be many different colors to create totally contrasting moods in our stripes. With the same warps of twelve colors or so, a red or blue or black weft would create amazing differences—from dark and mysterious purple blues to rich reddish pinks to sunny yellows—another of life's great color lessons.

We stayed in a Red Cross center about half an hour from the village. Wanting to please the children of the village, one day Brandon went to the nearest town to buy balloons, and blew them up on the way back so the jeep was full of color as he arrived. The kids saw it at once and went ballistic. The village elder had to calm them down and line them up so each one could get their balloon in an orderly fashion. They were dancing about and squealing with delight all afternoon. It's amazing how a bit of rubber and air can bring so much joy. In the West, it seems to take the most expensive athletic shoes or computer games to raise a little enthusiasm from the kids.

I was thrilled with the results of the weaving, and our sample bolt was a triumph. We had a celebration with speeches and thanks and food and songs. A little ancient fellow sang his heart out to us. The weavers, who had been so attractive in their outfits of T-shirts and long, colorful cloth wraps, attended in white nylon drip-dry shirts and dark trousers. It took both Brandon and I aback until we realized what looked so ordinary and dull to our eyes was the height of exotic smartness to them. These masculine, hardworking men would never understand why we liked their graceful *lunghis*.

We returned to England with our sample cloth and convinced Ken Bridgewater at Westminster Fibers in New England to order a bolt of each stripe combination. We waited months and no fabric came. A year later, we contacted Oxfam to complain, "Where is our order?" They went to the village and learned they had no money to buy the colors to get started, so they just ignored us. It turns out other companies had ordered yardage, then canceled, leaving them with no money and bolts of fabric to get rid of. So Oxfam gave them a starter fee, and our fabric samples arrived a few months later. Oxfam used some of the woven stripes to make duvet covers and a couple of shirts for their charity shops. I was disappointed after all our efforts that this was all they would use them for, so we gave a selection of the stripes to patchwork quilters like Karen Stone. Having one of the best color senses in the quilt world, she made some brilliant quilts with them in her fabulous style. I remember a rather ancient Byzantine use of husky browns, reds, and golds. This proved my woven stripes could be great in patchwork, which I was starting to really get into. We were off!

1, 4, 7, 12: Some of the stripes I designed for Indian weavers to make.
2, 9, 13: When I visited India in 1992 to start work with the weavers, they used the village streets to stretch out and starch the warp threads for my striped fabrics. **3:** A weaver chatting with Brandon.
5, 10: Roman and Venetian glass and the Roman Glass fabric it inspired me to design as my first quilt fabric print—it is still in my collection.
6: The Roman glass theme taken over to my knitting. **8:** Children in the weaving village in costumes to thank us for working there. **11:** A village woman winds the threads for our woven sample. **14, 15, 16, 17:** A few of my prints. Swiss Chard, was one of my earliest quilt fabrics with a large-scale design. **18:** My Indian woven stripes made into a quilt, nestled in a Virginia creeper at the American Museum in Bath.

11

12

13

14

15

16

17

18

After the stripes, Ken Bridgewater asked me to design a range of five printed quilt fabrics in five colorways each to go with them. I pulled out my garden catalogs and a picture of gazanias caught my eye. The intricate shapes and patterns the petals made would, I felt, be good for patchwork. My Small Pebbles print was next, then I remembered the Roman Glass vest I'd knitted and felt that would be perfect. The world agreed, and fifteen years later that Roman Glass fabric print is still very popular. But my biggest early attention-getter was the Swiss Chard print inspired by a Victorian botanical illustration.

That fall, we brought our fabric to the Houston quilt market (the Mecca for all things quilting) for the first time. Our stall was draped in Indian stripes, and we won best booth award. It was a great honor and a warm welcome to the world of quilts.

Brandon and I returned to our Indian village recently to find that, because of the work we had brought them, the weavers now had concrete floors and electricity. This amazed us. It meant they could work in all weather and not have to suspend weaving when the rains came, making their dirt floors unworkable.

1995 1999

My passion for patchwork quilts is ignited

Inspired by my interest in Indian textiles and further encouraged by Liza Prior Lucy, the Rowan rep who accompanied me on my first book tour in the United States, by 1995 I was totally caught up in patchwork design. Liza had started mentioning how exciting she was finding patchwork quilts in 1987, about two years after I met her. "You should get into this world," she kept saying to me. But at the time I was just getting over the workload that arrived with my book *Glorious Needlepoint*, so I was in no mood to take on a whole new craft. After she persisted, I said to her, "Isn't patchwork just cutting up old clothes and sewing them back together?"

"Oh, you are *so* wrong!" was her reply. She envisioned me bringing a fresh and unique color influence to the craft and doing my own range of fabrics.

Since I was not in the mood to take her ideas on at that moment, she started going through my knit books and making my motifs into patchwork blocks, which was not too difficult, as many of my geometric patterns in knitting came from old patchwork books. She would send me the blocks, and I'd comment that a patch here and there was too bright a white, or that a print needed to be in a larger scale. After a few of these exchanges, she wrote me, "See, you already are a patchwork designer."

Warming to the idea of doing patchwork by the mid-nineties, I flew to the States to work with Liza on our first serious quilts. I remembered that long-ago trip to Wales, when I slept under those overblown furnishing-fabric roses. Liza and I found some large-scale floral prints at furnishing-fabric shops and combined them with smaller prints in Liza's extensive stash of fabrics. Our first quilt was a simple nine-patch called Rosy, and we did versions of it in three different colorways. It was dead easy to sew with only two different square sizes.

At first, I would lay out the fabrics I wanted on the floor in folded parcels. Then Liza would photograph the arrangement and we'd move on to the next idea, confident the sequence was in the camera. But one morning, two days after I'd gone back to England,

Above: My first patchwork quilt, Rosy, was reminiscent of the English quilt I slept under in the seventies in Wales. **Opposite:** With Liza Prior Lucy. Out of the blue, a stranger offered to sell Liza this painting of mine at the same time that she was trying to convince me to take up patchwork design.

Liza's four-year-old daughter said, "Look Mom, I found a pretty ribbon." She was holding the opened camera with the film cascading out of it. So Liza had to try to remember what I had put together. Nevertheless, we somehow completed those first few quilts.

We started toying with the idea of doing a quilt book together, which was a big commitment on both our parts. Then something happened that felt too much like an omen for me to ignore. I had painted a large still life of kitchen items on a patchwork quilt and sold it to an American buyer in London in the late eighties. She took it to America and decorated a room around it. Just as Liza was wooing me into patchwork, she got a call from the owner of the painting asking if she was the Liza who knew the work of Kaffe Fassett. "Yes," she said, and when the woman told her she was selling his painting of a quilt, she replied, "It's of a patchwork? Just a moment, I have to ask my husband," as she held the phone to her chest and let out a whoop of joy. When she found out that the price was what the woman had paid for it, Liza jumped at the chance to buy it, sight unseen. It is one of my best efforts of that period, and the fact that this painting of a quilt came to Liza so serendipitously committed me to start my patchwork adventure.

Above: On the photo shoot for *Simple Shapes Spectacular Quilts*, published in 2010. **Above, right:** One of my quilts shot in Hastings, a town on England's south coast. I love how the quilt looks amidst these black houses. **Below:** Oriental carpets inspired my Turkish Delight quilt fabric. The stripiness of these big motifs echo the Indian stripes, right. **Right:** My hand-woven Indian stripes in their full glory, in this quilt from *Passionate Patchwork*, published in 2001.

We embarked on *Glorious Patchwork* and spent two creatively ecstatic years—1995 and 1996—designing, sewing, and quilting our first book's worth of quilts. I loved the hours we spent shopping for fabric; we made the quilts out of anything we could find. At that point, I had nothing but a few of my Indian woven fabric designs on the market.

Visiting Liza whenever I could in those months of intense quilt making, I became part of her family. Her husband, Drew, is a quiet man of few words, but those few can be very funny. Liza and Drew have two daughters, Alex and Elizabeth. Young Alex was as exquisite as a Velasquez portrait and as otherworldly to me. Elizabeth was a down-to-earth little old lady at four, when I first really got to know her. They both have an aptitude for the stage (not surprising considering their outgoing mum), and Liza has really nurtured this, finding a voice coach who has brought out the real talent in them.

Our work routine would go like this: I would usually arrive at Liza's in the evening, having thrown myself together in London and caught an early flight, then made the long drive from New York to New Hope, Pennsylvania, where Liza has her New England–style house. It was orderly for a family house, and as I entered, Liza would run up to her bedroom/workroom and fetch the latest finished quilt I had designed from those squares of fabric arranged on the floor.

She would proudly display the result, having gotten used to it as it grew, and loving it herself. I'd study it in the electric light, groggy with travel, and only see things not looking like I had envisioned them. "I'll look at it in the morning," I learned to say to a disappointed Liza. Next day, a lot fresher, I'd bounce down at 6 a.m. and start working. Liza would have me do research in her stashes of fabric and her vintage quilt books while she got her kids up, fed, and on the school bus.

She decided from the start that I wasn't safe to cut fabric with her lethal rotary blades and probably wouldn't be careful enough, either. Precision is everything in this game if you want a good, flat result when pieces are sewn together. By mid-morning, I'd have fabric strewn all through the once-tidy house. We'd have sewing machines roaring away as Bobbi Penniman, a brilliant quilt maker who lived nearby, threw herself into our project with enthusiasm. We would jump in the car on the second or third day and make the rounds of the fabric shops within a ten-mile radius of Liza's house, returning with inspiring new colors and patterns.

All the while, we were both building our dream of where the next quilt, then the next show, then the next book could go. We used the available fabrics designed and printed for our market, but we had an eye on the large-scale furnishing-fabric prints for more drama than what the commonly found quilt fabrics possessed. I quickly learned what prints were missing in our specialized world. The voluptuous scale of big, blousy florals was what really appealed to me, and these were hard to come by in a craft dominated by small-scale, cutesy prints.

However, I did love the reproduction prints on the market because I was so steeped in antique quilts. I would pore over books of vintage pieces trying to decipher what made them so magically appealing. How my enthusiasm would rise when I turned a page and there was another startlingly beautiful arrangement of squares or triangles in a harmony that took my breath away! So I'd look at the color and the little repeat prints of those, but I also noticed that some of the fabrics on larger squares or borders possessed bigger, sprawling prints that got my painterly fingers itching. Putting together our first book provided a very necessary grounding and research time for me.

Liza with her quick brain knew all the textile artists and companies by name and reputation and would fill me in. In our never-ending search for fabrics, we headed to New York City to Liza's all-time favorite store, ABC Carpet & Home, and, boy, did I learn to take notice of anything she pointed out after entering that palace of delights. The first massive floor was so full of the sort of things that fill my dreams that I found it hard to breathe: beautifully executed mosaic-covered furniture; chandeliers that made eccentric and delightful use of shells; glass flowers; and cabinets filled with silk brocades embroidered so colorfully I felt they had been designed with divine guidance. The color, extravagance, and downright beauty made me feel like a child in a fantasy candy store.

And that was only the first floor. There were five more, one entirely full of fabrics of such invention and gorgeousness that we literally couldn't choose what to buy on that first trip. Later, I got wonderful pieces there for our quilts, using their classic European toiles and lavish stripes and plaids to inspire many a project.

We went to ABC so often that the owner asked us if we wanted to have a shop within a shop. I became really excited by the idea of having a branch at ABC with my own designs. That dream soon ended when we were informed that we would need to make a million dollars a month or some such figure. "This is another world that could definitely age me overnight," I said to myself as I returned to my simple textile-creating life.

I did have a brief but earnest venture into retail in 1996 and 1997. It was scary enough to kill off the dream most artists and designers have of starting their own gallery or store so they can display their output to the world. It all started when antique seller June Henry approached me to go into business with her. She had asked me many times since I met her in the seventies with Richard. She was a blond beauty with a ladylike air and a definite flair for spotting good antiques on the cheap. She had had a few antique shops herself, but always dreamed of opening one with me.

The Kaffe Fassett Designs shop, which June Henry and I opened on a back street in Bath in 1996. Few customers could find it and we closed after two years.

We were both avid collectors, so it did seem a good idea. She loved my design work and wanted to start a shop combining my designs on pottery, tin ware, and textiles along with her antique items. She was able to get a lease on a shop in Bath, Somerset. Bath was a beautiful location in itself, but—big mistake numero uno—the shop was located on a back alley that had very little traffic.

June wanted to raise money from friends who were eager to be part of any business we would form, but I felt they would interfere, so I talked her out of too much financing. We'd try to get it going alone as much as possible—that was big mistake number two! We got a little pottery maker to produce china mugs and bowls for us, a tin company for boxes and trays, and another company for oilcloth table coverings, and we were off.

The shop, called Kaffe Fassett Designs, opened in 1996. I used every waking hour painting designs, making mosaic-covered furniture, painting murals for the shop space, and doing needlepoint footstools. June had many good ideas and contacts, and we did tons of work for this venture, as did Brandon and others at my studio. But the odds were against us. Even the tourist board of Bath, when asked where the Kaffe Fassett shop was, didn't know how to direct people to us. The ones that did find us would walk through the shop like it was a free exhibition, say how they loved it, and leave without buying even a postcard. It reminded me how the great Danish florist Tage Andersen charged people to enter his shop because so many came just to look. We should have done the same.

I'd call Liza in America to tell her our latest ploy to attract customers, and she would say in her matter-of-fact way, "It's still retail, Kaffe." She had owned and run a needlepoint shop in the eighties in Washington, D.C., so she had experience to back up her skepticism. After two years, we admitted defeat. I'd invested a huge chunk of my savings and creative energy, and June had, too. As Richard said, it was actually not a high price to pay to learn that I don't belong in retail. It definitely didn't feel good, but I know he was right.

With the attention and respect I'd had with shows in major museums in Norway, Sweden, Britain, and Holland, I still couldn't get a serious museum exhibition in my country of origin. I took this up with Lotus Stack, the curator of textiles at the Minneapolis Institute of Arts, when I was asked to give a lecture and show my slides there. "We talk about you in museums in the U.S., but we feel you are too popular," she said. "But don't give up on us." That was encouraging, and one day she called to ask if I had a show ready to display for the Christmas season of 1997. As luck would have it, my entire V&A exhibition was in storage, ready for shipping. Roxy Ballard was the museum's designer in residence, a tall, brilliant display artist who did me proud. She painted the rooms my show occupied in the museum eighteen different colors to create my color groupings; this setting showed off my work better than ever before. We used items from the Minneapolis museum's rich store of pottery, painted furniture, and textiles to augment our displays. A book on my studio, titled *Welcome Home: Kaffe Fassett* and published in 1999, shows the exhibition marvelously.

One of the brilliant sets for the exhibition at the Minneapolis Institute of Arts. My knitting and needlepoint mixed so happily with the museum's porcelains and furniture. After the show at the V&A Museum in 1988, my work slowly made its way around museums in Europe and finally hit Minneapolis for Christmas of 1997. This photo appeared in *Welcome Home*, published in 1999.

Sometime after Liza's and my first book collaboration, *Glorious Patchwork: More than 25 Glorious Quilt Designs,* was published in 1997, I went to visit my friend Candace Bahouth in her Somerset house and studio. It was an old converted chapel in the tiny village of Pilton, Somerset, on the edge of the farm that hosts the Glastonbury Festival every year. Candace is American and a hugely talented artist who made her name in Britain at the same time I did. Starting out as a tapestry weaver, she wove a postage stamp of the Queen and a portrait of the punk singer Johnny Rotten, among other iconic figures of our time. After that, she took up needlepoint and became one of the most successful of Hugh Ehrman's stable. She was also an established mosaic artist.

Candace's studio home was a treasure trove of her work and witty collections of kitschy found objects. A lot of her cabinets and sink surrounds were delightfully mosaicked in bright bits of china. I'd always comment how much I loved it all, and on that visit, she said, "Why don't we do a book on mosaics together?" I'd recently started doing some mosaic, and loved the idea of really getting stuck into more ambitious projects. Doing books or being promised an exhibition is my best way of giving myself license to work flat-out on projects that would seem indulgent otherwise.

Once my publisher gave the go-ahead for us to do our own individual mosaic designs in a combined book, Candace and I worked hard to meet our deadlines. Brandon and I mosaicked our front outdoor entranceway—I did massive hollyhocks on one side, and Brandon did diamonds of pooled color on the other side. We then tackled the back terrace, completing the tile floor in two days and covering the wall surrounding the window above the terrace in another two days. We also mosaicked two tables and a white bathroom. My medium was broken china for the most part, but I also used small shells on a swan urn and fake pearls on a lamp base.

The mural I did in 1998 for the outside wall of the theater at my old school, Happy Valley in Ojai, California, was finished just in time to put in the book. It was made up of pebbles and shells as well as broken tiles and china. Because the mural had to be completed quickly in the hot August sun with the aid of volunteers, I laid out everything on the floor beforehand. That was an arduous but fun communal collaboration. My sisters Holly and Kim drove down from Big Sur to help Brandon and me, and Gayle Ortiz advised on technique.

Candace did wonderful projects like vases, tabletops, and a glorious tapestry wingback chair covered in tiny broken matte tiles. Many people thought it was a chair covered in an antique woven tapestry.

The book came out in 1999 to good reviews, but not massive sales. However, it does still sell, and people often approach me for signatures in it at my other book signings and talks.

Steve Lovi alerted me to the treasure trove of delight to be found in English gardens. Grand or intimate, they often reach a high level of artistic expression. The patient attentiveness lavished on them year after year is one of the qualities I admire the most in the English. Their sense of history and climate and their use of stone add richness to their gardens. Imagine my delight, therefore, when I was invited in the autumn of 1996 to design a garden for the well-known Hillier nursery, to be their showpiece at the Chelsea Flower Show—Britain's most famous annual gardening exhibition, a five-day event on an eleven-acre site in the center of London.

1: The hollyhock mosaic I made at the entrance to my London house when I was working with textile and mosaic artist Candace Bahouth on our joint book *Mosaics*, published in 1999. 2, 4: Helpers working with me on the mosaic mural I designed in 1998 for the theater building at Happy Valley School, which I had attended in the fifties. 3: The finished theater mosaic. 5: A detail of an apple mosaic I designed for a mosaic-covered shelf. It was beautifully rendered for me by Sarah Kelly. 6: Candace Bahouth in her usual lush style among the yarns she employs so elegantly in her needlepoints for Ehrman kits. 7: Candace Bahouth's Trompe l'Oeil Chair done for *Mosaics*. 8: Candace's wonderful mosaic flowers executed in her brilliant, expressive way.

I was well into mosaic at that point, so the concept of my garden was to link plants and mosaic. It all had to be ready for the May 1998 show, so Brandon and I spent several months in 1997 and 1998 covering large clay drainpipes with bold patterns in broken tiles and pots. These became columns to support big terra-cotta pots overflowing with plants. I also designed a waterway lined with pottery shards and had mirrors and oblong planters covered in a rich, medium-to-dark palette of mosaic from ocher to maroons to cobalt, purple, and black. The planting was to be all dark-leafed and rich floral tones. My palette for it included bronze foliage and flowers in deep red, purple, burgundy, russet, orange, and amber, accented with fuchsia and magenta. I decided to separate the ground bedding plants with a lattice of coal to underscore the dark palette. It took a year for Hillier to prepare all the plants so they would be flourishing in time for the show. When it opened, Martha Stewart showed up to have a look at our garden and the British seemed to approve, awarding the display a gold medal. It featured heavily in the TV coverage of the event and made a good inclusion for Candace's and my book on mosaic.

A garden I designed for Hillier Garden Centre for the 1998 Chelsea Flower Show. It featured mosaic columns and containers that took my helpers and me months to complete. The garden palette was dark, so coal was used to separate the planting beds; my black mosaic swans looked brilliant in it.

Greg Doran, a director for the Royal Shakespeare Company, called one day in 1999 to ask if I would design sets and costumes for the millennium production of *As You Like It*. Wow, is the pope Catholic? Shakespeare! I instantly thought of the rich imagery of the Elizabethans—tapestries, bold carving, beading, and embroidery. Thrilling, but would a modern young director want all that richness, or would he be thinking modern dress, God help us!

Then Greg said the magic words: "I think it should feel like a stumpwork box." My favorite crafted objects from the Elizabethan period are the elaborate, intricately embroidered boxes in stumpwork featuring miniature padded fruit trees, animals, insects, and people in stylized landscapes. "I'm not really familiar with the technical requirements of stage design," I said. "Could I work with someone who knows the ropes?"

Greg put me in touch with the dynamic designer Niki Turner. At our first meeting, I asked what her work was like. "Oh, I think of the bare minimum required and then take something away."

Left: The patchwork robe I designed with Niki Turner for the Royal Shakespeare Company's performance of *As You Like It* in 2000. **Below:** Stitching their needlepoint tapestry, Rosalind and Celia on our set. My sketch for Rosalind's dress. The backdrop being painted in my Shakespearian flowers. **Overleaf:** Relaxing on my needlepoint cushions, Adrian Schiller, playing Touchstone, and director Greg Doran, who asked me to design the sets and costumes for *As You Like It*.

"Well, guess what? I'm oriental Russian opera!" I said. She gulped, and I thought, "This is going to be interesting."

I brought out my scraps of needlepoint canvas and a big pile of colored yarn and said, "Let's start by stitching some color stories." She looked at me, amazed, then started stitching, commenting, "I can't believe I am doing this!" We then dug into lots of books on the period and examined Elizabethan embroideries, deciding we wanted our Forest of Arden to have gigantic leaves painted to look like they were in the crewelwork of the time.

The costumes would be in big and exaggerated brocades and patchwork. I also designed a huge, multicolored knitted jacket for the court jester. When it came to color moods, we decided to start with the cold, forbidding court all in black, white, and gray, which would transform to spring and summer colors as the cast felt the freedom and love in the forest. Niki really got into the color, helping me design the bright patchwork, knitted, and hand-painted outfits for the forest romp and the magical wedding. She went on to do wonderful plays and operas full of the colors of Africa and India.

Working with the set painters at the RSC was richly fulfilling. They were always amused at my puppy-dog excitement at bringing a large production to life on a Stratford stage. The costume department had the best reaction: "Thank God you are doing the play in period. That's what we know how to do. The last Shakespeare was in modern dress, all black suits on a black set, boring for us!"

Our play opened in 2000 to mostly good reviews. One I remember fondly started, "This is *As You Like It*, as we like it!" Unfortunately, when the play transferred to London, they played it in a white theater, leaving out our embroidered forest. I was disappointed, but Prince Charles attended and said the costumes told the story as well as any set.

My best memory of this unforgettable period of my life was sitting through endless rehearsals of the play as it took shape, letting those wonderful lines wash over me, while stitching big needlepoint cushions of Elizabethan flowers for the play's lovers to lounge on. I even did miniatures of those oversized cushions in petit point to be used as pincushions or small bags for the Ehrman catalog.

As most Englishmen and women know, Shakespeare reveals much on each re-encounter. I walked the street at that time repeating his pithy words—rich, indeed!

One of my most satisfying trips in the nineties was to South Africa in 1999. I had had requests to go there for years, but had refused because of apartheid. Since Nelson Mandela was released in early 1990, I decided it was finally time to go. Brandon organized a lecture tour for 1996. After traveling to the key cities like Johannesburg, Durban, and Cape Town, Brandon remarked how few blacks there were in the country. "That's because we are only going to specially selected places," I explained. "A white bubble sealed off from the real world." We had only one workshop in the black townships on that first trip.

On our next trip in 1999, starting as we intended to continue, we were met at the airport by a barefoot Ndebele woman sporting the beaded donut-shaped leg, arm, and neck pieces. A bold red, black, and green blanket was draped over her shoulders. With our white guides and this exotic woman, we drove miles to her village, where we were met by a band of ladies dressed like her, blowing whistles and wearing policeman's peaked caps. They danced us from the main road up to the village where they treated us to their VIP banquet of Kentucky Fried Chicken.

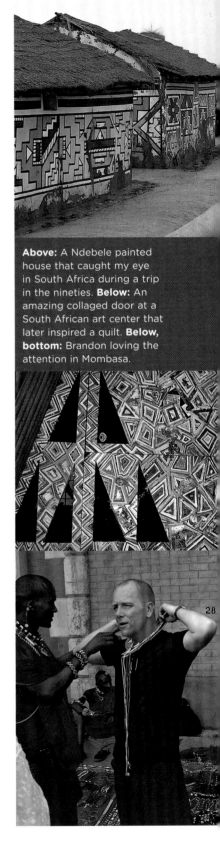

Above: A Ndebele painted house that caught my eye in South Africa during a trip in the nineties. **Below:** An amazing collaged door at a South African art center that later inspired a quilt. **Below, bottom:** Brandon loving the attention in Mombasa.

28

At another village, we met one of the dynamic women painters who was traveling the world drawing attention to their distinctive culture. Her house was painted in geometric patterns in pastels, black, and white. She had a big sign up saying "I am Ester ARTWOMAN." Brandon asked her if she ever took off her donut-shaped beaded neckpieces. "They are my wedding rings," she said. "So, no."

Being in South Africa confirmed my belief that often poor societies produce great creativity. The inventive ways of making do in India and Mexico were so magnified in South Africa. What Africans could do with tin, wire, old bottles, even plastic shopping bags was a sheer delight to behold. The patched houses in the townships lined with advertisements or product labels inspired me to no end.

Taking glorious color into the twenty-first century

During the first year of the twenty-first century, I was busy designing knitting and needlepoint as usual and was finishing off quilts with Liza for our next patchwork book, *Passionate Patchwork*, to be published in 2002. I also had an exhibition that year at the Steninge Slott Palace in Sweden.

Brandon had his hands full running the studio, scheduling lectures for me and workshops for himself, all while working on his first knitting book, *Brilliant Knits*. Richard had become a great rock for us, and still is. Living nearby, he comes by most days to see what we are working on. He always has insights that are invaluable to our creative work. Officially, he does all our contracts and keeps the books, but his objective eye is what really encourages us in our many projects.

Another positive force who resurfaced in my life at this time was Deirdre McSharry, who had been the editor in chief of the UK edition of *Cosmopolitan* for over thirteen years. I met her in the 1970s, when she did an article on me for *Cosmopolitan*. Throughout the years this passionate and beautiful Irish woman, with her wide view of the world arts movements, has always encouraged and championed my work.

Deirdre was now living in Bath and curating shows for the American Museum located on the edge of town. She had the museum invite me to participate in a group show in 2001 and two one-man shows there after that. Her faith in me paid off with record attendances at these exhibitions.

My love of big-scale projects never wanes, and the chance to do a large needlepoint panel in 2000 was eagerly taken up. A Shakespearean theater near the Lincolnshire town of Stamford commissioned me to design a piece to hang in their bar area. I quoted a price for the three-foot square they requested, but when I viewed the cream-colored bar, I saw at once it needed a larger piece to make a presence in the space. So I offered to do a nine-foot by six-foot tapestry for the same price. They wanted to have elements of their garden reflected in the room, and since the garden included hollyhocks, one of my favorite English plants, I jumped at the chance to tackle those bold shapes and glorious colorings in wool stitches.

Left and above: The Hollyhock Tapestry, a commission for the Stamford Shakespeare Company. How exciting it was to work on this big piece. These handsome plants demanded this nine-foot by six-foot scale. **Below:** My sketch for the hanging.

The next big needlepoint tapestry I took on was for a lady in England's West Country. She turned out to be an admirer of my needlepoint and had done a lot herself. She was decorating a barn on the property to be a summerhouse and wanted a dramatic piece for the end wall. Her furnishings were on the dark side, and she plainly loved color, as there were stained-glass windows, rich wall colorings, and pre-Raphaelite paintings throughout her house. So I arranged all my jewel-colored pots together and did a large four-foot-square painting of this still life, which I doubled in size for the tapestry. Of all my commissions, it was one of the most challenging and deeply satisfying to carry out. With the help of two stitchers, it took three months to complete. The silky depths of tone on those maroon, cobalt, jade, and turquoise pots was achieved through multiple shades of wool used in combination (several shades of thread in the needle at once). It was thrilling to inhabit that scaled-up, glowing world of color for the months of its growth in the studio.

Left: The Big Pots Tapestry, completed after months of stitching. **Above:** The painting on which I based the needlepoint. **Right:** In progress. **Below:** Working on it from my squared-off painting.

204

My usual designwork—hand knitting for Rowan, patchwork fabrics for Westminster Fibers, needlepoint for Ehrman and for one-off commissions, and patchwork for my books—continued to thrill me, but in 2001 I was happy for a new challenge. It was always curious to me how few interesting knits there were to be found in stores. I was becoming so aware of what machines could do if fed with good colors and yarn, yet one so rarely comes across anything of unusual quality.

One label, however, always caught my eye, and that was Peruvian Connection. I learned their sweaters were mostly hand knitted in Peru, and that the company was run by a very smart anthropologist from Kansas named Annie Hurlbut. Annie had gone to Peru to work in her field and had come home with some handsome handknits for friends. They were adored, and friends of friends begged for something similar the next time she went to Peru. She would return with cases of knits, and it was only a matter of time before she started asking the knitters to do different colors and shapes. The Peruvian Connection catalog was born. To my mind, it is the best hand knitting on the world market. The catalog is beautifully styled and photographed, and the designs get better and better.

When I first saw the catalog, I noticed that some of the Peruvian Connection designers were knocking off my designs to sell to her. I then heard from my friend Kay Kettles that she was designing for them, so I decided to call Annie up and offer to design for her directly. She was thrilled. We have had a successful collaboration ever since. They send me a huge box of the most sophisticated palette of yarns each season, I knit up sample swatches along with a sketch, and they work out the details.

The freedom to use as many colors as I like is great. I often work with twenty-five to thirty colors in a garment, and the thin yarns can be combined to create hundreds of hues. Knitting up swatches the size of a back of a garment for Peruvian Connection is one of my most joyous tasks. The colors they produce each season are the richest I've ever come across: chestnut brown, burnt maroons, smoky lavenders, and teal blues. Annie said of our collaboration, "This is a marriage made in heaven."

When *Saga* magazine sent Brandon and me down to Peru with a photographer to do a travel story, I got to meet some of the wonderful knitters who do our knitting and see how they spend up to a week weaving in all the ends on one of my multicolor knits. We also got to go up to Cusco and see how richly painted and decorated the churches are there and how many extensive museum collections there are of the ancient textiles and pottery. Again, I was struck by how rich everyday objects can be if we let artists have free rein to decorate the interiors we frequent. Imagine banks and hospital waiting rooms decorated with the same loving flair as those old churches are. Of course, the pottery and textiles of South America give me endless inspiration for my own work.

The same year I started working for Peruvian Connection,

Brandon suddenly felt the Rye house was too small. So he and I started a hunt in nearby Hastings, on England's southern coast. I was excited by the new plan, even though we had put so much into that little Rye house. All those tiles and murals! But we loved the idea of a bigger house, and houses in Hastings were not very expensive, so we were bound to get more space for the same price.

Two or three weekend searches went by with only dreary places to see, where there was always something not quite right. Then one weekend, as we were ending another fruitless

Above: Swatches for Peruvian Connection. **Below:** My first designs for Peruvian Connection. **Below, bottom:** One of my favorite designs for Peruvian Connection—the big flowers were inspired by a carpet design.

search, I noticed a house called The Hollies. "My sister's name!" I cried. "We have to check this out." So without a call to a real estate agent, we walked up the drive of The Hollies, and our mouths fell open. A large family Victorian manor, it was set in its own private gardens so it was not overlooked or bordered by any nearby properties. It welcomed us with open arms.

We couldn't resist knocking on the door. A handsome young man answered with his children and their toys about his legs. "Do come in," he said, and we did, greedy to see inside. Large wooden floorboards in the two main rooms grabbed me, as did the white marble fireplaces and sun streaming through the ample windows from the garden. We were in love before we even saw the five bedrooms and dining and kitchen area.

I told Brandon we had to have it. I'd pay two-thirds of it so we could go right ahead. Richard loaned us quite a bit of the down payment, interest-free, until we could sell the Rye house. Miraculously, it sold the next month to a fan of mine at our asking price, over two times what we had paid for it. It all happened so fast that Belinda and Yvonne were not at all sure they wanted to move so soon. They thought in a year or two maybe, but we were so gung-ho we jumped straight into it.

The morning we moved in, Brandon went shopping with Yvonne. He called me from a fish shop to say, "Turn on the TV! You won't believe what's happening!" I did and watched the second plane crash into the World Trade Center in New York—it was September 11, 2001.

After a bit, Belinda and Yvonne grew to love the house. We put in an old Aga stove, and I tiled the kitchen with blue and white tiles I made in Scotland at the Highland Stoneware pottery. I went all the way to the top of Scotland to make these tiles, painting every kitchen motif I could find on over five hundred tiles—cauliflowers, Brussels sprouts, loaves of bread, eggs, cats and dogs, and fruits and vegetables galore. It was a long task that took several trips to Scotland, but I loved it, and the results were very rewarding. David Grant, the founder of Highland Stoneware pottery, donated all the tiles to the project, for which Brandon and I did large mosaics outside two of his potteries, using their broken crockery.

There was a terrible sort of Greek mural all over the living room leftover from the days when it was a dance school, but we painted over most of it. I then totally reworked and softened the end wall so it had a romantic landscape with palms. In the dining room, I painted mock Chinese wallpaper with peony trees and birds on duck egg blue. Brandon and I went to Venice to find a chandelier to finish off the room. We could not find anything like the old flowery, pastel Venetian chandeliers I had in mind, so we made one up of several different chandeliers that almost fit the bill.

Brandon has thrown some great summer parties in that house. I am so glad for this haven he can retreat to on many weekends to recoup his energies. We often use the house to photograph our quilts, and it is sometimes featured in magazines. I love going there in the summer when it is warm enough to swim in the sea.

In 2008 I came up with the idea of doing a new quilt book that unpacked the ingenious use of basic geometry in quilt construction. I'd long been turned on by the endlessly inventive ways in which simple shapes were incorporated into vintage quilts—how squares or diamonds could be used to produce so many exciting and fresh effects just by adjusting their colors and the way they were laid out. It makes pouring over old quilt books endlessly fascinating. A harmony is achieved by the right placement of color and proportion that has the power to appeal, as a good work of art does down through the centuries.

Left, top: Mural in the living room at The Hollies, our home in Hastings on the south coast of England. **Left and above:** Jill Gordon helped me paint mock Chinese wallpaper in the dining room in the Hastings house. I also designed a set of needlepoint peony chairs for this room. **Right and below:** The blue-and-white tiles I designed for the Hastings kitchen. They were made in the kiln at Highland Stoneware pottery in Scotland.

Right: Bordered Diamonds from *Simple Shapes Spectacular Quilts*, which was published in 2010. I've taught workshops on this quilt all over the world. **Above and below:** The quilts in the book were inspired by the basic shapes that are in front of us if we open our eyes—like the mosaic outside my front door, a Peruvian knitted hat, and blue and white star tiles in Portugal.

The more I thought about it, the more I was convinced that this approach could stimulate an inspiring collection of quilts. But my publishers in England weren't so enthused. I hated to see this idea wither on the vine so I looked for another publisher. Melanie Falick at Stewart, Tabori & Chang showed great interest and liked my concept of also showing how basic shapes found in daily life—everything from paving stones to tires to watermelon slices—could also inspire quilt designs.

Making the quilts was thrilling. I went back to basics and my imagination became a fountain of ideas. Liza and I spent many happy days mocking up colors and patterns on our design wall in New Hope. As she would cut the shapes for our first concepts, I would plunder her collection of vintage quilt books to find ingenious uses of these shapes from the past. Often we'd combine ideas from two or three vintage quilts to arrive at our version, which we made fresh with new fabrics, a combination of my designs and fabrics from Liza's stash.

To find locations for photography I walked about a three mile radius around my London home, looking at industrial sights like railroad bridges, lumberyards, houses under construction, and playgrounds—turning away from the romantic, lush floral, and colorful locations I usually choose. I was amazed by the bounty I found.

When *Simple Shapes Spectacular Quilts* was launched in 2010, a young woman at one of my book signings gave me one of my favorite compliments ever. She stated simply, "Till now you've done recipe books—*this* is the art of cooking."

We used blogs on the Internet to publicize the launch. One blog invited quilters to submit photos of their creations made with my fabrics or quilt layouts. It unleashed an avalanche of creativity from my fans. I loved seeing what they did with the fabrics and geometry. Seeing so many of their creations and better understanding how they use my fabrics has influenced my approach to fabric design ever since.

Above: A brilliant example of geometric forms—pebble mosaic streets in Portugal—for *Simple Shapes Spectacular Quilts*. **Right:** The energy created by contrasting triangles is softened here in the Clay Tiles quilt by using many small-scale textured prints in earthy tones. This quilt is also from *Simple Shapes Spectacular Quilts*.

My painting ideas still swirl about in my head and, occasionally, materialize on canvas. After a trip to Australia in 2011, I received a commission to do a painting for Kim McLean, an acclaimed appliqué artist there. I felt joyous painting colors I thought she would enjoy—golden yellows, pinks, and lime green.

I still get a special thrill painting prints to be transformed into fabric and then once the fabrics are produced, cutting them apart to create quilts. Searching out locations to photograph the quilts is the final and very important part of this creative process. To find sympathetic colors, textures, and shapes that echo and expand the aesthetic of the quilt is very satisfying indeed.

In the fall of 2011 Debbie, Brandon, and I went to a small farming village in Bulgaria to photograph a collection of quilts for one of our Rowan books. Our only problem was too much bright sunlight. We could do some early morning shots against the rustic farmyards, but then had to wait out the days till the beautiful evening light appeared. The textures of old wood and stone and the colors of weathered paint, adobe bricks, and autumnal foliage were exactly right for the various color moods in our quilts, but we had to be patient. Our team spirit prevailed and we were more than happy when our art editor mounted our shots sympathetically on the pages of the book. Cropping and arranging the images we deliver in a sensitive way is an integral part of the process. Best of all, for me, is the opening chapter in each of the recent Rowan quilt books, where beautiful location shots set the scene.

Knowing appliqué artist Kim McLean loves oriental themes and colors as much as I do, I created a symphony of gold, pinks, and turquoise in this still life she commissioned.

As you can see, my creative work flourishes when I am involved in teamwork. When photographer Debbie Patterson, Pauline Smith, my editor for my annual *Rowan Patchwork and Quilting Book*, and Brandon go with me on the road to photograph my latest quilts, it's always a stimulating, warm time. Sally Harding has worked on editing my knitting, patchwork, and needlepoint books for years; as a fellow American, she has an innate understanding of what moves me in this English world. Another collaborator is Chris Wood, who does the vital job of art editor, laying out my books to make the images come alive on the page. She has overseen our annual *Rowan Patchwork and Quilting Book* and Brandon's *Brilliant Knits*, among others. Another recent collaboration has been with Philip Jacobs. This exciting textile designer combs early English and French fabric archives to produce classic floral, shell, and feather studies as quilt fabric. I pick prints each season and color Philip's artwork to fit in with my Kaffe Fassett Collective ranges. The large motifs on these chintzlike prints really appeal to quilters of a certain ilk. I feel at times like a movie director who has a favorite team for film after film.

Another aspect of teamwork is giving workshops in an attempt to pass on my enthusiasm to others—being an artistic hermit is not for me. The energy and focus of quilters is particularly refreshing. In my quilting workshops, we pin up a large piece of flannel, cut fabrics to the size required, and stick them to the flannel, rearranging to refine the color combos. The whole process of arranging the pieces for an entire quilt, ready to be pinned together and taken home, can be done in just a few hours. Because I enjoy this sense of instant gratification—and I enjoy the quilters' enthusiasm when they see a quilt idea come together so quickly—I decided to hand over knitting workshops to Brandon. With his eagle eye, Brandon picked up my knitting color workshop teaching skills almost overnight and was an immediate hit. His patience and caring demeanor are encouraging to knitters, whose samples grow more slowly on the needles. They love his humorous stories as well.

Left: Philip at his desk, working on another stunning floral for our quilt fabrics. He works from French and English archive sources.
Above, right: An example of the artwork Philip Jacobs gives me to do in my own colors for the Kaffe Fassett Collective fabric collections. This is for a fabric called Garden Party.
Above, left: My yellow and magenta version of Garden Party. **Right:** Another Jacobs print, Petunias, in one of my colorways.

I have given talks in many various and far-flung places, and I continue to do so because the feedback is so rewarding. A few of my lectures really stand out—one such was given in Vancouver, Canada. I told the enthused crowd there if only I could bottle their laughter and take it with me, I'd be made.

Quiet audiences have really tested me. It amazes me how some audiences are totally closed, not cracking a smile or a sigh of delight or "ugh" of disgust. Not everyone in my audiences is always friendly, either. At the height of my publicity, when I was attracting audiences of over a thousand, I gave a knitting talk in Aberdeen, Scotland. During the lecture, a small, fierce-looking woman in the front row (in a knitted hat) yelled out, "Can you knit a sock?" I had to admit I couldn't, which evoked a grim smile. But my favorite audience memory happened when I showed a long-sleeved top I'd knitted from cuff to cuff in one piece, commenting in jest, "Be sure to leave a hole for the neck."

A young woman with a Liverpool accent piped up, saying, "I knitted one of those and forgot to leave a hole for the neck."

"Oh, dear, what did you do?" I asked.

"Oh, I just burned a hole in it with the iron!" she replied.

Wonderful!

I'll never forget when Anne Marie Evans, a fabulous art teacher at a Leicester trade school, asked me to speak to her young catering class. Anne Marie was French and had visited the Dogon people in Africa, which caught my attention. As she guided me around the college, I was delighted to see what this inventive woman had inspired in her students. There were many displays, but the one that impressed me the most was a townscape made entirely of burnt toast cut into small squares. All the shading was done in toast tones. That sort of concept is right up my alley.

During my lecture, I strutted my stuff showing slides and knitted samples to a completely silent audience of students. I later told Anne Marie how disappointed I was and that it was no good talking to adolescents who obviously didn't get me. She called me two months later to ask if I'd talk to her more mature students—middle-aged women. "That's my audience. Of course I will," I agreed. I gave my talk, and as I packed up my samples to head home, Anne Marie asked if I could spare five minutes. She took me to a classroom, opened the door, and there were all the students from my previous audience, standing proudly behind their desks, a sweater on each one. They had not only knitted Fair Isle patterns, but they had hand-dyed the yarns with food products they cooked with. I was bursting with emotion and pride, and I learned not to judge an audience by their apparent nonreaction.

In addition to my lecture and workshop tours, I also continue to get

museum shows that take Brandon and me around the world. Many of these museum shows have had record attendances. It always surprises people how popular the needle arts can be. Interest is aroused first because I am a man doing these crafts and because of the bold color and the scale of the works, but ultimately I think the shows are successful because needlecraft is something everyone can do. Many people relate deeply to something when they have an understanding of how it is made.

Sweden is a country that really proves this point. Most Scandinavians can sew, knit, and embroider to a high standard, so they tap right into my world. I've had four museum shows there. One of the most exciting was in 2003 at the Röhsska Museum of Design and

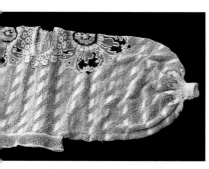

One of my early knit designs, knitted from cuff to cuff. When I showed a slide of it during a lecture in Liverpool, an audience member told me she copied it but forgot to leave an opening for the neck. To resolve, she said she burned a hole with her iron where the neckline was meant to be.

Decorative Arts in Gothenburg. The museum was vast, with many rooms at our disposal. We also could dot our work through the top floors of the five-story building. On the top floor was a huge bronze Buddha. The curators asked if I could make a piece of knitting to go on the Buddha, so I made him a gigantic knitted cap.

We told the curators we wanted to split up the show into color groups and paint the different parts rich colors like scarlet, cobalt, yellow, and even bold stripes. Patchwork quilts hung behind knitting and needlepoint pieces, and many antique items were brought up from the archives to enhance the show. We even had my paintings hanging in the restaurant.

The attendance that cold, dark winter was the best they had ever had. They hung huge, colorful banners outside the building to draw attention, and we placed wreaths of silk flowers around the two Chinese dog sculptures at the entrance. I wanted to paint them cobalt blue, but that was going too far for the museum's director. They even put huge posters along the sides of Gothenburg's trams.

I was going to give a talk there at the time of the St. Lucia Festival, which meant that I would be unable to get to church to see the procession of little singing girls—a great disappointment. That afternoon, as I started to go up to the stage to start my lecture, I noticed everyone was whispering and turning out lights in the theater of the museum. I heard a very faint sound of singing. Then the doors opened and in processed about twenty girls in white robes with wreaths of candles in their hair, singing like angels. They passed through the theater and out into the rest of the museum, so as I started my talk I could hear the enchanting echo of their high voices singing as they walked through the galleries of the institution. I had tears in my eyes as I somehow managed to continue and will never forget the rich treat they laid on for me.

I knitted a gigantic cap for the Buddha at the Röhsska Museum in Gothenburg, Sweden, for the exhibition of my textile work in winter 2003. The trolley cars in the city bore posters for the show—a blast of color in an austere Scandinavian winter.

Sitting in my studio after yet another trip, I'm amazed once more that what is produced in my low Afghani chair at the end of my chaotic studio, littered with yarns, fabrics, photos, and manuscripts, goes out and speaks to so many people. My work has never felt like drudgery or duty to me, and I'm still pinching myself to make sure that this life—making a living from something that gives me such deep satisfaction—isn't just a dream. Mostly, I'm delighted that people in this world of textile crafts ask Brandon and me to travel across the world to teach and pass on what we have learned on our colorful journey, marked with such highlights as my Victoria and Albert Museum show, the many other museum exhibition shows around the world, the books published and reprinted, and the kind words in so many articles and reviews.

But as detailed as this book is, I have only been able to include a sampling of the adventures I have experienced and people I have encountered—many of whom I'm able to keep in touch with over the Internet. Since I don't drive or do computers, I rely on Brandon and my part-time studio assistant, Katy Kingston, to keep a running dialogue with Pauline Smith, who brilliantly edits the annual Rowan patchwork book in Yorkshire, and with Liza Prior Lucy in Pennsylvania, so we can create quilts together from afar. There are so many others, like museum curators and shops that sponsor my talks and our workshops.

The Internet also keeps us in touch with the many fans and creative souls the world over who share their ideas and enthusiasm for what we produce. These are people like the brilliant American quilter Kathy Doughty, the owner of the Material Obsession shop near Sydney, Australia, who encourages her customers to use Kaffe Fassett Collective fabrics fearlessly. I often think of the many people like Kathy, whose belief in what my team and I create in north London gives us the enthusiasm to continue our satisfying work. Their sense of color and form gives us so many new ideas, proving what a collaborative craft quilting is.

Another boon at this stage of my life is getting visits from the growing tribe of my Californian family—my siblings' offspring. That they are now growing into creative people, too, is deeply satisfying and makes me hopeful for the future. My family recently expanded after I read a book called *Grace: An American Woman's Forty Years in China* about a cousin I was unaware of, written by another cousin, Eleanor McCallie Cooper. Eleanor has now introduced me to a large new family group of educators and writers in Chattanooga, Tennessee, a wonderful creative center. A great legacy from my dad.

Five generations of Fassett women—my sister Holly with her daughter Erin and her granddaughter Emily, and a portrait of my mother, Lolly, in the background, painted by her grandmother Jane Gallatin Powers.

As I finish this book, I am appalled at all the people I wanted to write about, who have made my life so rich and rewarding, but who couldn't be fit into the narrative. I could easily write several parallel books to include them and countless other inspirations. I would like to mention a few here:

The life-enhancing films that opened windows in my mind—*The Red Shoes*, Olivier's *Henry V*, Cocteau's *Beauty and the Beast*, *Moulin Rouge* (the 1952 version with José Ferrer), *The Wizard of Oz*, *West Side Story*, *My Brilliant Career*, *Billy Elliot*. The music that became my soundtrack—Bulgarian choral music, so many Joan Baez songs, Odetta, Daphnis and Chloe, Schoenberg's *Transfigured Night*, Offenbach, the Modern Jazz Quartet, the Beatles, Crosby, Stills and Nash, klezmer music, Songs of the Auvergne, and so many ethnic pieces I've forgotten the names of.

The many designers and teachers I have met along my journey who inspire so much talent to surface in others.

The manufacturers of textiles who believed in my designs and got them out into the world, like the Missonis, Peruvian Connection, Designers Guild, Pine Cone Hill, Renaissance Ribbons, Peking Handicraft, and Westminster Fibers.

All the collectors of my paintings, embroidery, and patchworks who put their money where their mouth is, giving me courage to continue, like Zoe Landers, who has the best of my pieces in her collection, making them look so happy together.

My extraordinary family, multiplying so fast I lose track, but whose lives keep a part of my heart in California.

To all those fabulous shop owners who supply our fix of color and pattern right across the world, and the manufacturers of yarn and printed fabric.

All the spectacular exhibitions of art and textiles, the BBC for mind-expanding television and radio, particularly BBC Radio 4, whose popular output of highly insightful plays, interviews, and discussion programs keep me informed and amused as I work. For the theater that has given me so many emotionally rewarding evenings.

Those fans the world over who conquered their shyness to tell me how inspired they were by my books, exhibitions, radio and TV appearances.

And, of course, all those who helped me in the making of my textiles and mosaic dreams. The sewers, quilters, needlepoint stitchers, and knitters.

Those museum curators and directors who took on showing my work. The journalists who wrote and broadcast about the exhibitions, making them the success they were, finding new ways to spread the word.

All the dedicated students who attend my classes and actually listen and apply themselves, filling me to the point of tears with their originality and passion; the audiences who turn out for my talks and ooh and aah and, best of all, laugh at my jokes—you have no idea how encouraging you all are and how you have kept the show on the road.

To all those world cultures who have inspired me with embroidery, mosaic, decorative painting, beading, and organic buildings. And all the sights that make traveling the magic experience it undoubtedly is. To the delicious food I've enjoyed on my travels and all the fabulous gardens—those gardens so close to the hearts of us textile makers—thanks to the passionate, patient devotion of their makers.

To all those hotels who made visiting them a bit more special. That touch of humor or fantasy that is balm for us tired travelers.

Overleaf: The studio set up with a collection of my paintings, plus some needlepoint pieces and a knitted blanket of striped squares. There are also three of Brandon's still lifes in the left-hand top and bottom corners and above the basket.

Lastly, to that amazing band of intelligent, hardworking people who publish the books we artists all love to pore over and work from in so many far-flung corners of this earth. Without these books, we would not be able to so easily tune in to the message and magic of color that is our lifeblood.

As I was putting the finishing touches on this book, the news reached me from San Francisco that Steve Lovi has died. This, of course, gives me pause. His towering existence affected all who met him, and I owe so much to the undivided attention he lavished on me while we produced the four books we collaborated on. In my eventful life, Steve's contribution is so much more than I've indicated here. It would take a whole other book to communicate the rich experiences we lived through and how much he taught me. Suffice it to say, he was my greatest teacher, and inspired me to be a far better artist and person than I would have been without his guidance.

I want to end this book with the glorious news that Brandon has had a rose named after me. It is humbling indeed and my gratitude is endless. I haven't seen it yet in the flesh but have been told it has a scent, which thrills me. And look at its rich pink coloring!

Left: *Rosa* 'Kaffe Fassett,' produced by Eurosa in Britain and due to be available in 2013.
Opposite: Steve Lovi sitting in his Notting Hill Gate flat in the seventies. I am amazed at the detail I caught in this painting.

Resources

Books by Kaffe Fassett

This is a selection of the first editions of major works by Kaffe Fassett.

1985

Glorious Knits, published by Clarkson Potter (UK edition: *Glorious Knitting*, Century Publishing, London)

1987

Glorious Needlepoint, published by Clarkson Potter (UK edition: *Glorious Needlepoint*, Century Hutchinson, London)

1988

Glorious Color: Sources of Inspiration for Knitting and Needlepoint, published by Clarkson Potter (UK edition: *Kaffe Fassett at the V&A*, Century Hutchinson, London)

1989

Family Album, published by Taunton Press (UK edition: *Family Album*, Century Hutchinson, London)

1991

Glorious Inspiration for Needlepoint and Knitting, published by Clarkson Potter (UK edition: *Glorious Inspiration: Kaffe Fassett's Needlepoint Source Book*, Century Editions, London)

1993

Kaffe's Classics: 25 Favorite Knitting Patterns for Sweaters, Jackets, Vests, and More, published by Little Brown & Co. (UK edition: *Kaffe's Classics: 25 Glorious Knitting Designs*, Ebury Press, London)

1995

Glorious Interiors: Needlepoint, Knitting and Decorative Design Projects for Your Home, published by Little Brown & Co. (UK edition: *Glorious Interiors*, Ebury Press, London)

1997

Patchwork: More than 25 Glorious Quilt Designs, by Kaffe Fassett with Liza Prior Lucy, published by Clarkson Potter (UK publisher: *Patchwork: Over 25 Glorious Quilt Designs*, Ebury Press, London)

1999

Mosaics, Inspiration and Original Projects for Interiors and Exteriors, by Kaffe Fassett and Candace Bahouth, published by Taunton Press (UK edition: *Mosaics, Inspiration and 24 Original Projects*, Ebury Press, London)

2001

Passionate Patchwork: Over 20 Original Quilt Designs, by Kaffe Fassett with Liza Prior Lucy, published by Taunton Press (UK edition: *Passionate Patchwork*, Ebury Press, London)

2003

Kaffe Fassett's Pattern Library: Over 190 Creative Knitwear Designs, published by Taunton Press (UK edition: *Kaffe Fassett's Pattern Library: Over 190 Original Knitting Motifs*, Ebury Press, London)

2005

Kaffe Fassett's Museum Quilts: Designs Inspired by the Victoria & Albert Museum, by Kaffe Fassett with Liza Prior Lucy, published Taunton Press (UK edition: *Kaffe Fassett's V&A Quilts: 23 Beautiful Patchworks Inspired by the Victoria and Albert*, Ebury Press, London)

2007

Kaffe Knits Again: 24 Original Designs Updated for Today's Knitters, published by Potter Craft (UK edition: *Kaffe Knits Again: 24 Updated Rowan Original Designs,* by Kaffe Fassett, Rowan Yarns)

2010

Kaffe Fassett's Simple Shapes Spectacular Quilts: 23 Original Quilt Designs, by Kaffe Fassett with Liza Prior Lucy, published by STC Craft / A Melanie Falick Book, an imprint of Stewart, Tabori & Chang and Abrams Books

Books About Kaffe Fassett

1999

Welcome Home, published by Martingale & Company; republished 2010 by Landauer Publishing

Recommended Reading

To learn more about my mother's and father's sides of the family

2009

My Nepenthe: Bohemian Tales of Food, Family, and Big Sur, by Romney Steele, published by Andrews McMeel

This book by my niece recounts the building of our family restaurant and our family's life in Big Sur.

2003

Grace: An American Woman's Forty Years in China, 1934–1974, by Eleanor McCallie Cooper, published by Soho Press

This is a book of my cousin Grace's adventures; she was a Southern belle who married a Chinese engineer and settled in China for the next 40 years. The book was written by another cousin, Eleanor McCallie Cooper.

Acknowledgments

I've produced many books in my time but this one has been by far the most demanding and difficult. The hardest part was deciding which elements of my complex story to put down; then to organize that into a coherent flow and, lastly, find hundreds of pictures to illustrate the tale. My two editors, Sally Harding and Betty Christiansen, fashioned my story into a readable script, while Brandon Mably and Katy Kingston sorted through literally thousands of uncatalogued slides to locate the masses of images that grace our book. Sally Cole sourced our library images, including celebrity shots and historical paintings. Tom Birmingham and Bruce Campbell shot Fassett-family paintings. Many other photographers contributed their images, including Brooke Elgie, Debbie Patterson, Sara Remington, Steve Lovi, Tessa Traeger, Anne James, Sheila Rock, Jon Stewart, Irving Schild, Michael Childers, and Drew Lucy. The Beatrice Wood Center for the Arts, Virginia Ironside, Natalie Rykiel, Missoni, Rowan Yarns, Peruvian Connection, Philip Jacobs, and Eurosa also provided photos. Renaissance Ribbons provided my ribbons when they were needed, and Liza Lucy was always on hand to send fabrics for scanning. My niece Romney Steele possessed an extensive archive that she had used in her brilliant book *My Nepenthe* and spent hours locating the many images I needed. Anna Christian arranged everything in her artful and delightful way. Richard Womersley, Erin Gafill, and Brandon Mably proofread and gave invaluable comments and encouragement. Jonny Pegg, my agent, arranged the contract. To all the above, a huge grateful thank you, and particularly to Melanie Falick for believing in this project and for the months she spent bringing it into the world.

Photo Credits

All photos courtesy of the Kaffe Fassett Studio archive, except those listed below. All Sara Remington photos listed also appeared in *My Nepenthe* by Romney Steele, published by Andrews McMeel in 2009.

Every effort has been made to locate and credit the appropriate rights holders. We apologize in advance for any unintentional omissions. Requests for changes will be considered by the publisher, and any necessary corrections or revisions will be amended in future reprints.

Page 2: Brandon Mably. **Page 5:** Debbie Patterson/Landauer Publishing. **Page 8:** Debbie Patterson. **Page 15:** (Nos. 3, 4) Sara Remington. **Page 18:** (Center) Koichi Kamoshida/Getty Images. **Page 22:** (No. 2) Sara Remington; (No. 4) Photograph by Morley Baer. ©2012 by the Morley Baer Photography Trust, Santa Fe. All reproduction rights reserved. **Page 23:** (No. 8) Sara Remington; (No. 7) Courtesy of the Fassett family. **Page 24:** Debbie Patterson. **Page 27:** (Right) Courtesy of the Fassett family; (Lower left) Jon Stewart. **Page 28:** (Bottom) Brandon Mably. **Page 31:** Courtesy Beatrice Wood Center for the Arts/Happy Valley Cultural Center. **Pages 32–33:** (Center) Photo from the book *The Story of Happy Valley* by Radha Rajagopal Sloss. Courtesy Beatrice Wood Center for the Arts/Happy Valley Cultural Center. **Page 34:** (Center—photo of Beatrice Wood in middle age) © Christopher Felver/Corbis; (Center—group photo) J. Krishnamurti, Radha Rajagopal, Beatrice Wood at Santa Barbara, 1938. Courtesy Beatrice Wood Center for the Arts/Happy Valley Cultural Center; (Bottom) Courtesy Beatrice Wood Center for the Arts/Happy Valley Cultural Center. **Page 39:** Sara Remington. **Page 46:** (Right) Bouquet of Wild Flowers (oil on canvas), Redon, Odilon (1840-1916)/Private Collection/Photo ©

Lefevre Fine Art Ltd., London/The Bridgman Art Library; (Bottom left) Debbie Patterson/Landauer Publishing. **Page 49:** Rex Features/CSU Archives/Everett Collection. **Page 52:** (No. 2) New York Daily News Archive; (No. 4) John Tresillian/New York Daily News Archive; (No. 9) Le Déjeuner, Pierre Bonnard/© The Gallery Collection/Corbis. **Page 55:** Michael Ochs Archives/Getty Images. **Page 57:** (No. 5) Sara Remington; (No. 3) Brooke Elgie. **Page 58:** (Center) Pierluigi Praturion/Rex Features. **Page 66:** Steve Lovi. **Page 74:** Courtesy of the Fassett family. **Page 75:** Courtesy of the Fassett family. **Page 78:** (Top right) Morandi, Giorgio (1890–1964), Still Life 1936/Scala, Florence; (Bottom right) PhotoLibrary; (Bottom left) Steve Lovi. **Page 83:** (Top) Steve Lovi. **Page 84:** Courtesy of Virginia Ironside. **Page 85:** Michael Childers. **Page 86:** The Kobal Collection/MGM. **Page 92:** (Nos. 3 and 4) Steve Lovi. **Page 93:** Tessa Traeger. **Page 94:** (Bottom left and center) Courtesy of the Missoni archive. **Page 97:** (Right) Steve Lovi. **Page 100:** (No. 2) Justin de Villeneuve/Getty Images; (No. 4) Sarah Moon/Vogue/Condé Nast Publications; (No. 3) Steve Lovi. **Page 101:** (No. 5) Vuillard, Édouard (1868–1940)/Scala, Florence. **Page 105:** Steve Lovi. **Page 107:** (Top left) Richard Womersley; (Top right) George Stroud/Hulton Archive/Getty Images. **Pages 110–111:** Gopi's Search for Krishna, Mehrangarh Museum Trust, Jodhpur, Rajasthan, India and His Highness Maharaja Gaj Singh of Jodhpur/Photo courtesy of the Arthur M. Sackler Gallery, Smithsonian Institution. **Page 115:** (Top left and top right) Steve Lovi. **Page 116:** Brandon Mably. **Page 118:** (All photos) Steve Lovi. **Page 119:** (No. 7) Steve Lovi. **Page 122:** Steve Lovi. **Page 125:** (All three photos on right) Steve Lovi. **Page 128:** Steve Lovi. **Page 130:** Steve Lovi. **Page 131:** (All photos) Steve Lovi. **Page 133:** Steve Lovi. **Page 134:** Steve Lovi. **Page 136:** (Nos. 1, 2, 5, 6) Steve

Lovi. **Page 138:** (Nos. 1, 2, 3, 4) Steve Lovi; (No. 5) Debbie Patterson. **Page 139:** (Nos. 6, 7, 9, 10, 13) Steve Lovi; (Nos. 8, 12) Debbie Patterson. **Page 140:** Steve Lovi. **Page 142:** (Top left) Rory Mitchell; (Bottom) Steve Lovi. **Page 144:** Drew Lucy. **Page 145:** Steve Lovi. **Page 147:** (Center) Courtesy of the Fassett family. **Page 149:** (No. 4) Koichi Kamoshida/Getty Images. **Page 152:** (Nos. 3, 7) Steve Lovi; (No. 4) Brandon Mably. **Page 154:** Steve Lovi. **Page 155:** (All photos) Anne James. **Page 156:** (Bottom) Reuters/Corbis; (Top) Brandon Mably. **Page 158:** (Left and right) Steve Lovi. **Pages 160–161:** (All photos) Steve Lovi. **Page 163:** Steve Lovi. **Page 166:** Debbie Patterson. **Page 167:** (Center left) Brandon Mably. **Page 169:** Courtesy of Natalie Rykiel. **Page 170:** (No. 1) Debbie Patterson/Landauer Publishing; (No. 2) Sheila Rock. **Page 172:** (Center bottom) Brandon Mably. **Page 173:** (Left) Brandon Mably. **Page 174:** (Center) Anne James. **Page 179:** (Left) Courtesy of Rowan Yarns. **Page 180:** Brandon Mably. **Page 182:** (Center) Steve Lovi. **Pages 184–185:** (All photos) Debbie Patterson. **Page 188:** (No. 4) Steve Lovi. **Page 189:** (No. 18) Debbie Patterson; (Nos. 11, 13) Brandon Mably. **Page 190:** Debbie Patterson. **Page 191:** Irving Schild. **Page 192:** (Center left, right top, and right bottom) Debbie Patterson. **Page 195:** Courtesy of Landauer Publishing. **Page 197:** (No. 1) Debbie Patterson; (No. 6) Clay Perry. **Page 198:** (All photos) Debbie Patterson. **Page 203:** (Top right) Brandon Mably. **Page 205:** (Center) Courtesy of Peruvian Connection. **Page 207:** (Top right) Jim Holden; (Left top and left bottom) Brandon Mably. **Page 208:** (Right) Jon Stewart. **Page 209:** (Right) Debbie Patterson; (Left) Brandon Mably. **Page 211:** (Left, top center, top right) Philip Jacobs. **Page 214:** Catherine Karnow/Corbis. **Pages 216–217:** Debbie Patterson/Landauer Publishing. **Page 219:** Courtesy of Eurosa.

Index